Anonymous

Sailing Directions for the North-American Pilot

Containing the Gulf and River St. Laurence, the whole Island of Newfoundland,

including the straits of Bell-Isle, and the coast of Labradore.

Anonymous

Sailing Directions for the North-American Pilot
Containing the Gulf and River St. Laurence, the whole Island of Newfoundland, including the straits of Bell-Isle, and the coast of Labradore.

ISBN/EAN: 9783337331634

Printed in Europe, USA, Canada, Australia, Japan

Cover: Foto ©Lupo / pixelio.de

More available books at **www.hansebooks.com**

Sailing Directions

FOR THE

NORTH-AMERICAN PILOT:

CONTAINING THE

GULF and RIVER St. LAURENCE,

The Whole Iſland of NEWFOUNDLAND,

INCLUDING

The STRAITS of BELL-ISLE,

AND

The COAST of LABRADORE.

GIVING A PARTICULAR ACCOUNT OF THE

BAYS, HARBOURS, ROCKS, LAND-MARKS, DEPTHS OF WATER, LATITUDES, BEARINGS, AND DISTANCE FROM PLACE TO PLACE; THE SETTING AND FLOWING OF THE TIDES, &c.

FOUNDED ON ACTUAL SURVEYS, TAKEN BY

SURVEYORS THAT HAVE BEEN EMPLOYED BY THE ADMIRALTY, AND OTHER OFFICERS IN THE KING's SERVICE.

PUBLISHED BY PERMISSION OF THE

RIGHT HONOURABLE THE LORDS COMMISSIONERS OF THE ADMIRALTY.

LONDON:

Printed for R. SAYER and J. BENNETT, Map and Print Sellers, in Fleet-Street.
MDCCLXXV.

Of whom may be had, bound together or ſeparately, all the Charts belonging to the above Directions.

CHARTS, *printed for and sold by* R. SAYER *and* J. BENNETT, Map *and* Print Sellers, No. 53, *in* Fleet-Street.

I. THE BRITISH CHANNEL; extending from Dover to the Isles of Scilly, on the English Coast; and from Cape Griz-nez to the Isle of Ouessant, on the French Coast. To which are added a Part of the German Sea; with the Entrance of the Thames, the Banks of Flanders, and the Straights of Dover: also the Bristol Channel, the Entrance of St. George's Channel, the South-West Coast of Ireland as far as Cape Clear, and Part of the Atlantic Ocean; laid down from authentic Surveys, both printed and manuscript, from all the Maps and Charts hitherto published in England, and particularly in Respect to the French Coast, from the large Topographical Map of France, surveyed by Order of that Government. The Whole regulated according to the Astronomical Observations of both Kingdoms. In Six large Sheets, near 7 feet long, and four feet wide. By the late Mr. Jefferys, Geographer to the King.

This Chart, having been above seven Years in compleating, and having undergone the Examination of many experienced Pilots, by whom it has been universally approved of, was presented to the DIRECTORS of the HON. the UNITED EAST-INDIA-COMPANY, who were pleased to grant the following Permission:

"*At a* COURT *of* DIRECTORS, *held on* Friday, *the 3d of* February, 1775.
" ORDERED, That Mr. ROBERT SAYER be permitted to dedicate a *very useful*
" CHART, which he is preparing, of the ENGLISH CHANNEL, to this Court.
"P. MICHELL, Secretary."

In great Forwardness, and will be published with all possible Dispatch;

II. A CHART OF THE ATLANTIC OCEAN, from the 57th Degree of Latitude North, to the Equator; with the accurate Delineation of the European, African, and American Coasts, between which it is comprehended; the true Position of all the Islands, Rocks, and Shoals, lying in that Ocean; the Soundings, Currents, and several other Particulars useful to Navigators.

The Whole founded upon Astronomical Observations and Nautical Surveys, made by English, French, Dutch, Spanish, and Portuguese Navigators, from the 15th Century to the Year 1770. In Four large Sheets, near Three Feet and One-half by Four Feet and One-half.

IV. THE WEST-INDIA PILOT, being an Accurate Description of the Coasts of those numerous Islands, which has been upwards of Twelve Years in compiling and rendering compleat.

This very extensive Work, whose Sailing Directions, by the most skilful Pilots, are now preparing for the Press, is compleated on Forty large Plates, and will be followed immediately by an Hydrographical Collection, on a very large Scale, of all the Roads, Bays, and Harbours of Note in the West-Indies, which will be rendered materially necessary for the Navigation of that Part of the World.

V. A CHART OF NORTH AND SOUTH AMERICA, comprehending the Atlantic and Southern Oceans, as well as the Pacific Ocean or South Sea; in which are inserted all the New Discoveries made by the late Circumnavigators in the South Sea, and by the Russian Officers between the North-East of Asia and America. In Six Sheets, with an Explanation in Letter-Press.

VI. THE EAST-INDIA PILOT; being an extensive Collection of Charts and Hydrographical Plans, improved from the latest Works of Monf. D'Apres, de Mannevillette, with many additional ones from original Drawings and Surveys, which were communicated to the Editor, or procured by him, at a great Expence, from the Dutch and others; with a Book of Sailing Directions by the most experienced Officers in the Hon. the East-India Company's Service.

N. B. This Work is nearly finished, and will be published in the Course of the Year.

VII. THE MEDITERRANEAN SEA, made from the Draughts of the Pilots of Marseilles, and corrected by the best Astronomical Observations, by Order of Monf. Le Comte de Maurepas. To which is annexed, A Draught of the Straights Mouth, with the Bays of Cadiz, Gibraltar, and Malaga; the Ports of Leghorne, Naples, Mahon, Smyrna, Thessalonica, Scandaroon, and Alexandria; with the Course of the Nile from thence to Grand Cairo. Printed on Three large Sheets.

VIII. THE GULFS OF FINLAND AND LIVONIA, with their respective Ports and Harbours; together with a large Plan of Kronstad and St. Petersburg. Printed on a large Sheet.

DIRECTIONS

For Navigating on Part of the

South Coast of Newfoundland.

N. B. *All Bearings and Courses hereafter-mentioned, are the true Bearings and Courses, and not by Compass.*

CAPE *Chapeaurouge*, or the Mountain of the *Red Hat*, is situated on the West-side of *Placentia Bay*, in the Latitude of 46° 53′ North, and lies nearly West 17 or 18 Leagues from Cape St. *Maries*; it is the highest and most remarkable Land on that Part of the Coast, appearing above the rest somewhat like the Crown of a Hat, and may be seen in clear Weather 12 Leagues. *[Cape Chapeaurouge.]*

Close to the Eastward of Cape *Chapeaurouge* are the Harbours of *Great* and *Little St. Laurence*. To sail into *Great St. Laurence*, which is the Wester-most, there is no Danger but what lies very near the Shore; taking Care with Westerly, and particularly S. W. Winds, not to come too near the *Flat Mountain*, to avoid the Flerrys and Eddy Winds under the high Land. The Course in is first N. W. till you open the upper Part of the Harbour, then N N. W. half W. the best Place for great Ships to anchor, and the best Ground is before a Cove on the East-side of the Harbour in 13 Fathom Water. A little above *Blue Beach Point*, which is the first Point on the West-side; here you lie only two Points open: You may anchor any where between this Point and the Point of *Low Beach*, on the same Side near the Head of the Harbour, observing that close to the West Shore, the Ground is not so good as on the other Side. Fishing Vessels lay at the Head of the Harbour above the Beach, sheltered from all Winds. *[Harbours of St. Laurence.]*

[4]

To sail into *Little St. Laurence* you must keep the West Shore on Board, in order to avoid a sunken Rock which lies a little without the Point of the *Peninsula*, which stretches off from the East-side of the Harbour: You anchor above this *Peninsula*, (which covers you from the Sea Winds) in 3 and 4 Fathom Water, a fine sandy Bottom. In these Harbours are good Fishing Conveniencies, and Plenty of Wood and Water. Ships may anchor without the *Peninsula* in 12 Fathom good Ground, but open to the S. S. E. Winds.

Sauker-Head.   *Sauker-Head* lies 3 Miles to the Eastward of Cape *Chapeaurouge*; it is a pretty high round Point, off which lie some sunken Rocks, about a Cable's Length from the Shore.

Garden Bank.   This Bank, whereon is from 7 to 17 Fathom Water, lies about half a Mile off from *Little St. Laurence*, with *Blue Beach Point* on with the East Point of *Great St. Laurence*.

Ferryland-Head.   *Ferryland-Head* lies S. W. 1 Mile from Cape *Chapeaurouge*; it is a high rocky Island, just separated from the Main: It and Cape *Chapeaurouge* are sufficient Marks to know the Harbours of St. *Laurence*.

Bay of Laun.   West 5 Miles from *Ferryland-Head*, lies the Bay of *Laun*, in the Bottom of which are two small Inlets, called *Great* and *Little Laun*. *Little Laun*, which is the Eastermost, lies open to the S. W. Winds, which generally prevails upon this Coast; and therefore no Place to anchor in. *Great Laun* lies in about N. by E. 2 Miles, is near half a Mile wide, whereon is from 14 to 3 Fathom Water. To sail into it, You must be careful to avoid a sunken Rock, which lies about a quarter of a Mile off from the East Point. The best Place to anchor is on the East side, about half a Mile from the Head, in 6 and 5 Fathom; the Bottom is pretty good, and you are shelter'd from all Winds, except S. and S. by W. which blow right in, and cause a great Swell. At the Head of this Place is a Bar Harbour, into which Boats can go at half Tide, and Conveniencies for a Fishery, and Plenty of Wood and Water.

Laun Islands.   Off the West Point of *Laun Bay* lay the Islands of the same Name, not far from the Shore; the Westermost and outermost of which lie W. Southerly 10 Miles from *Ferryland-Head*; near a quarter of a Mile to the Southward of this Island is a Rock whereon the Sea breaks in very bad Weather: There are other sunken Rocks about these Islands, but they are no Ways dangerous, being very near the Shore.

Taylor's Bay.   This Bay, which lies open to the Sea, lies 3 Miles to the Westward of *Laun* Islands; off the East Point are some sunken Rocks, near a quarter of a Mile from the Shore.

Point Aux Gaul.   A little to the Westward of *Taylor's Bay*, there stretches out a low Point of Land, called *Point Aux Gaul*; off which lies a Rock above Water, half a Mile

from

from the Shore, called *Gaul Shag Rock*; this Rock lies West three quarters South, 5 Leagues from *Ferryland-Head*; you have 14 Fathom close to the off Side of it, but between it and the Point are some sunken Rocks.

From *Point Aux Gaul Shag Rock*, to the Islands of *Lamelin*, is West three quarters N. 1 League; between them is the Bay of *Lamelin*, wherein is very shallow Water, and several small Islands and Rocks, both above and under Water, and in the Bottom of it is a Salmon River. *Lamelin Bay.*

The two Islands of *Lamelin* (which are but low) lie off the West Point of the Bay of the same Name, and lie West three quarters South, 6 Leagues from the Mountain of the *Red Hat*; but in steering along Shore make a W. by S. Course good, will carry you clear of all Danger. Small Vessels may anchor in the Road between these Islands in 4 and 5 Fathom, tolerably well shelter'd from the Weather: Nearly in the Middle of the Passage, going in between the two Islands, is a sunken Rock, which you avoid by keeping nearer to one Side than the other; the most Room is on the East-side. The Eastermost Island communicates with the Main at Low-water, by a narrow Beach, over which Boats can go at High-water, into the N. W. Arm of *Lamelin Bay*, where they lay in Safety. Here are Conveniencies for a Fishery, but little or no Wood of any Sort. Near to the South Point of the Westermost Island is a Rock pretty high above Water, called *Lamelin Shag Rock*; in going into the Road between the Islands, you leave this Rock on your Larboard Side. *Lamelin Islands.*

These Ledges lay along the Shore, between *Lamelin Islands* and *Point May*, which is 3 Leagues, and are very dangerous, some of them being 3 Miles from the Land. To avoid these Ledges in the Day-time, you must not bring the Islands of *Lamelin* to the Southward of Far, until *Point May*, or the Western Extremity of the Land bear N. by E. from you; you may then steer to the Northward with Safety, between *Point May* and G. en Island. In the Night, or foggy Weather, you ought to be very careful not to approach these Ledges within 20 Fathom Water, lest you get intangled amongst them. Between them and the Main are various Soundings from 10 to 5 Fathom. *Lamelin Ledges.*

All the Land about Cape *Chapeaurouge* and *Laun*, is high and hilly close to the Sea; from *Laun Island* to *Lamelin* it is of a moderate Height; from *Lamelin* to *Point May*, the Land near the Shore is very low, with sandy Beaches, but a little Way inland are Mountains. *Observations.*

The Island of St. *Peter*'s lies in the Latitude 46 Degrees 46 Minutes North, West by South, near 12 Leagues from Cape *Chapeaurouge*, and West by South half South 5 Leagues from the Islands of *Lamelin*; it is about 5 Leagues in Circuit, and pretty high, with a craggy, broken, uneven Surface. Coming from the Westward, as soon as you raise *Gallantry-Head*, which is the South Point of the Island, it will make in a round Hommock, like a small Island, and appears as if separated from St. *Peter*'s. On the East-side of the Island, a *Island of St. Peter's.*

little

[6]

little to the N. E. of *Gallentry-Head* lay three small Islands, the innermost of which is the largest, called *Dog-Island*; within this Island is the Road and Harbour of St. *Peter*'s; the Harbour is but small, and hath in it from 12 to 20 Feet Water; but there is a Bar across the Entrance, whereon there is but 6 Feet at Low-water, and 12 or 14 Feet at High water. The Road which lies on the N. W. Side of *Dog-Island* will admit Ships of any Burthen, but it is only fit for the Summer Season being open to the N. E. Winds; you may lay in 8, 10, and 12 Fathom, and for the most Part is a hard rocky Bottom; there is very little clear Ground; Ships of War commonly buoy their Cables; the best Ground is near the north Shore. Going in or out, you must not range too near the East-side of *Bear-Island*, which is the Easternmost of the three Islands above-mentioned, for Fear of some sunken Rocks which lie East about 1 Mile from it, and which is the only Danger about St. *Peter*'s, but what lay very near the Shore.

Island of Columbo.   This Island is of a small Circuit, but pretty high, and lies very near the N. E. Point of St. *Peter*'s; between them is a very good Passage, one third of a Mile wide, wherein is 12 Fathom Water. On the North-side of the Island is a Rock pretty High above Water, called *Little Columbo*; and about a quarter of a Mile N. E. from this Rock is a sunken Rock, whereon is 2 Fathom Water.

Island of Langley.   The Island of *Langley*, which lies on the N. W. Side of St. *Peter*'s, is about 8 Leagues in Circuit, of a moderate and pretty equal Height, except the N. End, which is a low Point, with Sand Hills along it; it is flat a little Way off the low Land on both Sides of it; but all the high Part of the Island is very bold too, and the Passage between it and St. *Peter*'s (which is 1 League broad) is clear of Danger. You may anchor on the N. E. Side of the Island, a little to the Southward of the *Sand Hills*, in 5 and 6 Fathom, a Fine Sandy Bottom, sheltered from the Southerly S. W. and N. W. Winds.

Island of Miquelon.   From the North Point of *Langley*, to the South Point of *Miquelon* is about 1 Mile; it is said that a few Years since they join'd together at this Place by a Neck of Sand, which the Sea has washed away and made a Channel, wherein is 2 Fathom Water. The Island of *Miquelon* is 4 Leagues in Length from North to South, but of an unequal Breadth; the Middle of the Island is high Land, called the high Land of *Dunn*; but down by the Shore it is low, except Cape *Miquelon*, which is a lofty Promontory at the Northern Extremity of the Island.

Dunn Harbour.   On the S. E. Side of the Island, to the Southward of the High Land, is a pretty large Bar Harbour, called *Dunn Harbour*, which will admit Fishing Shallops at half Flood, but can never be of any Utility for a Fishery.

Miquelon Rock and Bank.   *Miquelon Rock* stretches off from the East Point of the Island, under the high Land 1 Mile and a quarter to the Eastward, some are above and some under Water; the outermost of these Rocks are above Water, and you have 12 Fathom close to them, and 18 and 20 Fathom 1 Mile off. N. E. half N. 4 or 5 Miles from these Rocks lies *Miquelon Bank*, whereon is 6 Fathom Water.

The

[7]

The Road of Miquelon (which is large and spacious) lies at the North-end, and Road of Miquelon on the East side of the Island, between Cape Miquelon and a very remarkable round Mountain near the Shore, called Chapeaux: Off the South Point of the Road are some sunken Rocks, about a quarter of a Mile from the Shore, but every where else it is clear of Danger. The best Anchorage is near the Bottom of the Road in 6 and 7 Fathom, fine sandy Bottom; you lay open to the Easterly Winds, which Winds seldom blow in the Summer.

Cape Miquelon, or the Northern Extremity of the Island is high bluff Land; Cape Miquelon. and when you are 4 or 5 Leagues to the Eastward or Westward of it, you would take it for an Island, by Reason the Land at the Bottom of the Road is very low.

The Seal Rocks are two Rocks above Water, lying 1 League and a half off Seal Rocks. from the Middle of the West-side of the Island Miquelon; the Passage between them and the Island is very safe, and you have 14 or 15 Fathom within a Cable's Length all round them.

This Island, which is about three-quarters of a Mile in Circuit, and low, lies Green Island. N. E. 5 Miles from St. Peter's, and nearly in the Middle of the Channel, between it and Point May on Newfoundland; on the South-side of this Island are some Rocks both above and under Water, extending themselves 1 Mile and a quarter to the S. W.

Description of Fortune Bay.

Fortune Bay is very large; the Entrance is form'd by Point May and Pass Island, which are 12 Leagues N. by E. and S. by W. from each other, and it is about 23 Leagues deep, wherein are a great many Bays, Harbours, and Islands.

The Island of Brunet is situated nearly in the Middle of the Entrance into Island of Fortune Bay; it is about 5 Leagues in Circuit, and of a tolerable Height; the Brunet. East end appears, at some Points of View, like Islands, by reason it is very low and narrow in two Places. On the N. E. Side of the Island is a Bay, wherein is tolerable good Anchorage for Ships in 14 and 16 Fathom, shelter'd from Southerly and Westerly Winds; you must not run too far in for fear of some sunken Rocks in the Bottom of it, a quarter of a Mile from the Shore; opposite this Bay, on the South-side of the Island, is a small Cove, wherein small Vessels and Shallops can lay pretty secure from the Weather, in 6 Fathom Water; in the Middle of the Cove is a Rock above Water, and a Channel on each Side of it. The Islands lying at the West-end of Brunet, called Little Brunets, afford indifferent Shelter for Shallops in blowing Weather; you may approach these Islands, and the Island of Brunet, within a quarter of a Mile all round, there being no Danger but what lay very near the Shore.

Plate

[8]

Plate Iſlands. *Plate Iſlands* are three Rocks of a moderate Height, lying S. W. 1 League from the Weſt-end of *Great Brunet*. The Southermoſt and outermoſt of theſe Rocks lay W. by S. half S. 11 Miles from Cape *Miquelon*, and in a direct Line between *Point May* and *Paſs Iſland*, 17 Miles from the former, and 19 from the latter; S. E. a quarter of a Mile from the *Great Plate* (which is the Northern-moſt) is a funken Rock, whereon the Sea breaks, which is the only Danger about them.

Obſervations. There are ſeveral ſtrong and irregular Settings of the Tides or Currents about the *Plate* and *Brunet Iſlands*, which ſeem to have no Dependency on the Moon, and the Courſe of the Tides on the Coaſt.

Iſland of Segona. The Iſland of *Segona*, which lies N. N. E. two Leagues from the Eaſt-end of *Brunet*, is about 3 Miles and a half in Circuit, of a moderate Height, and bold too all round; at the S. W. End is a ſmall Creek that will admit Fiſhing Shallops; in the Middle of the Entrance is a funken Rock, which makes it exceeding narrow, and difficult to get in or out, except in fine Weather.

Point May. *Point May* is the Southern Extremity of *Fortune Bay*, and the S. W. Extremity of this Part of *Newfoundland*; it may be known by a great Black Rock, nearly joining to the Pitch of the Point, and ſomething higher than the Land, which makes it look like a black Hommock on the Point; near a quarter of a Mile right off from the Point, or this round black Rock, are three funken Rocks, whereon the Sea always breaks.

Dantzick Coves. Near 2 Miles North from *Point May*, is *Little Dantzick Cove*, and half a League from *Little Dantzick* is *Great Dantzick Cove*; theſe Coves are no Places of Safety, being open to the Weſterly Winds; the Land about them is of a moderate Height, bold too, and clear of Wood.

Fortune. From *Dantzick Point* (which is the North Point of the Coves) to *Fortune* the Courſe is N. E. near 3 Leagues; the Land between them near the Shore is of a moderate Height, and bold too; you will have in moſt Places 10 and 12 Fathom two Cables Length from the Shore, 30 and 40 one Mile off, and 70 and 80 two Miles off. *Fortune* lies North from the Eaſt-end of *Brunet*; it is a Bar Place that will admit Fiſhing Boats at a quarter Flood; and a Fiſhing Village ſituated in the Bottom of a ſmall Bay, wherein is Anchorage for Shipping in 6, 8, 10, and 12 Fathom; the Ground is none of the beſt, and you lay open to near half the Compaſs.

Grand Bank. Cape of *Grand Bank* is a pretty high Point, lying 1 League N. E. from *Fortune*; into the Eaſtward of the Cape is *Ship Cove*, wherein is good Anchorage for Shipping, in 8 and 10 Fathom, ſhelter'd from Southerly, Weſterly and N. W. Winds. *Grand Bank* lies E. S. E. half a League from the Cape; it is a Fiſhing Village, and a Bar Harbour, that will admit of Fiſhing Shallops at a quarter Flood; to this Place and *Fortune*, reſort the Crews of Fiſhing Ships, who lay

their

their Ships up in Harbour *Britain*. From the Cape of *Grand Bank* to Point *Enragee*, the Course is N. E. a quarter E. 8 Leagues, forming a Bay between them, in which the Shore is low, with several sandy Beaches, behind which are Bar Harbours that will admit Boats on the Tide of Flood, the largest of which is *Great Garnish*, 5 Leagues from *Grand Bank*; it may be known by several Great Gar- Rocks above Water lying before it; 2 Miles from the Shore, the outmost of nish. these Rocks are steep too, but between them and the Shore are dangerous sunken Rocks. To the Eastward, and within these Rocks is *Frenchman's Cove*, wherein Frenchman's you may anchor with small Vessels, in 4 and 5 Fathom Water, tolerably well Cove. sheltered from the Sea Winds, and seems a convenient Place for the Cod Fishery: The Passage in is to the Eastward of the Rocks that are the highest above Water; between them and some other lower Rocks lying off to the Eastward from the East Point of the *Cove*, there is a sunken Rock nearly in the Middle of this Passage, which you must be aware of. You may anchor any where un- Anchorage. der the Shore, between *Grand Bank* and *Great Garnish* in 8 and 10 Fathom Water, but you are only sheltered from the Land Winds.

Point Enragee is but low, but a little way in the Country is high Land; Point Enra- this Point may be known by two Hummocks upon it close to the Shore, but gee. you must be very near, otherwise the Elevation of the high Lands will hinder you from discovering them; close to the Point is a Rock under Water.

From *Point Enragee* to the Head of the Bay, the Course is first N. E. a quarter E. 3 Leagues to *Grand Jervey*; then N. E. by E. half E. 7 Leagues and a half to the Head of the Bay; the Land in general along the South Side is high, bold too, and of an uneven Height, with Hills and Vallies of various Extent; the Vallies for the most Part cloathed with Wood, and watered with small Rivulets.

Seven Leagues to the Eastward of *Point Enragee*, is the Bay *L'Argent*, where- Bay L'Argent; in you may anchor in 30 or 40 Fathom Water, sheltered from all Winds.

The Entrance of Harbour *Millee* is to the Eastward of the East Point of Harbour Mil- *L'Argent*; before this Harbour and the Bay *L'Argent* is a remarkable Rock, lee. that at a Distance appears like a Shallop under Sail. *Harbour Millee* branches into two Arms, one laying into the N. E. and the other towards the E. at the upper Part of both is good Anchorage, and various Sorts of Wood. Between this Harbour and *Point Enragee*, are several Bar Harbours in small Bays, wherein are sandy Beaches, off which Vessels may anchor, but they must be very near the Shore to be in a moderate Depth of Water.

Cape Millee lies N. N. E. half E. 1 League from the afore-mentioned *Shallop* Cape Millee. *Rock*, and near 3 Leagues from the Head of *Fortune Bay* is a high reddish barren Rock. The Width of *Fortune Bay* at *Cape Millee* doth not exceed half a League, but immediately below it, it is twice as wide, by which this Cape may easily be known; above this Cape the Land on both Sides is high, with

B steep

steep craggy Cliffs. The Head of the Bay is terminated by a low Beach, behind which is a large Pond or Bar Harbour, into which Boats can go at quarter Flood. In this and all the Bar Harbours between it and *Grand Bank*, are convenient Places for building of Stages, and good Beaches for drying of Fish, for great Numbers of Boats.

Grand L'Pi- *Grand L'Pierre* is a good Harbour, situated on the North Side of the Bay,
erre Harbour. half a League from the Head, you can see no Entrance until you are abreast of it; there is not the least Danger in going in, and you may anchor in any Depth from 8 to 4 Fathom, sheltered from all Winds.

English Har- *English Harbour* lies a little to the Westward of *Grand L'Pierre*, it is very
bour. small, and fit only for Boats and small Vessels.

Little Bay de To the Westward of *English Harbour* is a small Bay called *Little Bay de Leau*,
Leau. wherein are some small Islands, behind which is Shelter for small Vessels.

New Harbour. This Harbour is situated opposite *Cape Millee*, to the Westward of *Bay de Leau*; it is but a small Inlet, yet hath good Anchorage on the West Side in 9, 8, 7, and 5 Fathom Water sheltered from the S. W. Winds.

Harbour Harbour *Femme*, which lies half a League to the Westward of *New Harbour*,
Femme. lies in N. E. half a League, it is very narrow, and hath in it 23 Fathom Water; before the Entrance is an Island, near to which are some Rocks above Water: The Passage into the Harbour is to the Eastward of the Island.

Brewer's One League to the Westward of *Harbour Femme*, is a small Cove called
Hole. *Brewer's Hole*, wherein is Shelter for Fishing Boats; before this Cove is a small Island near the Shore, and some Rocks above Water.

Harbour la This Harbour is situated one Mile to the Westward of *Brewer's Hole*, be-
Coute. fore which are two Islands, one without the other; the outermost, which is the largest, is of a tolerable Height, and lies in a Line with the Coast, and is not easy to be distinguished from the Main in sailing along the Shore. To sail into this Harbour, the best Passage is on the West Side of the outer Island, and between the two; as soon as you begin to open the Harbour, you must keep the inner Island close on Board, in order to avoid some sunken Rocks that lay near a small Island, which you will discover between the N. E. Point of the outer Island, and the opposite Point on the Main; and likewise another Rock under Water, which lays higher up on the Side of the Main; this Rock appears at Low Water. As soon as you are above these Dangers, you may steer up in the Middle of the Channel, until you open a fine spacious Bason, wherein you may anchor in any Depth from 5 to 17 Fathom Water, shut up from all Winds; the Bottom is Sand and Mud. In to the Eastward of the outer Island, is a small Cove fit for small Vessels and Boats, and Conveniencies for the Fishery.

This

[11]

This Harbour lies 4 Miles to the Westward of Harbour *La Conte*, and N. E. by N. 5 Leagues from *Point Enragee*; it may be known by a small Island in the Mouth of it, called *Gull Island*; and half a Mile without this Island, is a Rock above Water, that hath the Appearance of a small Boat. There is a Passage into the Harbour on each Side of the Island, but the broadest is the Westermost. Nearly in the Middle of this Passage, a little without the Island, is a Ledge of Rocks, whereon is two Fathom Water; a little within the Island on the S. E. are some sunken Rocks, about two Cables Length from the Shore, laying off two sandy Coves; some of these Rocks appear at Low-water. On the N. W. Side of the Harbour, two Miles within the Island is *Morgan's Cove*, wherein you may anchor in 15 Fathom Water, and the only Place you can anchor, unless you run into, or above the *Narrows*, being every where else very deep Water. This Harbour runs five Leagues into the Country, at the Head of which is a Salmon Fishery. Long Harbour.

A little to the Westward of *Long Harbour* is *Bell Bay*, which extends three Leagues every Way, and contains several Bays and Harbours. On the East Point of this Bay is *Hare Harbour*, which is fit only for small Vessels and Boats, before which are two small Islands, and some Rocks above and under Water. Bell Bay, and its contain'd Bays and Harbours. Hare Harbour.

Two Miles to the Northward of *Hare Harbour*, or the Point of *Bell Bay*, is *Mall Bay*, being a narrow Arm, laying in N. E. by N. 5 Miles, wherein is deep Water, and no Anchorage until at the Head. Mall Bay.

Rencontre Islands lie to the Westward of *Mall Bay*, near the Shore; the Westermost, which is the largest, hath a Communication with the Main at low Water: In and about this Island are Shelter for small Vessels and Boats. Rencontre Islands.

Bell Harbour lies one League to the Westward of *Rencontre* Islands: The Passage into the Harbour is on the West Side of the Island; in the Mouth of it, as soon as you are within the Island, you will open a small Cove on the East Side, wherein small Vessels anchor, but large Ships must run up to the Head of the Harbour, and anchor in 20 Fathom Water, there being most Room. Bell Harbour.

Lally Cove lies a little to the Westward of *Bell Harbour*; it is a very snug Place for small Vessels, being covered from all Winds behind the Island in the Cove. Lally Cove.

Lally Head is the West Point of *Lally Cove*; it is a high bluff white Point: To the Northward of the Head is *Lally Cove back Cove*, wherein you may anchor in 16 Fathom Water. Lally Cove Back Cove.

Two Miles to the Northward of *Lally Cove Head*, is the Bay of the East, and Bay of the North; in both is deep Water, and no Anchorage, unless very near the Shore. At the Head of the North Bay is the largest River in *Fortune Bay*, and seems a good Place for a Salmon Fishery. Bay of the East, and Bay of the North.

B 2 The

[12]

Bay of Cinq Ifles. The Bay of *Cinq Ifles* lies to the Southward of the North Bay; and opposite to *Lally Cove Head* there is tolerable good Anchorage for large Ships on the S. W. Side of the Islands in the Bottom of the Bay. The North Arm is a very snug Place for small Vessels; at the Head of this Arm is a Salmon River.

Corben Bay. A little to the Southward of the Bay of *Cinq Ifles* is *Corben Bay*, wherein is good Anchorage for any Ships in 22 or 24 Fathom Water.

Bell and Dog Islands. South-East about two Miles from *Lally Cove Head*, are two Island about a Mile from each other; the North-eastermost is called *Bell Island*, and the other *Dog Island*; they are of a tolerable Height, and bold too all round.

Between *Dog Island* and *Lord and Lady Island*, which lies off the South Point of *Corben Bay*, is a sunken Rock, (somewhat nearer to *Lord and Lady*, than *Dog Island*) whereon the Sea breaks in very bad Weather, and every where round it very deep Water. About a Quarter of a Mile to the Northward of the North End of *Lord and Lady Island*, is a Rock that appears at low Water.

Bande de La-rier Bay and Harbour. *Bande de La'rier* Bay lies on the West Point of *Bell Bay*, and N. N. W. half W. near 3 Leagues from *Point Enragee*, it may be known by a very high Mountain over the Bay, which rises almost perpendicular from the Sea, called *Iron Head*. *Chappel Island*, which forms the East Side of the Bay, is high Land also. The Harbour lies on the West Side of the Bay, just within the Point, formed by a narrow low Beach; it is very small, but a snug Place, and conveniently situated for the *Cod Fishery*. There is a tolerable good Anchorage along the West Side of the Bay, from the Harbour up towards *Iron Head* in 18 and 20 Fathom Water.

Bande de La-rier Bank. The Bank of *Bande de La'rier*, whereon is no less than 7 Fathom, lies with the Beach of *Bande de Laurier* Harbour, just open of the West Point of the Bay, and *Poxy Point* on with the North End of St. *Jaques* Island.

St. Jaques. Two Miles to the Westward of *Bande de La'rier*, is the Harbour of St. *Jaques*, which may be easily known by the Island before it. This Island is high at each End, and low in the Middle, and at a Distance looks like two Islands, it lies N. god. E. 8 and a half Leagues from the Cape of *Grand Bank*, and N. E. by E. 7 Leagues from the East End of *Brunet*. The Passage into the Harbour is on the West Side of the Island; there is not the least Danger in going in, or in any Part of the Harbour; you may anchor in any Depth from 17 to 4 Fathom.

Blue Pinion. Two Miles to the Westward of St. *Jaques* is the Harbour of *Blue Pinion*; it is not near so large, or so safe as that of St. *Jaques*; near to the Head of the Harbour, on the West Side, is a Shoal, whereon is two Fathom at Low Water.

English Cove. A little to the Westward of *Blue Pinion* is *English Cove*, which is very small, wherein small Vessels and Boats can anchor; before it, and very near the Shore, is a small Island.

Bexy

[13]

Boxy Point lies S. W. by W. a quarter W. two Leagues and a half from St. *Jaques* Island, N. N. E. near 7 Leagues from the Cape of *Grand Bank*, and N. E. half E. 13 Miles from the East End of *Brunet* Island; it is of a moderate Height, the most advanced to the Southward of any Land on the Coast, and may be distinguished at a considerable Distance; there are some sunken Rocks off it, but they lay very near the Shore, and are no ways dangerous.

_{Boxy Point.}

N. N. E. three Miles from *Boxy* Point, is the Harbour of *Boxy*; to sail into it you must keep *Boxy* Point just open of *Fryer's* Head; (a black Head a little within the Point) in this Direction you will keep in the Middle of the Channel between the Shoals which lay off from each Point of the Harbour, where the Stages are; as soon as you are within these Shoals, which cover you from the Sea Winds, you may anchor in 5 and 4 Fathom Water, fine sandy Ground.

_{Boxy Harbour.}

West 1 Mile from *Boxy* Point is the Island of St. *John's*, which is of a tolerable Height, and steep too, except at the N. E. Point, where is a Shoal a little way off.

_{St. John's Island, Head, Bay and Harbour.}

N. W. half a League from St. *John's Island*, is St. *John's Head*, which is a high, steep, craggy Point. Between St. *John's Head* and *Boxy Point* is St. *John's Bay*, in the Bottom of which is St. *John's Harbour*, wherein is only Water for Boats.

On the North Side of St. *John's Head* are two rocky Islands, called the *Gull* and *Shag*; at the West End of these Islands are some sunken Rocks.

_{Gull and Shag.}

One League and a half to the Northward of St. *John's Head* is the *Great Bay de Leau*, wherein is good Anchorage in various Depths of Water, sheltered from all Winds. The best Passage in is on the East Side of the Island, laying in the Mouth of it; nothing can enter in on the West Side but small Vessels and Shallops.

_{Great Bay de Leau.}

To the Westward of *Bay de Leau*, 3 Miles N. N. W. from St. *John's Head* is *Little Bay Barrysway*, on the West Side of which is good Anchorage for large Ships in 7, 8, or 10 Fathom Water; here is good Fishing Conveniencies, with plenty of Wood and Water.

_{Little Bay Barrysway.}

Harbour Briton lies to the Westward of *Little Bay Barrysway*, North 1 League and a half from the Island of *Sagena*, and N. by E. from East End of *Brunet*. The two Heads, which from the Entrance of this Harbour or Bay are pretty high, and lay from each other E. N. E. and W. S. W. above 2 Miles; near the East Head is a Rock above Water, by which it may be known: There are no Dangers in going in until you are the Length of the South Point of the S. W. Arm, which is more than a Mile within the West Head; from off this Point stretches out a Ledge of Rocks N. E. about two Cables Length; the only Place for King's Ships to anchor is above this Point, before the S. W. Arm in

_{Harbour Briton.}

16 or 18 Fathom Water, mooring nearly East and West, and so near the Shore as to have the East Head on with the Point above-mentioned; the Bottom is very good, and the Place convenient for wooding and watering. In the S. W. Arm is Room for a great Number of Merchant Ships, and many Conveniencies for Fishing Vessels.

South West Arm.

Opposite to the S. W. Arm is the N. E. Arm, or *Jerseyman*'s Harbour, which is capable of holding a great Number of Ships, securely shelter'd from all Winds. To sail into it you must keep the Point of *Thompson*'s *Beach* (which is the Beach Point, at the Entrance into the S. W. Arm) open of *Jerseyman*'s *Head*, (which is a high bluff Head at the North Entrance into *Jerseyman*'s *Harbour*) this Mark will lead you over the Bar in the best of the Channel, where you will have 3 Fathom at low-water; as soon as you open the Harbour, haul up North, and anchor where 'tis most convenient in 8, 7 or 6 Fathom Water, good Ground, and shelter'd from all Winds. In this Harbour are several convenient Places for erecting many Stages, and good Beach room. *Jerseymen* generally lay their Ships up in this Harbour, and cure their Fish at *Fortune* and *Grand Bank*.

Jerseyman's Harbour.

From Harbour *Briton* to the W. End of *Brunet*, and to the *Plate Islands*, the Course is S. W. by S. 6 Leagues and a half to the Southermost *Plate*. From the *Harbour Briton* to Cape *Miquelon* is S. W. a quarter W. 10 Leagues. From the West Head of *Harbour Briton* to *Cannaigre Head*, the Course is W. by S. distant 2 Leagues; between them are *Gull Island* and *Deadman's Bay*. *Gull-Island* lies close under the Land, 2 Miles to the westward of Harbour *Briton*. *Deadman's Bay* is to the westward of *Gull-Island*, wherein you may anchor with the Land Winds. Between *Harbour Briton* and *Cannaigre Head*, is a Bank stretching off from the Shore between 2 and 3 Miles, whereon is various Depths of Water from 34 to 4 Fathom. Fishermen say that they have seen the Sea break in very bad Weather, a good Way without *Gull-Island*.

Gull Island, and Deadman's Bay.

Cannaigre Head, which forms the East Point of the Bay of the same Name, lies North Easterly 3 Leagues and a half from the West end of *Brunet*; it is a high craggy Point, easy to be distinguished from any Point of View. From this Head to *Bassterre* Point, the Course is W. by N. half N. 2 Leagues, and likewise W. by N. half N. 3 Leagues and a half to the Rocks of *Pass Island*; but to give them a Birth make a W. by N. Course good. Between *Cannaigre Head* and *Bassterre Point* is *Cannaigre Bay*, which extends itself about 4 Leagues in Land, at the Head of which is a Salmon River. In the Mouth of the Bay lay the Rocks of the same Name above Water; you may approach these Rocks very near, there being no Danger but what discovers itself. The Channel between them and the North Shore is something dangerous, by reason of a Range of Rocks which lie along Shore, and extend themselves 1 Mile off.

Cannaigre Head.

Cannaigre Bay.

Cannaigre Rocks.

Cannaigre Harbour, which is very small, with 7 Fathom Water in it, is within a Point on the South Side of the Bay, 5 Miles above the Head: The Passage into the Harbour is on the S. E. Side of the Island, lying before it. Nearly in the

Cannaigre Harbour.

the Middle of the Bay, abreaſt of this Harbour, are two Iſlands of a tolerable Height; on the South-ſide of the Weſtermoſt Iſland, which is the largeſt, are ſome Rocks above Water.

This Cove is on the N. W. Side of the Bay, bears North, Diſtance about 4 Miles from the Head, and Eaſt 2 Miles from the W. End of the *Great Iſland*. In it are good Fiſhing Conveniencies, and Anchorage for Veſſels in 6 and 5 Fathom Water, but they will lay open to the ſoutherly Winds. Between the S. W. Point of this Cove and *Baſstarre Point*, which is 5 Miles Diſtance, lays the Range of Rocks before-mentioned. Dawſon's Cove.

Baſstarre Point, which forms the Weſt Point of *Cannaigre Bay*, is of a moderate Height, clear of Wood, and bold too, all the Way from it to *Paſs-Iſland*, which bears N. W. by W. 1 League from *Baſstarre Point*. Baſstarre Point.

The Land on the North-ſide of *Fortune Bay*, for the moſt Part, is hilly, riſing directly from the Sea, with craggy, barren Hills, which extends 4 or 5 Leagues inland, with a great Number of Rivulets and Ponds. The Land on the South-ſide of *Fortune Bay*, has a different Appearance to that on the North-ſide, being not ſo full of craggy Mountains, and better cloathed with Woods, which are of a ſhort bruſhy Kind, which makes the Face of the Country look green. Obſervations.

Paſs Iſland lies N. 16° 30′ Eaſt, 7 Leagues and a half from Cape *Miquelon*; it is the N. W. Extremity of *Fortune Bay*, and lies very near the Shore, is more than 2 Miles in Circuit, and is pretty high. On the S. W. Side are ſeveral Rocks above Water, which extend themſelves 1 Mile from the Iſland; and on the N. W. Side is a ſunken Rock, at a quarter of a Mile from the Iſland: The Paſſage between this Iſland and the Main, which is near two Cables Length wide, is very ſafe for ſmall Veſſels, wherein you may anchor in 6 Fathom, a fine ſandy Bottom. This Iſland is well ſituated for the Cod Fiſhery, there being very good Fiſhing Ground about it. Paſs Iſland.

In the Night-time, or in foggy Weather, Ships ought to place no great Dependance on the Soundings in *Fortune Bay*, leſt they may be deceived thereby; for you have more Water in many Parts near the Shore, and in ſeveral of its contained Bays and Harbours, than in the Middle of the Bay itſelf. On the Soundings.

Deſcription of *Hermitage Bay*.

From *Paſs Iſland* to *Great Jarvis Harbour*, at the Entrance into the Bay of *Deſpair*, the Courſe is N. by E. a quarter E near three Leagues; and from *Paſs Iſland* to the Weſt End of *Long iſland*, the Courſe is NNE. 8 Miles, between them is the Bay of *Hermitage*, which lies in ENE. 8 Leagues from *Paſs Iſland*, with very deep Water in moſt Parts of it.

Fox Islands.	The two *Fox Islands*, which are but small, lie nearly in the Middle of *Hermitage Bay*, 3 Leagues and a half from *Pass Island*; near to these Islands is good Fishing Ground.
Hermitage Cove.	*Hermitage Cove* is on the South-side of the Bay, opposite to *Fox's Islands*. To sail into it, you must keep between the Islands and the South Shore, where there is not the least Danger; in this Cove is good Anchorage for Shipping in 8 and 10 Fathom Water, and good Fishing Conveniencies, with Plenty of Wood and Water.
Long Island.	*Long Island*, which separates the Bay of *Despair* from *Hermitage*, is of a triangular Form, about 8 Leagues in Circuit, of a tolerable Height, is hilly, uneven, and barren. The East Entrance into the Bay of *Despair* from *Hermitage Bay*, is by the West-end of *Long Island*; about half a Mile from the S. W. Point of the said Island, are two Rocks above Water, with deep Water all round them.
Long Island Harbour.	This Harbour lies on the South Side of *Long Island*, 2 Miles and a half from the West-end; before which is an Island, and several Rocks above Water; there is a narrow Passage into the Harbour on each Side of the Island; this Harbour is formed by two Arms, one laying into the North, and the other to the Eastward; they are both very narrow, and have in them from 42 to 7 Fathom Water; the East Arm is the deepest, and the best Anchorage.
Round Harbour.	This Harbour, wherein is 6 Fathom Water, lies near 2 Miles to the Eastward of *Long Island Harbour*, is also in *Long Island*; it will only admit very small Vessels, by reason the Channel going in is very narrow.
Picarre.	*Harbour Picarre* lies N. by W. half a League from *Little Fox Island*, (which is the Westermost of *Fox Islands*;) to sail into it you must keep near the West-point, to avoid some sunken Rocks off the other, and anchor in the first Cove on the East-side in 9 or 10 Fathom, sheltered from all Winds.
Galtaus.	This Harbour, which is but small, lies near the East-point of *Long-Island*; at the Entrance is several rocky Islands. The best Channel into the Harbour is on the West-side of these Islands, wherein is 4 Fathom Water, but in the Harbour is from 15 to 24 Fathom. Here are several Places proper for erecting of Stages; and both this Harbour and *Picarre* are conveniently situated for a Fishery, they lying contiguous to the Fishing Ground about *Fox Islands*.
Passage of Long Island.	Between the East end of *Long Island* and the Main, is a very good Passage out of *Hermitage Bay*, into the Bay of *Despair*.

Description of the Bay of *Despair*.

The Entrance of the Bay of *Despair* lies between the West-end of *Long-Island* and *Great Jervis Island*, (an Island in the Mouth of the Harbour of the same Name;) the Distance from one to the other is 1 Mile and a quarter, and in the Middle between them is no Soundings with 280 Fathoms.

[17]

The Bay of *Defpair* forms two capacious Arms, one extending to the N. E. 8 Leagues, and the other to the Northward 5 Leagues: In the North Arm is very deep Water, and no Anchorage, but in the fmall Bays and Coves which lay on each Side of it. At the Head of the Bay of the Eaft, which is an Arm of the North Bay, is a very fine Salmon River, and plenty of Wood. In the N. E. Arm of the Bay of *Defpair* are feveral Arms and Iflands, and tolerable good Anchorage in fome Parts of it. *Little River* and *Conne River* are counted good Places for Salmon Fifheries: About thefe Rivers and the Head of the Bay are great plenty of all Sorts of Wood common to this Country, fuch as Fir, Pine, Birch, Witch-Hafle, Spruce, &c. All the Country about the Entrance into the Bay of *Defpair*, and for a good way up it, is very mountainous and barren, but about the Head of the Bay it appears to be pretty level, and well cloathed with Wood.

Great Jervis Harbour is fituated at the Weft Entrance into the Bay of *Def-* Great Jervis *pair*, is a fnug and fafe Harbour, with good Anchorage in every Part of it, in 16, Harbour. 18 or 20 Fathom, though but fmall, will contain a great Number of Shipping, fecurely fheltered from all Winds, and very convenient for wooding and watering. There is a Paffage into this Harbour on either Side of *Great Jervis Ifland*, the fouthermoft is the fafeft, there being in it no Danger but the Shore itfelf. To fail in on the North Side of the Ifland, you muft keep in the Middle of the Paffage, until you are within two fmall Rocks above Water near to each other on your Starboard Side, a little within the North Point of the Paffage; you muft then bring the faid North Point between thefe Rocks, and fteer into the Harbour, in that Direction will carry you clear of fome funken Rocks which lie off the Weft Point of the Ifland; thefe Rocks appear at Low-Water. The Entrance into this Harbour may be known by the Eaft End of *Great Jervis Ifland*, which is a high fteep craggy Point, called *Great Jervis Head*, and is the North Point of the South Entrance into the Harbour.

Bonne Bay lies one League to the Weftward from *Great Jervis-Head*, and Bonne Bay. North 7 Miles from *Pafs Ifland*, there are feveral Iflands in the Mouth of it, the Weftermoft of which is the largeft and higheft. The beft Paffage into the Bay is to the Eaftward of the largeft Ifland, between it and the two Eaftermoft Iflands; which two Iflands may be known by a Rock above Water off the South Point of each of them. The Bay lies in N. N. W. 4 Miles, and is near half a Mile broad in the narroweft Part; there is no Danger going in, but what fhews itfelf; you may go on either Side of *Drake Ifland*, which is a fmall Ifland nearly in the Middle of the Bay; between this Ifland, and two fmall Iflands, lying on the Weft Side of the Bay within *Great Ifland*, is Anchorage in 20 and 30 Fathom, but the beft Place for large Ships is at the Head of the Bay in 12 or 14 Fathom clear Ground, and convenient for wooding and watering. On the Weft Side of the Bay, a-breaft of *Drake Ifland*, is a very fnug Harbour for fmall Veffels, wherein is 7 Fathom Water, and good Conveniencies

C for

for a Fishery; off the South Point of the Entrance are some sunken Rocks about a Cable's Length from the Shore. On the N. W. Side of the great Island, within the two small Islands is very good Anchorage in 16, 20 and 24 Fathom Water, sheltered from all Winds. The Passage into this Place to the Westward of the great Island from the Sea is very dangerous, by reason there are several sunken Rocks in the Passage, and shallow Water; but there is a very good Passage into it from the Bay, passing to the Northward of the two small Islands, between them and the West Shore. In sailing in or out of the Bay you must not approach too near the South Point of the *Great Island*, because of some sunken Rocks, which lie a Quarter of a Mile from the Shore.

Musketa Cove.
A little to the Westward of *Bonne Bay*, between it and *Facheux* is *Musketa Cove*, a small Inlet wherein is from 30 to 47 Fathom Water.

Bay of Facheux, and Bay of the Dragon.
The Entrance to the Bays of *Facheux* and *Dragon*, lies West 4 Miles from *Bonne Bay*, and N. W. by N. near 3 Leagues from *Pass Island*; this Entrance is very conspicuous at Sea, by which this Part of the Coast is easily known. *Facheux*, which is the Eastermost Branch, lies in North 2 Leagues, and is one-third of a Mile broad in the narrowest Part, which is at the Entrance, with deep Water in most Parts of it. One Mile up the Bay on the West Side is a Cove, wherein is Anchorage in 10 Fathom, with gradual Soundings into the Shore, and a clear Bottom; and farther up the Bay, on the same Side, are two other Coves wherein is Anchorage, and plenty of Wood and Water. *Dragon Bay* lies in W. N. W. one League, and is near half a Mile broad, wherein is 60 and 70 Fathom Water, and no Anchorage till you come to the Head, and then you must be very near the Shore to be in a moderate Depth of Water.

Little Hole and Richard's Harbour.
One Mile to the Westward of *Facheux* is *Little Hole*, wherein is Shelter for Shallops. And one League to the Westward of *Facheux* is *Richard*'s Harbour, a snug Place for small Vessels, and fishing Shallops, wherein is not more than 23 Fathom. The East Point of this Harbour is a very conspicuous high Head, lying W. half S. 7 Miles from *Bonne Bay*, and N. W. a Quarter W. 3 Leagues from *Pass Island*.

Hare Bay.
W. by N. one League and a half from *Richard*'s Harbour, is *Hare Bay*, which lies in North about 5 Miles, is about one-third of a Mile broad in the narrowest Part, with very high Land on both Sides, and deep Water close home to both Shores in most Parts of it. Near one Mile up the Bay, on the East Side, is a small Cove wherein is Anchorage in 20 Fathom, with gradual Soundings into the Shore; and one League up the Bay, on the West Side, is a very good Harbour, wherein is good Anchorage in 8, 10, 12 and 15 Fathom, and plenty of Wood and Water.

W. by N. 4 Miles from *Hare Bay*, and one League N. by W. from *Hare's-* Devil Bay.
Ears Point is *Devil's Bay*, a narrow Inlet lying in to the Northward one League,
wherein is deep Water, and no Anchorage till you come clofe to the Head.

The Bay of *Recontre*, which lies to the Northward of *Hare's-Ears* Point lies Bay of R:-
in W. by N. 2 Leagues, it is near half a Mile broad in the narroweft Part, with contre.
deep Water in moft Parts of it. To anchor in this Bay, you muft run up above
a low woody Point on the South-fide, then haul under the South Shore until you
are landlocked, and anchor in 30 Fathom Water.

Hare's-Ears Point is a pretty large Point, with a ragged Rock upon it, that Hare's-Ears
from fome Points of View looks like the Ears of a Hare; it lies Weft Southerly Point.
11 Miles from the Point of *Richard's Harbour*, and W. by N. half N. 6 Leagues
from *Pafs Ifland*; off this Point is a Fifhing Bank that extends a Mile from the
Shore, whereon is from 20 to 36 Fathom Water.

One Mile to the Northward of *Hare's-Ears* Point, at the S. W. Entrance into New Har-
Recontre, is *New Harbour*, a fmall Harbour, wherein is Anchorage for fmall bour.
Veffels in 16 Fathom Water, and good Conveniencies for a Fifhery.

Weft 2 Miles from *Hare's-Ears* Point is the Bay of *Chaleur*, which lies in firft Bay of Cha-
N. W. then more Northerly, in the whole 2 Leagues; it is about half a Mile leur.
broad, and hath very deep Water in moft Parts. At the North Entrance into
the Bay, clofe to the Shore, is a fmall Ifland of a tolerable Height; and half a
League within the Ifland, on the N. E. Side of the Bay, is a Rock above Wa-
ter; a little within this Rock, on the fame Side, is a fmall Cove with a fandy
Beach, off which you may anchor in 28 Fathom, a Cable's Length from the
Shore.

W. S. W. near half a League from the Bay of *Chaleur*, is the Bay *Francois*, Bay Francois
which is a fmall Inlet, lying in N. N. W. half W. one Mile; it is near a quarter
of a Mile broad at the Entrance, and 17 Fathom deep; but juft within is 50
and 60 Fathom; at the Head is from 30 to 20 Fathom, good Anchorage, and
Conveniencies for a Fifhery.

W. S. W. 4 Miles from the Bay *Francois*, on the Eaft-fide of Cape *La Hune*, Oar Bay.
lies *Oar Bay*; off the Eaft Point of the Entrance is a low rocky Ifland, clofe to
the Shore; from this Point, to the Entrance into the Bay of *Defpair*, the Courfe
is W. three-quarters N. 9 Leagues. In the Mouth of this Bay is a rocky Ifland,
and a Paffage on each Side of it. The Bay lies in firft N. N. E. near one
League, then North 2 Miles; it is one-third of a Mile broad in the narroweft
Part, with deep Water clofe to both Shores all the Way up; the leaft Water is

at the Entrance. At the Head is a small snug Harbour, fit only for small Vessels, and Fishing Shallops, wherein is 5 Fathom Water. At the West-side of the Entrance into the Bay N. W. by N. from the Rocky Island before-mentioned, is a small snug Cove, call'd *Cul de Sac*, wherein is 3 and 4 Fathom Water, and good Shelter for Fishing Vessels.

Cape La Hune.

Cape la Hune is the Southermost Point of Land on this Part of the Coast, and lies in the Latitude of 47 D. 31 M. 42″ North. West half North from *Pass Island*, and N. W. half N. 10¼ Leagues from Cape *Miquelon*; it may be easily known by its Figure, which much resembles a Sugar Loaf; but in order to distinguish this, you must approach the Shore at least within 3 Leagues, (unless you are directly to the Eastward or Westward of it) otherwise the Elevation of the high Land within it will hinder you from distinguishing the Sugar Loaf Hill; but the Cape may always be known by the high Land of *La Hune*, which lies one League to the Westward of it; this Land rises directly from the Sea, to a tolerable Height, appears pretty flat at Top, and may be seen in clear Weather 16 Leagues.

Penguin Islands.

South 29 D. W. 3 and half Leagues from Cape *La Hune*, and North 61 D. West near 10 Leagues from Cape *Miquelon* lies the *Penguin Islands*, which are a Parcel of barren Rocks laying near to each other, and altogether about 2 Leagues in Circuit; you may approach these Islands in the Day time to half a League all round, there being no Danger at that Distance off. On the S. W. Side of the large Island, which is the highest, is a small Cove, wherein is Shelter for Fishing Shallops, and good Conveniencies for a Fishery, and there is good Fishing Ground about the Islands.

Whale Rock.

East 3 D. North, 7 Miles from the *Penguin* Islands, and South 9 D. East 3 Leagues from Cape *La Hune* is a dangerous Rock, whereon the Sea generally breaks; it is about one hundred Fathom in Circuit, with 10 12, and 14 Fathom Water close to all round it. From this Rock stretches out a narrow Bank one League to the Westward, and half a League to the Eastward, whereon is from 24 to 58 Fathom, a rocky and gravelly Bottom. In the Channel between the Shore and this Rock, also between the Shore and the *Penguin* Islands is 120 and 130 Fathom Water, a muddy Bottom, and the same Bottom, and nearly the same Depth of Water one League without them.

La Hune Bay.

Round the West Point of Cape *La Hune* is *La Hune Bay*, which lies in North near 2 Leagues, and is about one-third of a Mile broad in the narrowest Part, which is at the Entrance, with deep Water in most Parts of it. In sailing in or out of the Bay you must keep the Cape, or East Shore on board, in order to avoid a sunken Rock, which lies off the West Point of the Entrance

into

into the Bay, near one third Channel over. Two Miles up the Bay, on the East-side, is *Lance* Cove, wherein is Anchorage in 16 and 14 Fathom Water, clear Ground, and good Conveniencies for a Fishery; one Cable's Length off from the South Point of the Cove, (which is low) is a small Shoal, whereon is one and half Fathom, and between it and the Point 5 Fathom Water. To sail into the Cove, keep the Point of the Cape, or East Entrance into the Bay open of a red Cliff Point on the same Side, (off which is a Rock above Water) until a round Hill you will see over the Valley of the Cove be brought on the North-side of the Valley; you will then be above the Shoal, and may haul into the Cove with Safety. There is a narrow Bank, which stretches quite across the Bay, from the South Point of the Cove, to a Point on the opposite Shore, whereon is from 27 to 45 Fathom.

La Hune Harbour, wherein is only room for the Admittance of small Vessels La Hune open to the Westerly Winds, lies half a League to the Westwards of Cape *La Harbour. Hune*, before which is an Island close under the Shore. The Passage into the Harbour is on the N. W. Side of the Island; there is no Danger in going in, and you must anchor close up to the Head in 10 Fathom Water. This Harbour is well situated for a Fishery, there being good Fishing Ground about it, and other Conveniencies, such as a large Beach, quite a-cross from the Head of the Harbour to *La Hune Bay*, which is eight hundred Feet, exposed to an open Air, which is a great Advantage for drying of Fish.

Between *Cape La Hune* and *Little River*, the Land is tolerable high, and the Two Islands Shore forms a Bay, wherein lie several small Islands and Rocks above Water; and Magnetic the outermost of which lies North 3 Leagues from the *Penguin Islands*; near Rocks. these Rocks, and within them are sunken Rocks, and foul Ground: The Passage is very safe between the Rocks and the *Penguin Islands*.

W. by S. 4. Leagues from Cape *La Hune*, is the Entrance of *Little River*, Little River. which may be known by the Land near it, which forms a very conspicuous Point on the Coast, and tolerable high; the River is about one hundred Fathom broad at the Entrance, and 10 Fathom deep, and affords good Ancherage, a little way up it in 10, 8, and 7 Fathom Water; its Banks are tolerable high, and cloathed with Wood.

South a quarter East 2 Leagues from the Entrance of *Little River*, N. W. Little River half N. 2 Leagues and a half from the *Penguin Islands*, and E.S.E. half E. 3 Rocks. Leagues and half from the Isles of *Ramea*, lie the *Little River Rocks*, which are just above Water, and of a very small Circuit, with very deep Water all round them.

The Isles of *Ramea*, which are of various Extent both for Height and Cir- Ramea Isles. cuit, lay N. W. half N. near 6 Leagues from the *Penguin Islands*, and one League
from

from the Main; they extend Eaft and Weft 5 Miles, and North and South 2 Miles; there are feveral Rocks and Breakers about them; but more on the South Side than the North; the Eaftermoft Ifland, which is the largeft, is very high and hilly; and the Weftermoft, called *Columbe*, is a remarkable high round Ifland, of a fmall Circuit, near to which are fome rocky Iflands, and funken Rocks.

The Harbour of *Ramea*, (which is a fmall commodious Harbour for Fifhing Veffels,) is form'd by the Iflands, which lie between Great *Ramea* and *Columbe*, the Entrance from the Weftward (which is the broadeft) lies Eaft from *Columbe*, give the South Point of the Entrance a fmall Birth (off which are fome Rocks above Water) and fteer N. E. into the Harbour, keeping in the Middle of the Channel, which is more than a Cable's Length broad in the narroweft Part, and anchor in *Ship Cove*, which is the fecond on the N. W. Side in 5 Fathom, clear Ground. and fhelter'd from all Winds. To fail into it from the Eaftward, keep the North fide of *Great Ramea* on board until you are at the Weft-end thereof, then fteer S. W. into the Harbour, keeping in the Middle of the Channel, wherein is 3 Fathom at Low-water, and anchor as above directed. In this Harbour, and about thefe Iflands are feveral convenient Places for erecting of Stages, and drying of Fifh, and feem well fituated for that Purpofe.

Fifhing Bank.
S. E. half S. 4 Miles from *Ramea*, are 2 Rocks above Water, clofe to each other, called *Ramea Rocks*: S. W. one League from thefe Rocks is a fmall Fifhing Bank, whereon is 6 Fathom Water; it lies with the Rocks above-mentioned, on with the Weft Entrance of *Little River*, bearing N. E. and *Ramea Columbe* on with a high Saddle Hill, (called *Richard's Head)* on the Main within the Ifles of *Burges*, bearing nearly N. W. Nearly in the Middle between *Ramea* and the *Penguin Iflands*, 2 Leagues from the Land, is a Fifhing Bank whereon is from 50 to 14 Fathom. To run upon the fhoalyeft Part of this Bank, bring the two *Ramea Rocks*, (which lie S. E. half S. from *Ramea Iflands*,) on with the S. W. Part of the Iflan's, or between them and *Columbe*, and the Entrance into *Little River* to bear N. by E. half E.

Old Man's Bay.
Four Miles to the Weftward of *Little River*, and N. E. by E. from *Ramea Iflands*, lies *Old Man's Bay*, which lies in North 7 Miles, and is a Mile broad at the Entrance, with deep Water in moft Parts of it. N. E. half a League up the Bay, on the Eaft-fide, is *Adam's Ifland*, behind which is Anchorage in 30 and 40 Fathom, but the beft Anchorage is at the Head of the Bay, in 14 and 16 Fathom.

Mufketa Harbour.
Half a League to the Weftward of *Old Man's Bay*, and N. E. from *Ramea Ifles*, is *Mufketa Harbour*, which is a very fnug and fafe Harbour, that will hold a great Number of Shipping in perfect Security; but it is difficult to get in or out unlefs the Wind is favourable, by reafon the Entrance is fo very narrow

(being

(being but 48 Fathom broad) and the Land high on both Sides; the S. E. Point of the Entrance into the Harbour is a high white Rock; near a Cable's Length from this white Rock, or Point is a black Rock above Water, on the South-side of which is a funken Rock, whereon the Sea breaks: From this black Rock to the narrow Entrance into the Harbour is N. W. one-third of a Mile. In sailing in or out of the Harbour, give the black Rock a small Birth, and keep the West-side most on board, it being the safest. If you are obliged to anchor, you must be very brisk in getting a Rope on Shore, lest you tail upon the Rocks. In the Harbour is from 18 to 30 Fathom, every where good Anchorage, and Plenty of Wood and Water, and Fishing Conveniencies. In the *Narrows* is 12 Fathom bold to both Shores there; with Southerly and Easterly Winds it blows right in, with Northerly Winds out, and with Westerly Winds it is either calm or blows in variable Puffs.

This Harbour, which is formed by an Island of the same Name, lies N. E. Fox Island by N. from *Ramea Isles*, and half a League to the Westward of *Musketa Har-* Harbour. *bour*; between them are several rocky Islands, and some funken Rocks. This Harbour may be known by a high white Rock, lying South half a Mile from the outer Part of the Island. There are two Passages into the Harbour, one on each Side of the Island, and no Danger in either of them but what discovers itself; it is a small commodious Harbour for the Fishery, wherein is 6, 8, and 10 Fathom Water, and some Beach.

White Bear Bay lies 2 Miles to the Westward of *Fox Island Harbour*, and White Bear North one League from *Ramea Isles*; there are several Islands in the Mouth of Bay. it. The best Passage into the Bay is to the Eastward of all the Islands; it lies in N. E. by E. half E. 4 Leagues, and is near half a Mile broad in the narrowest Part, with high Land on both Sides, and deep Water close to both Shores in most Parts of it, until you are 8 Miles up it, you will then rise the Ground at once to 9 Fathom, and will afterwards have gradual Soundings up to the Head, and good Anchorage. A little way inland from the Head of the Bay, you have a very extensive Prospect of the interior Part of the Country, which appears to be all a barren Rock of a pretty even Height, and watered by a great Numbr of Ponds, with which the who'e Country very much abounds. On the S. W. Side of *Bear Island* (which is the Eastermost and largest in the Mouth of the Bear Island Bay) is a small Harbour, lying in E. N. E. half a Mile, wherein is from 10 to Harbour. 22 Fathom Water. Before the Mouth of which are funken Rocks that doth not break but in bad Weather. At the West Entrance into *White Bear Bay* is a high round white Island; and S S. W. half a Mile from the *White Island* is a black Rock above Water. The best Passage into the Bay from the Westward is on the West-side of this Rock, and between the *White Island* and *Bear Island*; there are funken Rocks half a League to the Westward of the *White Island*, some of which are above a Mile from the Shore.

Five

Red Island Harbours.

Five Miles to the Westward of *White Bear Bay*, and N. by W. three-quarters W. from *Ramea Columbe*, are two small Harbours, called *Red Island Harbours*, form'd by an Island of the same Name, lying close under the Land; that lying to the Westward of the Island is the largest and best, wherein is from 10 to 6 Fathom good Anchorage. To sail into it, keep the Island close aboard; the outer Part of which is red steep Cliffs.

Burgeo Isles.

N. W. by W. 3 Leagues from *Ramea Columbe*, lay the *Burgeo Isles*, which are a Cluster of Islands extending along the Shore, East and West about five Miles, forming several snug and commodious Harbours amongst them for Fishing Vessels, and are well situated for that Purpose, there being good Fishing Ground about them. To sail into *Burgeo* from the Eastward, the safest Passage is on the N. E. Side of *Boar Island*, which is the Northermost, and lies N. W. from *Ramea Columbe*; S. E. by E. half a League from this Island is a Rock that uncovers at Low-water, on which the Sea generally breaks: You may go on any Side of this Rock, there being very deep Water all round it; as soon as you are to the N. W. of it, keep the North-side of *Bear Island* on board, and steer W. by S. half S. for *Grandy's Cove*. The North Point of which is the first low Point on your Starboard Bow, haul round that Point, and anchor in the Cove in 14 Fathom, and moor with a Fast on Shore; but the best Place for great Ships to anchor is betwixt *Grandy's Cove*, and a small Island lying near the W. Point of *Boar Island*, in 20 or 24 Fathom good Ground, and shelter'd from all Winds. To sail into *Grandy's Cove* from the Westward, within the Islands, it is dangerous, unless well acquainted, by reason of sunken Rocks in the Passage; but there is a good Passage from the Southward between *Burgeo Columbe*, which is a high round Island, and *Recontre*, (which is the highest of all the Islands) you must steer in North-West, between the Rocks above Water lying to the Eastward of *Columbe*, and then to the Southward of *Recentre*; as soon as you are within these Rocks keep the Islands on board: There are several safe Passages in from the Southward and Eastward, between the Islands, and good Anchorage; and in bad Weather all the sunken Rocks discover themselves, and you may run in any where without fear; these Isles do not abound with either Wood or Water.

Wolfe Bay.

This Bay lies in N. E. half N. one League, the Entrance is N. E. 2 Miles from *Bear Island*, and 2 Miles to the Westward of *Fox Island* Harbours; the E. Point of the Entrance is low ragged Rocks, off which is a sunken Rock, a quarter of a Mile from the Shore, whereon the Sea breaks in bad Weather. Near the Head of the Bay is tolerable good Anchorage, and Plenty of Wood and Water.

King's Harbour.

Round the West Point of *Wolfe Bay* is *King's Harbour*, which lies in N. E. by N. three-fourths of a Mile, before the Mouth of which is a Cluster of little Islands, one of which is pretty high. To sail into it, keep the East Point of

the

the Iflands on board, and fleer N. W. by N. and N. N. W. for the Entrance of the Harbour, and anchor under the Eaft Shore in 9 Fathom Water.

On the South Side of the Iflands, before *King's Harbour*, and N. N. E. one Ha Ha, Mile from *Bear Ifland* is the Entrance into the *Ha Ha*, which lies in Weft one Mile, is about a quarter of a Mile broad, wherein is from 20 to 10 Fathom, and good Anchorage in every Part of it. Over the South Point of the Entrance into this Harbour is a high green Hill ; and a Cable's Length and a half from the Point is a funken Rock that always fhews itfelf. Over the Head of the *Ha Ha* is *Richard's Head*, mentioned as a Mark for running upon *Ramea Shoal*.

Four Miles to the Weftward of the *Burgeo Ifles* is the great *Barryfway Point*, Great Barry-which is a low white rocky Point, and N. W. by N. half a League from this fway, Point is the Weft Entrance into the great *Barryfway*, wherein is Room and Depth of Water for fmall Veffels. Between the *Burgeo Ifles* and the *Great Barryfway Point* are feveral funken Rocks, fome of which are half a League from the Shore.

N. W. by W. half W. 4 Leagues from the *Burgeo Ifles* is the Bay of *Connoir*, Bay of Con-the Eaft Point of which is fomething remarkable, rifing with an eafy Afcent to a noir. moderate Height, and much higher than the Land within it ; the Top of it is green, but down by the Shore is white ; the Weft Point of the Bay is low and flat, to the Weftward of which are feveral fmall Iflands : The Bay lies in N. by E. one League from the Entrance to the middle Head, which lies between the two Arms, and is half a League broad, with 14, 12, 10, and 8 Fathom clofe to both Shores, good Anchorage and clear Ground, open to the S. S. W. and Southerly Winds ; but the N. E. Arm affords Shelter for fmall Veffels from all Winds. To fail into it, keep the Starboard Shore beft on board, and anchor before a fmall Cove on the fame Side near the Head of the Arm, in 3 Fathom and a half ; towards the Head of the Arm, on the N. W. Side, is a Bank of Sand and Mud, whereon one might run a Ship, and receive no Damage.

Two Leagues to the Weftward of *Connoir*, lies the Bay of *Cutteau*, wherein is Cutteau Bay. only Shelter and Depth of Water for fmall Veffels and Fifhing Shallops ; in failing in or out of the Bay, keep the Weft Point clofe on board, in order to avoid the many funken Rocks in the Mouth of it.

Round the Weft Point of *Cutteau* is *Cinq Serf*, wherein are a great many Iflands Cinq Serf. which form feveral fmall fnug Harbours, wherein is Room and Depth of Water fufficient for Fifhing Veffels, with Conveniencies for Fifheries. Right off *Cinq Serf*, about half a League from the Shore, is a low rocky Ifland. The fafeft Paffage into the largeft Harbour is to the Weftward of this Rock, keeping pretty near it, and fteer in N. E. half E. keeping the S. E. Shore on board, until you are abreaft of a fmall woody Ifland, which is the Eaftermoft but one, and lies about a quarter of a Mile to the N. E. of a white Rock in the Middle of the Paffage, then haul fhort round this Ifland, and anchor behind it in 7 Fathom Water,

Water, cover'd from all Winds, or you may continue your Courſe up to the Head of the Arm, and anchor in 4 Fathom.

Grand Bruit.   Four Miles to the Weſtward of the rocky Iſland off *Cinq Serf*, is the Harbour of *Grand Bruit*, which is a ſmall commodious Harbour, and well ſituated for a Fiſhery ; it may be known by a very high remarkable Mountain over it, half a League inland, which is the higheſt Land on all the Coaſt ; down which runs a conſiderable Brook, which empties itſelf in a Caſcade into the Harbour of *Grand Bruit*. Before the Mouth of the Harbour are ſeveral ſmall Iſlands, the largeſt of which is of a tolerable Heighth, with three green Hillocks upon it. A little without this Iſland is a round Rock, pretty high above Water, called *Columbe* of *Grand Bruit*; and a quarter of a Mile to the Southward of this Rock, is a low Rock ; in the direct Line between this low Rock and the rocky Iſland off *Cinq Serf*, half a League from the former, is a ſunken Rock, whereon the Sea doth not break in fine Weather. The ſafeſt Paſſage into *Grand Bruit*, is to the N. E. of this Rock, and of the Iſlands lying before the Harbour between them and the three Iſlands (which are low, and lay under the Shore) and after you are to the Northward of the ſunken Rock above-mentioned, there is no Danger but what ſhews itſelf. The Paſſage into the Harbour is very narrow, but bold to both Sides. The Harbour lies in North half a Mile, and is a quarter of a Mile broad in the broadeſt Part, wherein is from 4 to 7 Fathom Water.

Rotte.   To the Weſtward of *Grand Bruit*, between it and *La Poil Bay*, lies the Bay of *Rotte*, wherein are a great many Iſlands and ſunken Rocks. The Southermoſt Iſland is a remarkable high round Rock, called *Columbe* of *Rotte*, and lies W. by N. 9 Leagues from the Southermoſt of the *Burgeos*. Between this Iſland and *Grand Bruit* is a Reef of Rocks, ſome above and ſome under Water, but do not lay to the Southward of the direct Line between the Iſlands. Within the Iſles of *Rotte* are Shelter for Shipping. The ſafeſt Paſſage in, is to the Weſtward of the Iſlands between them and the Iſland called *Little Ireland*, which lies off the Eaſt Point of *La Poil Bay*.

La Poil Bay.   The Bay of *La Poil*, which is large and ſpacious, with ſeveral commodious Harbours, lies Weſt 10 D. North, 10 Leagues from the Southermoſt of the *Burgeos*; W. by N. 14 Leagues from the Iſles of *Ramea*, and near 12 Leagues to the Eaſtward of Cape *Ray*. It may be known by the high Land of *Grand Bruit*, which is only five Miles to the Eaſtward of it ; and likewiſe by the Land on the Eaſt-ſide of the Bay, which riſes in remarkable high craggy Hills. One Mile S. S. W. from the Eaſt Point lies *Little Ireland*, a ſmall low Iſland invironed with ſunken Rocks, ſome of which are one-third of a Mile off ; N. N. W. half a Mile from this Iſland is a ſunken Rock that ſhews itſelf at Low-water, which is the only Danger going into the Bay, but what lies very near the Shore.

Great Harbour.   Two Miles within the Weſt Point of the Bay, and N. N. W. half W. two Miles from *Little Ireland*, is *Tweeds*, or *Great Harbour*, the South Point of which is

low ;

low; it lies in West one Mile, and is a Cable's Length and a half broad in the narrowest Part. To sail into it, keep the North Shore on board, and anchor near the Head of the Harbour in 18 or 20 Fathom clear Ground, and shelter'd from all Winds. In this Harbour are several Conveniencies for erecting of Stages, and drying of Fish. Half a Mile to the Northward of *Great Harbour*, is *Little Harbour*, the North Point of which is the first high bluff Head on the West-side of the Bay, (called *Tooth's Head*); the Harbour lies in West one Mile, is not quite two Cables Length broad in the broadest Part. To sail into it, give the South Point a small Birth, and anchor about half way up the Harbour, in 10 Fathom Water before the Stage, which is on the North-side. Little Harbour.

Opposite to *Tooth's Head*, on the East Side of the Bay, is *Gally Boys Harbour*, a small snug and commodious Harbour for Ships bound to the Westward: Near the South Point of the Harbour are some Hillocks close to the Shore; but the North Point is high and steep, with a white Spot in the Cliff. In sailing in or out of the Harbour, keep the North-side on board; you must anchor as soon as you are within the inner South Point, in 9 or 10 Fathom good Ground, and shelter'd from all Winds. Gally Boys Harbour.

Two Miles to the Northward of *Tooth's Head*, on the same Side of the Bay, is *Broad Cove*, wherein is good Anchorage in 12 and 14 Fathom Water. Off from the North Point of the Cove, stretches out a Bank into the Middle of the Bay, whereon is from 20 to 30 Fathom, a stony and gravelly Bottom. One Mile to the Northward of *Gally Boys Harbour*, between two sandy Coves on the East-side of the Bay; and near two Cables Length from the Shore, is a sunken Rock that just uncovers at Low-water. Broad Cove.

Two Leagues up the Bay, on the East-side, is the N. E. Arm, which is a spacious, safe, and commodious Harbour. To sail into it, give the low sandy Point on the S. E. Side a small Birth, and anchor above it where you please, in 10 Fathom Water, good holding Ground, and shelter'd from all Winds, and very convenient for wooding and watering. N. E. Arm.

A little within the West Point of *La Poil Bay*, is *Indian Harbour*, and *de Plate*, two small Coves conveniently situated for a Fishery, and into which small Vessels can go at High-water. Indian Harbour and de Plate.

From *Little Ireland Island* to *Harbour La Cove*, and *Moine Bay*, the Course is W. 3 quarters S. 4 Leagues; between them lies the Bay of *Garia*, and several small Coves, wherein are Shelter for small Vessels, and Conveniencies for Fisheries; before which are several small Islands, and sunken Rocks lying along the Shore, but none of them lie without the above Course. In bad Weather the sunken Rocks all discover themselves. To sail into the Bay of *Garia*, which lies Midway between *Poil* and *Harbour La Cove*, you will, in coasting along Shore, discover a white Head, which is the South Point of an Island lying under the Land, Bay of Garia.

off the East Point of the Bay, a little to the Westward of two green Hillocks on the Main, you must bring this white Point to bear North, and steer in directly for it; keep between it and the several Islands that lie to the S. W. from it. From this white Point, the Course into the Bay is N. W. by N. keeping the East Point on board, which is low. In this Bay is Plenty of Timber, not only for erecting of Stages, but large enough for building of Shipping.

La Moine Bay and Harbour La Coue.   The S. W. Point of the Entrance into *Harbour La Coue*, call'd *Rose Blanche Point*, (near to which are Rocks above Water) is tolerable high, and the Land near the Shore over *Harbour La Coue* and *La Moine Bay* is much higher than any Land near them, by which they may be known. *La Moine Bay* lies in N. N. E. 3 quarters E. one League and a half, and is a quarter of a Mile broad in the narrowest Part. Off the East Point are some small Islands, and Rocks above Water. To sail into it, keep the West Point on board until you have entered the Bay, then edge over to the East Shore, and steer up to the Head of the Bay, where there is good Anchorage in 10 and 11 Fathom, and Plenty of Wood and Water. Your Course into *Harbour La Coue*, which lies at the West Entrance into *La Moine Bay*, is N. W. between a Rock above Water in the Mouth of the Harbour, and the West-shore; as soon as you are within the Rock, haul to the Westward, into the Harbour, and anchor in 8 or 6 Fathom Water, and moor'd with a Fast on Shore; or you may steer into the Arm, which lies in N. E. by N. from the Harbour, and anchor in 20 Fathom, shelter'd from all Winds. *Harbour La Coue*, is a small snug Harbour for small Vessels, and well situated for a Fishery, where there has been one for several Years.

Rose Blanche.   Round to the Westward of *Rose Blancke Point*, is the Harbour of the same Name, a small snug Harbour, well situated for a Fishery, with good Conveniencies. The Channel into the Harbour is between the Island lying off the West Point, and *Rose Blanche Point*; you must give the Island a good Birth, because of some sunken Rocks which lie on the East-side of it, and keep the West-side of a small Island, which lies close under *Point Blanche*, close on board, and anchor within the N. E. Point of the said Island, in 9 Fathom Water. To sail into the N. W. Part of the Harbour is dangerous, unless acquainted, by reason of several small Islands, and sunken Rocks in it.

Mull Face.   This is a small Cove 2 Miles to the Westward of *Rose Blanche Point*, wherein is Anchorage for small Vessels in 4 Fathom. Off the West Point of the Cove are 2 small Islands, and several sunken Rocks. The Passage in, is to the Eastward of the Islands and sunken Rocks.

Burnt Isles.   Two Leagues to the Westward of *Rose Blanche Point* are the *Burnt Isles*, which lie close under the Shore, and are not to be distinguished from it, behind which are Shelter for small Vessels, and good Fishing Conveniencies. Off these Islands are sunken Rocks, some of which are half a Mile from the Shore.

Three

Three Leagues and a half to the Westward of *Rose Blanche Point*, is *Conny* Conny Bay *Bay*, and *Otter Bay*; in the latter is good Anchorage for Shipping in 7, 8 and 9 and Otter Bay. Fathom, but it is dangerous going in, because of several sunken Rocks without the Passage, which in fine Weather do not shew themselves.

West 3 Quarters South, 4 Leagues from *Rose Blanche Point*, are the *Dead* Dead Isles. *Islands*, which lay close under the Shore; in the Passage between them and the Main is good Anchorage for Shipping, in 6, 7 and 8 Fathom, sheltered from all Winds, but it is very dangerous going in unless well acquainted, by reason of several sunken Rocks lying in both the East and West Entrance. The Entrance from the Eastward may be known by a very white Spot on one of the Islands: Bring this white Spot to bear N. W. by N. and steer in for it, keeping the Rocks on the Starboard Hand nearest on Board, and leave the Island on which the white Spot is on your Larboard Side. The West Entrance may be known by a tolerable high white Point on the Main, a little to the Westward of the Islands, on the West Part of this Point is a green Hillock; keep this white Point close on Board, until you are within a little round Rock, lying close to the Westermost Island, at the East Point of the Entrance; then haul over to the Eastward for the *Great Island*, (on which is a high Hill) and steer in N. E. by E. half E. keeping the little Rock before-mentioned in Sight.

From the *Dead Isles* to *Port aux Basque*, the Course is West 4 Miles: Between Port aux them lie several small Islands close under the Shore, and sunken Rocks, some of Basque. which are half a Mile from the Shore. *Port aux Basque*, which is a small commodious Harbour, lies 2 Leagues and a half to the Eastward of *Cape Ray*. To steer in for it, bring the *Sugar Loaf* over *Cape Ray* to bear N. W. half W. or the West End of the *Table Mountain*, to bear N. W. Steer in for the Land, with either of them as above, and you will fall directly in with the Harbour. The S. W. Point of which is of a moderate Height, and white, called *Point Blanche*, but the N. E. Point is low and flat, close to which is a black Rock above Water, in order to avoid the outer Shoal (on which is 3 Fathom,) and which lies East 3 Quarters of a Mile from *Point Blanche*, keep the said Point on Board, and bring the Flag Staff which is on the Hill, that is over the West Side of the Head of the Harbour, on with the S. W. Point of *Road Island*, and keep in that Direction will carry you in the Middle of the Channel, between the East and West Rocks; the former of which always shew themselves, and which you leave on your Starboard Hand. You must continue this Course up to *Road Island*, and keep the West Point on Board, in order to avoid the *Frying-Pan Rock*, which stretches out from a Cove on the West Shore, opposite the Island; and as soon as you are above the Island, haul to the N. E. and anchor between it and *Harbour Island*, where it is most convenient in 9 or 10 Fathom good Ground, and sheltered from all Winds; this is what is called the *Road*, or *Outer Harbour*, and is the only anchoring Place for Men of War; but fishing Ships always lie up in the *Inner Harbour*. To sail into it, you must steer in between the West Shore, and the S. W. End of *Harbour Island*, and anchor behind the said Island, in 3 or 4 Fathom. In some Parts of this Harbour Ships can

can lie there Broadfide fo near the Shore as to reach it with a Plank. This Harbour hath been frequented by Fifhermen for many Years, and is well fituated for that Purpofe, and has excellent Conveniencies.

Little Bay. One Mile to the Eaftward of *Port Aux Bafque* is *Little Bay*, a narrow Creek lying in N. E. near half a League, wherein is Room and Depth of Water fufficient for fmall Veffels.

Grand Bay. Two Miles to the Weftward of *Port Aux Bafque* is *Grand Bay*, in and before which are feveral Iflands and funken Rocks, the outermoft of which are not above a quarter of a Mile from the Shore, on which the Sea generally breaks. In this Bay is Anchorage for fmall Veffels, but not Water fufficient for large Ships. From *Port Aux Bafque*, to *Cape Ray*, the Courfe is Weft one League to Point *Enragee*, then N. W. one League and a half to the Cape; off Point *Enragee* (which is a low Point,) and to the Eaftward of it are fome funken Rocks one Mile from the Shore, on which the Sea breaks.

Cape Ray. Cape *Ray* is the S. W. Extremity of *Newfoundland*, fituated in the Latitude 47 D. 37 M. North: The Land of the Cape is very remarkable near the Shore, it is low, and three Miles inland is a very high *Table Mountain*, which rifes almoft perpendicular from the low Land, and appears to be quite flat at Top, except a fmall Hillock on the S. W. Point of it. This Land may be feen in clear Weather 16 or 18 Leagues. Clofe to the Foot of the Table Mountain, between it and the Point of the Cape, is a high round Hill, refembling a Sugar Loaf (called the *Sugar-Loaf of Cape Ray*) whofe Summit is fomething lower than the Top of the Table Mountain; and to the Northward of this Hill, under the *Table Mountain*, are two other Hills refembling Sugar-Loaves, which are not fo high as the former; one or another of thofe *Sugar-Loaf* Hills are from all Points of View feen detached from the *Table Mountain*. On the Eaft Side of the Cape between it and *Point Enragee*, is a fandy Bay, wherein Shipping may anchor with N. W. northerly, and N. E. Winds, but they muft take care not to be furprized there with the S. W. Winds which blow right in, and caufe a great Sea, and the Ground is not the beft for holding, being all a fine Sand. Towards the Eaft Side of this Bay is a fmall Ledge of Rocks, one Mile from the Shore, on which the Sea doth not break in fine Weather. The beft Place for great Ships to anchor is to bring the Point of the Cape to bear W. by N. and the high white Sand Hill in the Bottom of the Bay N. N. E. in 10 Fathom Water, but fmall Veffels may lie much farther in. You muft take Care not to run fo far to the Eaftward as to bring the End of the *Table Mountain* on with the Sand Hill, in the Bottom of the Bay, for fear of the Ledge of Rocks before-mentioned. W. by N. half N. near one Mile from the Point of the Cape is a fmall Ledge of Rocks, whereon the Sea always breaks; and one Mile to the Northward of the Cape, clofe under the Land, is a low rocky Ifland, in the Channel between the Ledge and the Cape; alfo between it and the Ifland is 14 and 15 Fathom, but it is not fafe for Shipping, on account of the Tides, which run here with great Rapidity. The Soundings under 100 Fathoms do not

extend

[31]

extend above one League from the Land to the Weſtward and Northward of the Cape, nor to the Southward and Eaſtward of it, except on a Bank which lies off *Port aux Baſque*, between 2 or 3 Leagues from the Land, whereon is from 70 to 100 Fathom good fiſhing Ground. S. E. by E. half E. 8 Leagues from *Port aux Baſque*, in the Latitude of 47 D. 14 M. North is a Bank whereon is 70 Fathom. *Note*, The true Form and Extent of theſe Banks are not yet ſufficiently known to be laid down in the Draft.

From *Cape Ray* to *Cape Anguille*, the Courſe is North 16 D. Weſt, diſtant 6 Leagues; *Cape Anguille* is the Northermoſt Point of Land you can ſee, after paſſing to the Northward of *Cape Ray*. In the Country, over the Cape is high *Table Land*, covered with Wood; between the high Land of the two Capes, the Land is low, and the Shore forms a Bay, wherein are the *Great* and *Little Rivers of Cod Roy*; the great River, which is the Northermoſt, is a Bar Harbour, and will admit Veſſels of 8 and 10 Feet Draft at high Water, and in fine Weather. It is a good Place for a Salmon Fiſhery, and for building of ſmall Veſſels and Boats, &c. there being plenty of Timber. You may approach the Shore between the two Capes to half a League, there being no Danger that Diſtance off.

Cape Anguille.
Rivers of Cod Roy.

The Iſland of *Cod Roy* lies two Miles to the Southward of Cape *Anguille*, cloſe under the high Land, it is a low flat green Iſland, of near two Miles in Compaſs, it forms (between it and the Main) a ſmall ſnug Harbour for fiſhing Shallops, and is frequented by Veſſels of 10 and 12 Feet Draft, but they lie aground the greateſt Part of the Time, there being not much above that Depth of Water in the ſafeſt Part of the Harbour at high Water; the Channel in is from the Southward, wherein is 2 Fathom at low Water. In that from the Northward is not above three Feet; this Harbour is very convenient for the Fiſhery, with good Beaches for drying of Fiſh.

Iſland of Cod Roy.

In the Road of *Cod Roy* is very good Anchorage for Shipping in 8, 7, and 6 Fathom, a Clay Bottom, ſheltered from the N. W. northerly and S. E. Winds; the beſt Place is to bring the South Point of the Iſland to bear Weſt, and the Point of the Beach on the Inſide of the Iſland, at the South Entrance into the Harbour on with a Point on the Main to the Northward of the Iſland, you will then be in 7 Fathom, and nearly half a Mile from the Shore. One League to the Southward of *Cod Roy* is a high bluff Point, called *Stormy Point*, off which ſtretches out a Shoal half a Mile; this Point covers the Road from the S. E. Winds, and it is good anchoring any where along the Shore, between it and the Iſland.

Cod Roy Road.

The Iſland of St. *Paul* lies S. 53 D. W. 13 Leagues and a half from *Cape Ray* in *Newfoundland*, and N. 42 D. E. 3 Leagues from the North Cape, in the Iſland of *Cape Breton*, in the Latitude 47 D. 12 M. 30 S. N. it is about 5 Miles in Compaſs, (including the ſmall Iſland at the N. E. End of it) with three high Hills upon it, and deep Water cloſe to the Shore all round.

Iſland of St. Paul.

Cape

[32]

Cape North. *Cape North* is a lofty Promontory at the N. E. Extremity of the Island *Cape Breton*, in the Latitude of 47 D. 5 M. North, the Entrance into the Gulf of St. *Laurence* is formed by this Cape, and *Cape Ray*; they lie from each other N. 52 D. E. and S. 52 D. W. distant 17 Leagues; in the Channel between them is no Ground under 200 Fathom.

Tides and Currents. A S. E. Moon makes high Water by the Shore in most Places in the Chart, and flows up and down, or upon a Perpendicular seven or eight Feet; but it must be observed, that they are every where greatly governed by the Winds and Weather. On the Sea Coast between Cape *Chapeaurouge* and St. *Peter*'s, the Current sets generally to the S. W. On the South Side of *Fortune Bay* it sets to the Eastward, and on the North Side to the Westward. Between Cape *La Hune* and Cape *Ray*, the Flood sets to the Westward in the Offing, sometimes two or three Hours after it is high Water by the Shore; but this Tide or Current (which is no where strong but at *Cape Ray*) is very variable, both with respect to its Course and Velocity, sometimes it sets quite the contrary to what might be expected from the common Course of the Tides, and much stronger at one Time than another, which Irregularities cannot be accounted for with Certainty, but seem to depend mostly on the Winds.

N. B. The *Burgeo Isles*, by an Observation of the Eclipse of the Sun, on the 5th of *August* 1766, are 3 h. 50 m. 4 sec. or 57 d. 31 m. West, from the Meridian of *London*.

From this Observation the Longitude of the following Places are deduced, and their Latitudes are from astronomical Observations made on Shore, except that of *Cape Race*, which was observed at Sea; some one of those Places being generally the first that Ships make bound to the Southern Parts of *Newfoundland*, or into the Gulf or River of St. *Laurence*, or from which they take their Departure, at leaving those Parts; it is hoped the determining their true Position will prove useful to Navigators.

	Latitude	Longitude
Burgeo Isles	47 36 N.	57 31 W.
Cape Ray	47 37	59 8
Island of St. *Paul*	47 12	59 57
Cape North, the N. E. Extremity of Cape Breton	47 5	60 8
Island of Scatarie, which lies off the S. E. Point of Cape Breton	46 1	61 57
Island of St. *Peter*'s	46 46	56 5
Cape Chapeaurouge, or the Mountain of the Red Hat	46 53	55 17
Cape Race	46 40	52 38
St. *John*'s	47 34	52 18

F I N I S.

DIRECTIONS

FOR

Navigating the Weſt Coaſt of *NEWFOUNDLAND*,

with a C H A R T thereof.

N. B. *All Bearings and Courſes hereafter-mentioned, are the true Bearings and Courſes, and not by Compaſs.*

CAPE *Anguille* lies 6 Leagues to the Northward of Cape *Ray*, N.E. by N. 17 Leagues, from the Iſland of St. *Paul*, and is in the Latitude of 47° 55′ North, it is high Land cover'd with Wood; 2 Miles to the Southward of this Cape lies the ſmall Iſland and Harbour of *Cod-Ray* before deſcribed. From Cape *Anguille* to Cape St. *George*, the Courſe is N. ¾ E. diſtant 11 Leagues; theſe two Capes form the Bay of St.*George*, which lies in N.E. 18 Leagues from the former, and Eaſt 15 from the latter; at the Head of this Bay, on the South-ſide round a low Point of Land, is a very good Harbour wherein is good Anchorage in 8, 10, or 12 Fathom Water. In ſeveral Parts about this Harbour are convenient Places for Fiſhing Works, with large Beaches, and good Fiſhing Ground in the Bay, which early in the Spring abound with Fiſh, and formerly was much frequented; a very conſiderable River empties itſelf into the Head of this Bay, but it is not navigable for any thing but Boats, by Reaſon of a Bar a-croſs the Entrance, which lies expoſed to the Weſterly Winds. On the North-ſide of this Bay, before the *Iſthmus* of *Port-a-Port*, is good Anchorage in 7 or 8 Fathom Water, with Northerly Winds; from off this Place ſtretches out a Fiſhing Bank two-thirds a-croſs the Bay, whereon is from 7 to 18 Fathom Water, a dark ſandy Bottom.

Cape Anguille.

Bay and Harbour of St. George.

Cape

Cape St. George and Red Island.

Cape St. *George* lies in the Latitude of 48d. 23m. it may be easily known, not only by its being the N.Point of the Bay of the same Name, but by the steep Clifts on the North Part of it, which rises perpendicular from the Sea to a considerable Hight, and by *Red Island* which lies 5 Miles to the Northward of the Cape, and half a Mile from the Shore: This Island is about one League in Circuit, and tolerable high, and the steep Clifts round it are of a reddish Colour. Under the N.E. end of the Island, and before a sandy Cove on the Main, which lies just to the Northward of the steep Clifts is Anchorage in 12 or 14 Fathom Water, you are there covered from the S.W.Winds by the Island, and from the Southerly and Easterly Winds by the Main, but there is no riding here with Northerly and N.W. Winds; this Place formerly was much frequented by Fishers.

Courses along Shore between Red Island and Point Rich.

From *Red Island* to *Long Point*, at the Entrance into the Bay of *Port-a-Port*, the Course is N. 52d East, distant 7 Leagues and a half. From *Red Island* to *Guernsey Island* in the Mouth of the Bay of *Islands*, the Course is N.E. ¾ N. 15 Leagues and a half. From *Red Island* to Cape St. *Gregory*, the Course is N.E. ¾ N. 20 Leagues. From *Red Island* to the Bay of *Ingornachoix*, the Course is N.N.E ½ E. distant 48 Leagues; and from *Red Island* to *Point Rich*, the Course is N. 29d. East, distant 48 Leagues and 2 Miles.

Bay of Port-a-Port.

The Land between *Red Island*, and the Entrance into *Port-a-Port*, is of a Moderate Height, or rather low, with sandy Beaches, except one remarkable high Hillock (called *Round-head*,) close to the Shore, and is 2 Leagues to the N.E. of *Red Island*; but up in the Country over *Port-a-Port*, are high Lands, and if you are 4 Leagues at Sea, you will not discern the *Long Point* of Land, which forms the Bay of *Port-a-Port*: This Bay is Capacious, being near 5 Miles broad at the Entrance, and lies into the Southward 4 Leagues, with good Anchorage in most Parts of it. The West Point of the Bay (called *Long Point*,) is a low rocky Point, from which stretches out a Reef of Rocks N.E. near 1 Mile; S.E. by S. 4 Miles from *Long Point*, and half a League from the East Shore, lies *Fox Island*, which is small, but tolerable high, from the North End of this Island stretches out a Shoal near 2 Miles to the Northward, called *Foxes Tail*; nearly in the Middle of the Bay, between the Island and the West-Shore, lies the Middle Ground, on one Place of which near the S.W. End is not above 3 or 4 Feet Water, at Low-Water; at the Head of the Bay, is a low Point, called *Middle Point*, it stretching out into the Middle of the Bay; from off this Point is a Shoal Spit, which extends near 2 Miles to the Northward, Part of which drys at Low-Water: From the Head of the East Bay over to the Bay of St *George*, is little more than a quarter of a Mile, this *Isthmus* is very low with a Pond in the Middle of it, into which the Sea washes in Gales of Winds from the Southward at high Tides. On the East-side of the *Isthmus* is a tolerable high Mountain, which appears flat at Top, and rises directly from the *Isthmus*, on the North-side of this

Mountain,

Mountain; and about 5 Miles from the *Isthmus* is a conspicuous Valley or Hollow, which together with *Fox Island*, serves as a leading Mark for coming in and out of this Bay, as is hereafter described: Two Leagues to the N.E. from the Entrance of this Bay, and half a League from the Shore lies *Shag Island*, which appears at a Distance like a high Rock, and is easy to be distinguished from the Main; West 1 League from the *Shag Island*, lies the Middle of *Long-Ledge*; which is a narrow Ledge of Rocks stretching N.E. and S.W. 4 Miles, the N.E. Part of them are above Water; the Channel into the Bay of *Port-a-Port*, between the S.W. End of this Ledge, and the Reef off the West Point of the Bay is 1 League wide. To sail into *Port-a-Port*, coming from the S.W. come not nearer the Pitch of the *Long-Point* of the Bay, then 1 Mile and a half, or haul not in for the Bay, until you have brought the Valley in the Side of the Mountain before mentioned, (which is on the East-side of the *Isthmus*) over the East-end of *Fox Island*, or to the Eastward of it, which will then bear S.S. E. ½ E. you will be then clear of the *Long-Point* Reef, and may haul into the Bay with Safety; coming from the N.E. and without the *Long Ledge*, or turning into the Bay in order to keep clear of the S.W. Point of the *Long Ledge*, bring the *Isthmus* or the Foot of the Mountain, (which is on the East-side of the *Isthmus*) open to the Westward of *Fox Island*, near twice the Breadth of the Island, (the Island will then bear S. ½ E.) you may haul into the Bay with this Mark, and when *Shag Island* is brought on with the Foot of the high Land, which is on the South-side of *Coal River*, and will then bear E. by N. ¼ N. you will be within the *Long Ledge*; there is a safe Passage into the Bay, between the *Long Ledge* and the Main, passing on either Side of *Shag Island*, taking Care to avoid a small round Shoal which lies S.W. 1 Mile from the Island, on which is 2 Fathom and a half Water. To sail up to what is called the *West Bay*, and into *Head Harbour* (which are the safest Anchorages, and the best Places to Wood and Water at) keep the West-Shore on board, and in turning between it and the Middle Ground, observe on standing over to the Middle to put about as soon as you shoalden your Water to 8 Fathom, you may stand to the Spit of the Middle Point, to 6 or 5 Fathom. To sail up to what is called the *East Road*, which lies between *Fox Island* and the East-Shore; observe about one League N.E. from the Island is a high Bluff-Head, being the South Part of the high Land that rises steep directly from the Shore, keep this Head bearing to the Southward of East until the *Isthmus* is brought to the Eastward of *Fox Island*, which will then bear S.S.W. you will then be within the Shoal, (called *Fox's Tail*) and may then haul to the Southward, and Anchor any where between the Island and the Main: To sail up to the East Bay passing between the Island and the East-Shore, observe the foregoing Directions; and after you are above the Island, come not nearer the Main then half a Mile until you are abreast of a Bluff Point above the Island, called *Road Point*, just above which in 12 Fathom is the best Anchorage with N.E. Winds; and to sail up to this Anchorage between the Middle Ground and the *Fox's Tail*, bring the said Point on with the S W.

Point

(6)

Point of the Ifland, this Mark will lead you up in the fair Way between the two Shoals. What is called the *Weſt Road*, lies before a high Stone Beach, about 2 Miles within *Long Point*, where you ride fecure with Wefterly and N.W. Winds in 10 or 12 Fathom Water, the faid Beach is fteep too, and is an excellent Place for landing and drying of Fifh, for which it has been formerly ufed; there is likewife a good Place at the North-end of *Fox Ifland* for the fame Purpofe; and the whole Bay and adjacent Coaft abound with Cod, and extenfive Fifhing Banks lays along the Sea Coaft.

Bay of Iflands. From the *Long Point*, at the Entrance of *Port-a-Port* to the Bay of *Iflands*, the directCourfe is N. 35 d. Eaft diftant 8 Leagues, but coming out of *Port a-Port*, you muſt firſt ſteer North for one League or a League and a half, in order to clear the *Long Ledge*, then N.E. by N. or N.E; the Land between them is of confiderable height rifing in craggy barron Hills directly from the Shore. The Bay of *Iflands* may be known by the many Iflands in the Mouth of it, particularly the three named *Guernſey Ifland*, *Tweed Ifland*, and *Pearl Ifland*, which are nearly of equal height with the Lands on the Main; if you are bound for *York* or *Lark Harbours* which lay on the S.W. Side of this Bay, and coming from the Southward, ſteer in between *Guernſey Ifland* and the South Head, either of which you may approach as near as you pleafe; but with S.S.W. and Southerly Winds, come not near the South Head for fear of Calms and Gufts of Wind under the high Land, where you cannot Anchor with Safety; you may ſail in or out of the Bay by ſeveral other Channels formed by the different Iflands, there being no Danger but what fhews itfelf, except a ſmall Ledge of Rocks which lies half a Mile from the North *Shag Rock*, and in a Line with the two *Shag Rocks* in one, if you bring the South *Shag Rock* open on either Side of the North Rock you will be clear either to the Eaftward or Weftward of the Ledge. The fafeft Paffage into this Bay from the Northward is between the two *Shag Rocks*, and then between *Tweed Ifland* and *Pearl Ifland*. From *Guernſey Ifland* to *Tortoife Head* (which is the North Point of *York Harbour*, and the S.E. Point of *Lark Harbour*,) the Courfe is S. by E. 5 Miles; *Lark Harbour* lies in S.W. near 2 Miles, and is one third of a Mile broad in the narroweft Part which is at the Entrance.

Lark Harbour. To ſail into it with large Ships keep the Larboard Shore on board, but with fmall Veſſels there is no Danger, you may Anchor with a low Point on the Starboard-fide bearing Weft, N.W. or North, and ride fecure from all Winds.

York Harbour. From *Tortoife Head* into *York Harbour* the Courfe is S.W. near 1 League; between the faid Head and *Governor's Ifland* which lies before the Harbour is good Room to turn, and Anchorage all the Way, but regard muft be had to a Shoal which ſpits off from a low Beach Point (called *Sword Point*) on the Weft-end of *Governor's Ifland*; to avoid which keep a good Part of *Seal Ifland* open to the Northward of *Governor's Ifland* until you are above this Point, in

turning

turning up the Harbour, ſtand not nearer the next Point on the Iſland (off which it is flat) then to bring *Tortoiſe Head* touching *Sword Point*, the beſt Anchorages is to keep *Tortoiſe Head* open of the ſaid Point and Anchor in 10 Fathom along the ſandy Beach on the Main ; farther up within the Iſland is too deep Water for anchoring all the Way through the Paſſage within the Iſland. This Harbour is very convenient to Wood and Water at. W.S.W. and S.W. Winds blows here ſometimes with great Violence, occaſioned by the Nature of the Lands, there being a Valley or low Land between this Harbour and *Coal River* which is bounded on each Side with high Hills, this cauſeth theſe Winds to blow very ſtrong over the low Land

Harbour Iſland lies at the Entrance of the *River Humber* and S.E. 7 Miles from *Guernſey Iſland*, at the S.W. Point of which is a ſmall ſnug Harbour (called *Wood's Harbour*) wherein is 5 and 4 Fathom Water, but the Entrance is too narrow for Strangers to attempt, and but 2 Fathom deep. Harbour Iſland.

The *River Humber* at about 5 Leagues within the Entrance, it becomes narrow, and the Stream is ſo rapid in Places for about 4 Leagues up to a Lake, that it is with great difficulty a Boat can be got up it ; and at ſome Times quite impracticable ; this Lake which ſtretches N.E. $\frac{1}{2}$ N. is in Length 7 or 8 Leagues, and from 2 to 5 Miles broad. The Banks of this River, and the Shores of the Lake are well clothed with Timber, ſuch as are common in this Country. This River is ſaid to abound with Salmon, in which has been formerly a very great Salmon Fiſhery. River Humber.

The *North* and *South Arms* are only long Inlets, in which is very deep Water, until you come to their Heads. North and South Arm's,

A little within the Entrance of the *North Arm*, on the Starboard-ſide, is a ſmall Cove, wherein a Veſſel might Anchor in 30 Fathom Water ; 1 League within the Entrance of the *South Arm* on the Starboard-ſide is a ſandy Cove (being the ſecond on that Side) wherein is Anchorage in 16 Fathom Water, and good Place to Wood and Water at ; haul into the Cove until the Weſt Point of it is brought on with the North Point of the Entrance of this Arm, and there Anchor ; if you miſs laying hold of this Anchoring Ground, there is a very good Harbour at the Head of the S.E. Branch of this Arm ; on the Eaſt-ſide of *Eagle Iſland* between the *North* and *South Arms* is Anchorage in 8, 10, or 12 Fathom Water. Under the North-ſide of *Harbour Iſland* is good Anchorage with S.W. Winds ; at a quarter of a Mile from the Iſland you will have a muddy Bottom. Oppoſite to the S.E. end of *Harbour Iſland* on the South-ſide of this Bay is *Frenchman's Cove*, wherein is good Anchorage in 20, 16, or 12 Fathom Water ; it is very probable that none of theſe Anchorages will ever be frequented by Shipping ; yet it is neceſſary to point them out, as it may happen that in coming into the Bay with a Gale of Wind at S.W. it may blow ſo hard out of *York Harbour* that no Veſſel can carry ſail to Work into Anchoring Ground ; at ſuch Times they will be glad to get to an Anchor in any Place of Safety. Anchorage's,

The

The Bay of *Islands* has been much frequented, formerly for the Cod Fishery, the best Place for Fishing Ships to erect Stages, and keep Boats, is in *Small Harbour* which lies a little without the *South Head*, and the large Beach on *Sword Point* on *Governor's Island*, is an excellent Place for drying of Fish.

From Bay of Islands to Bonne Bay.

From *Guernsey Island* to *Bonne Bay*, the Course is first N.N.E. 6 Leagues, then N.E. 3 Leagues. The Land near the Shore from the North *Shagg Rock*, to Cape St. *Gregory* is low, along which lay sunken Rocks, some of which are a quarter of a Mile from the Shore, but a very little Way in Land,

C. St. Gregory.

it riseth into a Mountain terminating at Top, in round Hills; from Cape St. *Gregory* to *Bonne Bay*, the Land riseth in Hills, directly from the Sea to a considerable height. Cape St. *Gregory* is high, and the Northermost Land you can see, when coasting along Shore between *Red Island* and the Bay of *Islands*.

Bonne Bay.

Bonne Bay may be easily known if you are not above 4 or 5 Leagues off at Sea by the Lands about it, all the Land on the S.W. side of the Bay being very high and hilly, the Land on the NE. Side, and from thence along the Sea-Coast to the Northward is low and flat, but about 1 League up in Land are a range of Mountains which run parallel with the Sea-Coast; you cannot distinguish the low Land if you are 6 or 7 Leagues off at Sea. Over the South-side of this Bay is a very high Mountain terminating at Top in a remarkable round Hill, which is very conspicuous when you are to the Northward of the Bay. This Bay lies in S.E. 2 Leagues, then branches into two Arms, one tending to the Southward and the other to the Eastward, the best Anchorage is in the Southern Arm; small Vessels must Anchor just above a low woody Point (which is on the Starboard-side of the Bay at the Entrance into this Arm,) before a sandy Beach in 8 or 10 Fathom Water, about a Cable's length from the Shore; but large Ships must run higher up unless they moor to the Shore, they cannot Anchor in less than 30 or 40 Fathom, but at the Head of the Arm where there is but 24 Fathom; notwithstanding the great depth of Water you lay every where in perfect Security and very convenient to Wood and Water, there being great Plenty of both. To sail into the East Arm keep the S.E. Point or Starboard shore on board; short round that Point is a small snug Cove wherein is good Anchorage in 16 or 18 Fathom Water, and moor to the Shore; a little within the North Point of this Arm is a very snug Harbour for small Vessels, wherein is 7 and 6 Fathom Water. In sailing in or out of this Bay with S W. Winds come not near the Weather Shore for fear of being becalmed under the high Land, or meeting with heavy Gusts of Wind which is still worse, and the depth of Water is too great to Anchor.

Bonne Bay to Point Rich.

From *Bonne Bay* to *Point Rich*, the Course along Shore is N.N.E. distant 24 Leagues; but in coming out of the Bay you must first steer N.N.W. and N. by W for the first 3 Leagues in order to get an Offing. 10 Miles to the Northward of *Bonne Bay* is a pretty high white Point (called

Martain

(9)

Martin Point) 3 quarters of a Mile right off from this Point is a small Ledge of Rocks whereon the Sea breaks : One League to the Northward of *Martin Point*, is a low white rocky Point (called *Broom Point*) half a Mile SW. from this Point lies a sunken Rock that seldom shews itself. On the N.E. Side of *Broom Point* lies the Bay of St. *Paul*, wherein Vessels may Anchor with Southerly and Easterly Winds, but lies quite exposed to the Sea Winds. *Martin Point. Bay of St. Paul.*

One League to the Northward of the Bay of St *Paul* is a pretty high Point of Land (called *Cow Head*) it will have the Appearance of an Island being only joined to the Main by a very low and narrow Neck of Land ; three quarters of a Mile off this Head lies *Stearing Island*, which is low and rocky, and the only Island on the Coast between the Bay of *Islands* and *Point Rich*. On the South-side of *Cow Head* is *Cow Cove*, wherein is Shelter for Vessels with Easterly and Northerly Winds ; and on the North-side of this Head is *Shallow Bay*, wherein is Water sufficient for small Vessels, and good Fishing Conveniencies ; at the N.E. Entrance into this Bay are a Cluster of rocky Islands, which range themselves N.E. and S.W. and at the S.W. Entrance are two Rocks close to each other, which generally shew themselves, they lay a full Cable's length from the Shore ; and there is a Channel into the Bay on either Side of them. In sailing in or out of this Bay, you may go on either Side of *Stearing Island* which lies right before it, but come not too near the N.E. end, there being sunken Rocks off that End. This Place is the best situated for a Fishery of any on the Coast, there being excellent Fishing Ground about it. *Cow Head and Stearing Island. Cow Cove and Shallow Bay.*

From *Stearing Island* to *Point Rich* the Course is N. 20d. 45m. E. Distance 17 Leagues. From *Shallow Bay* to the South Part of *Ingornachoix Bay*, is nearly a straight Shore all the Way, and neither Creek or Cove, where a Vessel can Shelter her self from the SeaWinds ; there are some small sandy Bays where Vessels may Anchor with the Land Winds ; 6 Leagues to the Northward of *Stearing Islands*, and about half a Mile in Land, is a remarkable Hill (called *Portland*, it makes not unlike *Portland* in the *English* Channel, and alters not in its Appearance from any Point of View. *Shallow Bay to Ingornachoix Bay.*

Hawke's Harbour and *Port Saunders* are safe and commodious Harbours situated in the Bay of *Ingornachoix* S.E. 2 Leagues from *Point Rich* ; at the Entrance of these Harbours lies an Island (called *Keppel Island*) which is not easily to be distinguished by Strangers from the Main, the Channel into *Hawke's Harbour* (which is the Southermost) lies between the Island, and the South Shore, on the Starboard-shore entring into this Harbour, and opposite to the West-end of the Island, begins a Shoal which streches up along that Shore 1 Mile, the Middle of which runs out into the Harbour two thirds the breadth thereof, great Part of this Shoal dries at Low-Water. Your Course into the Harbour is East, keeping Mid Channel, or rather nearest to *Keppel Island* until the East-end thereof, which is a low *Hawke's Harbour and Port Saunders.*

B

low ftone Beach) bears N. by E. or N. then fteer S.E. ½ E. for a fmall Ifland you will fee up the Harbour, keeping the N.E. or Larboard Shore pretty well on board, and fteer for the faid little Ifland, as foon as you have brought the Point at the South Entrance of the Harbour to bear W. by N. ¼ N. and are the Length of the S.E. Point of a Bay which is on the Starboard-fide of the Harbour, you will then be above the Shoal, and may Anchor in 12 Fathom Water, or you may run within half a Mile of the fmall Ifland and there Anchor, where you will lay convenienter to take in Wood and Water. To fail into *Port Saunder's*, there is not the leaft Danger, leave *Keppel Ifland* on your Starboard-fide and Anchor as foon as you are half a Mile within the Entrance in 10 or 11 Fathom Water; but if you run up towards the Head of this Harbour keep the Larboard Shore on board in order to avoid a Ledge of Rocks which lies nearly in the Middle of the Harbour. This is the beft Harbour for Ships to lay in that are bound to the Southward, as the other is for thofe bound to the Northward; all the Lands near thefe Harbours are in generally low and covered with Wood. You may occafionally Anchor without thefe Harbours in the Bay of *Ingronachoix*, according as the Winds are.

Point Rich. *Point Rich* lies in the Latitude of 51d. 41m. 30fec. it is the S.W. Point of a *Peninfula*, which is almoft furrounded by the Sea, it is every where of a moderate and pretty equal height, and is the moft remarkable Point of Land along the Weft-fide of *Newfoundland* it projecting out into the Sea farther than any other from whence the Coaft each Way takes a different Direction.

Two Miles N.E. from *Point Rich* is the Harbour of *Port-aux-Choix*, it is but fmall yet will admit of Ships of large Burthen, but they muft moor Head and Stern, there not being room to moor otherwife. To fail into it keep the Starboard Shore on board, and Anchor juft above a fmall Ifland which lies in the Middle of the Harbour. In this Harbour, and in *Boat Cove* which lies a little to the Northward are feveral Stages and good Places for drying of Fifh.

Old Port aux-Choix. Round the N.E. Point of the *Peninfula* lies the Harbour of *Old Port aux-Choix*, which is a fmall but fafe Harbour, in the Entrance of which lies a fmall Ifland called *Harbour Ifland*, and between this Ifland and the Weft Point of the Harbour, are Rocks, fome above and fome under Water. To fail into this Harbour on the Weft-fide of the Ifland, keep the Ifland clofe on board; but to fail in on the Eaft-fide give the N.E. Point of this Ifland a fmall birth; you may Anchor any where on the S.E. or Larboard-fide of the Harbour, but come not near the N.W. or Starboard-fide, there being a Shoal of Sand and Mud all along that Side.

From

From *Point Rich* to the *Twin Islands* (which are low, and the outermost Islands in the Bay of St. *John*) the Courfe is N.N.E. Diftance 4 Leagues, and from the *Twin Islands* to *Point Ferolle* the Courfe is N.E. ½ N. 11 Miles.

The Bay of St. *John* lies between *Point Rich* and *Point Ferolle*; there are in Bay St John. it a great many Islands and funken Rocks; the only Ifland of any extent is that of St. *John* which lies NE. 3 Leagues from *Point Rich*; on the S.W. Side of this Iſland is a fmall Harbour which ſeems not badly fituated for the Cod-Fifhery, and it hath good Conveniencies for that Purpoſe, but it is not a good Place for Shipping, they would be too much expoſed to the S.W. Winds, which fends in a great Sea. On the S.E. Side of this Iſland oppoſite to the Weſt-end of *Head Iſland*, is a fmall Bay wherein is Anchorage in 16 or 14 Fathom Water, and ſheltered from moſt Winds, and is the only Anchoring Place in the whole Bay.

From the South Part of *Point Ferolle* ftretches out a Ledge of Rocks S.S W. Ferolle Ledge near 1 League; and along the Shore to the River of *Caſtors* (which is in the Bottom of St. *John's Bay*) are funken Rocks 2 Miles off.

Over the Middle of the Bay of St. *John* is high Table Land, which is High Land of very fteep on that Side next the Bay, and terminates that Chain of Mountains St. John which runs parailel with the Sea-Coaft from *Bonne Bay*.

The Courfe of the Tides along this Coaft are greatly govern'd by the Tides. Winds, but when not interrupted by ftrong Gales of long continuance; a S.E. by S. or S.S.E. Moon makes High-Water, and flows up and down, or upon a perpendicular 7 or 8 Feet.

F I N I S.

DIRECTIONS

FOR

Navigating on Part of the N.E. Side of *NEWFOUND-LAND*, and in the Streights of *BELL-ISLE*.

N. B. *All Bearings and Courses hereafter-mentioned, are the true Bearings and Courses, and not by Compass.*

ON the N.E. Coast of *Newfoundland*, about 2 Leagues from the Main, are two Islands, the Northermost of which is called *Groias*, the North-end of this Island is in the Latitude of 51° 00′ North; at about 2 Miles Distance from this North-end are some Rocks high above Water. Isle Groias.

The Harbour of *Croque* bears N.W. by W. half W. 2 Leagues from the North-end of *Groias* Island, the Entrance is not easily distinguished by Strangers till you draw near it, then you will discover a small Island, or Rock, close to the South-head of the Harbour, you may stand boldly in with the Land, there being no Danger but what shews itself, and lies very near Shore; as soon as you are within the Heads you will open the two Arms, that to the S.W. is not safe to Anchor in, being foul Ground, and open to the N.E. Winds; you may run up into the N.W. Arm until you are Landlock'd, and Anchor where you please, from 16 to 10 Fathom Water, every where very good Ground. This is an excellent Harbour very convenient for the Fishery, and plenty of Wood and Water. Croque.

From the North-end of *Groias* Island, along the Coast to the *White Islands*, the true Course is N. by E. 12 Leagues, but to give these Islands, and the *Braha Shoal* a proper Birth, make a N.N.E. Course. Course from Groias to the White Islands.

A 2 Between

       Between *Croque* and the Bay of *Griguet* are several good Harbours, with
       excellent Fishing Conveniencies, particularly *Great* and *Little St. Julian's*,
       Grandsway, *Waterman's-Cove*, *Whites-Arm*, *Zealot*, *Feshot*, *Goose-Cove*, *Crai-*
       miliere, *St. Anthony*, and *St. Lunare*, which are not yet accurately survey'd,
       but are laid down in the Chart according to good Sketches and Obfervations,
       taken by Officers of the King's Ships on that Station ; there is no Danger on
Braha Shoal. the Coast but what lies very near the Shore, except the small Shoal of *Braha*,
       which lies directly off the Bay of the same Name, 4 Miles from the Land, on
       which the Sea breaks in bad Weather.

Griguet Bay   The Bay of *Griguet* is situated on the N.E. Coast of *Newfoundland*, in the
and its con- Latitude of 51° 32′ North; it is form'd by *Stormy Cape* to the North, and
tain'd Har- *White Cape* to the South, and contains several good Harbours for Shipping of
bours and
Islands.   all Kinds, wherein are many Fishing Conveniencies.

Camels Island. This Island lies in *Griguet* Bay, it is very high in the Middle, like the Back
       of a Camel, and in sailing along the Shore is difficult to be distinguished from
       the Main.

North Har- The North Harbour lies within *Stormy Cape*, at the Entrance of which is a
bour.   Rock above Water ; you may go on either Side of this Rock, it being bold
       too all round, and Anchor near the Head of the Harbour in 6 Fathom Water;
       in the Entrance that leads to the N.W. and S.W. Harbours, is a small rocky
       Island, which makes the Passage into those Harbours narrow ; the safest Paf-
       fage is to the Northward of this Island, giving the Point at the Entrance of the
       N.W. Harbour a little Birth ; as soon as you are within the Island you will
       open the two Harbours ; that of the N.W. which is the largest runs in N.W.
N.W. Har- near 2 Miles ; to sail up to the Head of the Harbour, the West-side is the
bour.   safest ; you will at first have 14, 16, and 18 Fathom Water, and after you
       are a little within the Point will meet with a Bank, whereon is 7 and 8 Fathom;
       being over it, you will again have 16 and 17 Fathom, and as you approach
       the Head, will shoalen your Water gradually to 5 Fathom, every where good
       anchoring and shelter'd from all Winds.

S.W. Har-   The S.W. Harbour runs in near 2 Miles behind *Camel's Island*, it is but a
bour.   narrow Arm, and hath in it from 10 to 4 Fathom Water ; there is a Shoal at
       the Entrance, but neither it, or the Harbour are yet sufficiently examin'd to
       give any Direction about it here.

Griguet   The two Islands of *Griguet* lay on the outside of *Camel's Island*, and together
Islands.   form between them several small, but very snug Harbours for Fishing Vessels.

Harbour Lit- From *Stormy Cape* to *Cape de Grat*, on the Island of *Quirpon* is N. by E.
tle Quirpon. distant 3 Miles and a half; between which is the Harbour of *Little Quirpon*,
       form'd by the Island of that Name; there is no Danger going in, but the
       Shore itself; its a small safe snug Harbour, where Fishing Ships Moor Head
       and Stern.

                                         Quirpon

[5]

Quirpon Ifland, which is the S.E. Point that forms the Entrance of the Streights of *Bell-Ifle*, is barren and mountanious; *Cape de Grat* on the S.E. Side, and the higheft Part of this Ifland may be feen in clear Weather 12 Leagues. *Ifland Quirpon.*

Thefe Iflands lay between *Griguet* and *Cape de Grat*, about 2 Miles and a half from the Land, they are but fmall and of a moderate Height; on the infide of them are fome Rocks, both above and under Water, but not dangerous as they difcover themfelves even in fine Weather; and the Paffage between them and the Main, which is half a League wide, is very fafe. *White Iflands.*

Thefe Coves lay on the S.E. fide of the Ifland of *Quirpon*, and to the Northward of *Cape de Grat*, in the Mouth of which are fome fmall Iflands and Rocks above Water; behind thefe Iflands are Shelter for Shipping in 4 Fathom Water, and convenient Places for Fifhing. *De Grat and Pidgeon Coves.*

The Paffage into this Harbour is on the N.W. fide of the Ifland of the fame Name, between it and *Graves*'s Ifland, which is an Ifland in the Mouth of the Harbour; in approaching the Entrance you may make as free as you pleafe with the Ifland *Quirpon*, there being no Danger but what fhews itfelf until you come to the Entrance of the Harbour, where there are Shoals on your Larboard-fide, which you avoid by keeping *Black-head* upon *Quirpon* open of all the other Land, until *Cape Raven* is brought over *Noddy-Point*, then haul in for the Harbour, keeping about half a Cable's Length from the Point of *Graves*'s Ifland; it is every where good Anchoring within the faid Ifland, and Room and Depth of Water for any Ships, and good Ground; the beft Place is in 9 Fathom Water up towards the upper End of *Graves*'s Ifland, abreaft of *Green* Ifland, which lies about the Middle of the Harbour. The Paffage to the inner Harbour on either Side of *Green* Ifland, is very good for Ships of a moderate Draft of Water, through which you will carry three Fathom; and above the Ifland is exceeding good Anchoring in 7 Fathom; there is a Paffage into this Place through little *Quirpon*, but it is too narrow and intricate for Veffels to attempt, unlefs well acquainted: In and about *Quirpon* are excellent Conveniences for great Number of Ships, and good Fifhing Grounds about thofe Parts: All the Land about *Griguet* and *Quirpon* is Mountanious, and appears a Barren Rock. *Harbour of Great Quirpon.*

This Harbour which lies a little to the W.ward of *Quirpon*, runs in S.S.W. between *Noddy Point* and *Cape Raven*, which form the Entrance of the Harbour; there is no Danger in going in; the Paffage in is on the Weft-fide of a fmall Ifland that lies about three-quarters of a Mile within the Heads, and you Anchor as foon as above it in 5 Fathom Water; or with fmall Veffels you may run up into the Bafon, and Anchor in 2 and a half or three Fathom; within the Ifland on the Eaft-fide of the Harbour is a Stage, and very convenient Room s for many Fifhing Ships. *Noddy Harbour.*

In

[6]

Gull Rock, Maria Ledge, and N.W. Ledge.
In turning up towards *Quirpon* and *Noddy Harbour*, you may stand pretty near to the *Gull Rock* and *Maria Ledge*, which are above Water, and both of them about half a League from the Land of *Quirpon*; the Passage between them is also half a League wide, and very safe, taking Care only to keep near to *Gull Rock* to avoid the N.W. Ledge, which Ledge doth not appear but in bad Weather; in the Passage between the N.W. Ledge and the Main, are many Rocks and shallow Water.

Sacred Islands.
The Course from *Bauld Cape*, which is the northern Extremity of *Quirpon*, to the *Great Sacred Island*, is West 2 Leagues; this Course will carry you the same Distance without *Gull Rock*, as you pass without *Bauld Cape*. Little Sacred Island lies E.S E. from the Great Island 1 Mile, the Passage between them is very safe, and you may sail round them both; they are high and bold:

Sacred Bay.
Within them, to the S.W. is *Sacred Bay*, which is pretty large, wherein are a great Number of small Islands and Rocks above Water; the Land at the Bottom of this Bay is covered with Wood: This Place is resorted to only for Wood for the Use of the Fishery at *Quirpon*, *Griguet*, and Places adjacent, where Wood is scarce.

Cape Onion.
From *Great Sacred Island* to Cape *Norman* the Course is West 13 Miles, and to *Cape Onion*, is S.W. by W. 2 Miles; this Cape is the North Point of *Sacred Bay*, it is pretty high and steep, near to which is a very remarkable Rock, called the *Mewstone*, like the *Mewstone* in *Plymouth Sound*; to the Southward of the *Mewstone* is a small Cove, where a Vessel may lie in Safety.

Burnt Cape.
From *Cape Onion* to *Burnt Cape*, the Course is W.S.W. Distance 5 Miles; the Shore between them is bold, and of a moderate Height; *Burnt Cape* appears white, and rises gradually from the Sea to a tolerable Height: On

Bay of Ha Ha.
the East Side of the Cape lies the Entrance to the Bay *Ha-Ha*, which runs in S.S.W. 2 Miles; when within *Burnt Cape*, you may anchor in six or seven Fathom, open only to N.E. Winds; or you may run up into the Harbour, where you lie land-lock'd in 3 Fathom. Here is good Conveniencies for Fishing-Ships, and Plenty of Wood for their Use. *Cape Norman*, from *Burnt*

Bay of Pistolet.
Cape bears N.W. by W. ¾ W. 7 Miles. Between them is the Bay of *Pistolet*, which runs in S.S.W. and extends several Miles every Way, with good anchoring in most Parts of it, particularly on the West-side, a little above the Islands, which lie on the same Side in 5 Fathom Water. The Shore about this Bay is tolerably well covered with Wood, Boats frequently come here for Wood from *Quirpon*.

Cook's Harbour.
This is a small Harbour within the Islands, at the N.W. Part of *Pistolet* Bay, and 2 Miles to the S.E. of *Cape Norman*; to sail into it, you must take Care and give the *Norman* Ledges which lie E.N.E. 1 Mile off the North Point, a good Birth. In going along Shore, the Mark to keep without these Ledges is, to keep all the Land of *Burnt Cape* open without the outermost Rocks, which lie on the South Side of the Entrance to this Harbour; if you are going in, as soon as you judge yourself to be to the Southward of the *Norman* Ledges

[7]

Ledges you muſt ſteer in for the Harbour, leaving the Iſlands on your Larboard-ſide; you muſt keep the South Shore cloſe on board, for fear of a Ledge of Rocks which ſpits out from a ſmall rocky Iſland, on the other Side; as ſoon as you are within that Iſland, you muſt haul over for the North Shore, and anchor in 4 or 5 Fathom Water. In this Harbour might be made ſeveral very convenient Fiſhing-Rooms, and in the Coves between it and *Cape Norman* might be built Stages for the Boats to reſort to, and to cure Fiſh.

Cape Norman is the Northermoſt Point of Land in *Newfoundland*, lies in the Latitude of 51 Deg. 38 Min. 23 Sec. North, it is of a moderate and even Height, and a barren Rock for ſome Miles in the Country. From *Cape Norman* a W.S.W. Courſe, between 9 and 10 Leagues, will carry you a League without *Green Iſland*; all the Shore between them is bold, and of a moderate and equal Height for ſeveral Miles into the Country; but a good way inland is a Chain of high Mountains, lying parallel with the Coaſt. Between 3 and 4 Miles to the Weſtward of the Cape is a Cove, wherein ſmall Veſſels and Boats may lie very ſecure from all Winds, except N.E.; from this Place to *Green Iſland* there is no Shelter on the Coaſt. In turning between *Cape Norman* and *Green Iſland* in the Night, or Foggy Weather, you may ſtand in for the Land with great Safety, into 25 Fathom Water, until you are nearly the Length of *Green Iſland*; you will then have that Depth of Water very near the Shore, and likewiſe on the outſide of the Iſland itſelf.

Cape Norman.

Boat Harbour.

This Iſland lies three Quarters of a Mile from the Main, is two thirds of a Mile in Length, very low, narrow, and agreeable in Colour to the Name it bears; from the Eaſt End ſtretches out a Ledge of Rocks, three Quarters of a Mile to the Eaſtward, whereon the Sea breaks in bad Weather. The Channel between the Iſland and the Main, wherein is 4 and 5 Fathom Water, is very ſafe, and where Veſſels may anchor, if they find Occaſion: The only Winds that can make a Sea here, are from the W.S.W. and E.N.E; to go in from the Weſtward, keep the Point of the Iſland on board for the deepeſt Water, which is 4 Fathom, and going in from the Eaſtward, keep the Main on board. The Diſtance from this Iſland to the oppoſite Part of the Coaſt of *Labradore*, called *Caſtles*, or *Red Cliffs*, doth not exceed 3 Leagues and an half; they bear from each other N.W. and S.E. and is the narroweſt Part of the Streights of *Bell-Iſle*.

Green Iſland.

From *Green Iſland* to *Flower Ledge* (which lies near half a League from the Shore) a W.S.W. Courſe 3 Leagues will carry you half a League without the Ledge; from *Flower Ledge* to the Bay of *St. Barbe*, the Courſe is S.S.W. 5 Miles, and to Point *Ferolle* S.W. ¼ S. 7 Leagues. Five Miles to the Weſtward of *Green Iſland* is *Sandy Bay*, wherein ſmall Veſſels might ride in 3 and 4 Fathom Water, with Southerly and S.W. Winds. Between *Green Iſland* and *Sandy Bay* is *Double Ledge*, which ſtretches off from the Shore near half a Mile, whereon is 8 and 9 Feet Water.

Courſes from Green Iſland to Ferolle Point.

Sandy Bay.

Double Ledge.

Savage

Savage, Mistaken, and Nameless Coves.	*Savage Cove*, which is 2 Miles to the Westward of *Sandy Bay*, is small, will admit only small Vessels and Boats, in the Mouth of which is a small low Island; the Passage in (which is very narrow) is on the East-side of the Island, and you must anchor as soon as you are within it, in 2 and a half, and 2 Fathom Water. One Mile to the Westward of this Cove is *Mistaken Cove*, which is something larger than *Savage Cove*, but not near so good, being shoal Water in every Part of it. *Nameless Cove* lies 1 Mile farther to the Westward, wherein is very shoal Water, and several sunken Rocks. One Mile right off
Flower Ledge and Grenville Ledge.	from the East Point of this Cove lies *Flower Ledge*, Part of which just appears at Low-water; you will have 10 Fathom Water close to the off Side of it. Between it and *Mistaken-Cove*, half a Mile from the Land, lies *Grenville-Ledge*,
Flower Cove and Seal Islands.	whereon is 6 Feet Water. *Flower-Cove* (wherein is 2 Fathoms and a half Water) lies just to the Southward of *Nameless Cove*; it may be known by some White rocky Islands called *Seal-Islands*, lying a little to the Westward of it; you must not come too near the outermost of these Islands, for fear of some sunken Rocks near it. A little within the Entrance lies a Rock above Water, and a Channel on each Side of it: This Cove lies in East, as doth *Nameless-Cove*, and you must mind not to mistake one for the other. Between *Seal-Islands* and the Main is a Passage for Boats, and Conveniences for a Seal Fishery.
Anchor Point.	From *Seal-Islands* to *Anchor-Point*, which is the East Point of the Bay of St. *Barbe*, the Course is S.W. by S. 1 League; there is no Danger but what lies very near the Shore, until you are the Length of the Point, where lies a rocky Island, from which stretches out a Ledge of Rocks S.S.W. one third of a Mile, which you must be mindful of in going in or out of the Bay of *St. Barbe*. A
Anchor Cove.	little within *Anchor Point* is *Anchor-Cove*, wherein is 3 Fathom Water; it is so very small that there is no Room in it to bring a Ship up, unless it be little Wind or Calm; the safest way is to Anchor without and warp in; there is Room in it for one Ship, and is a very snug and convenient Place for one Fishing Ship, and for a Seal Fishery.
Bay St. Barbe.	The Bay of *St. Barbe* lies between *Anchor-Point* and *St. Barbe-Point*, which is the S.W. Point of the Bay; they lay from each other S. by E. and N. by W. half a League; it lies in S.E. about 2 Miles from *Anchor-Point*. To sail into the Bottom of the Bay or Harbour, you must give *Anchor-Point* a good Birth, and all the East-side of the Bay to avoid the sunken Rocks, which lay along that Shore; the Bay will not appear to be of any Depth, and you must be well in before you can discover the Entrance into the Harbour, which is but narrow; you must then steer in S.S.E. keeping in the Middle of the Channel, and Anchor as soon as you are within the two Points, in a small Cove on the West-side in 5 Fathom Water; the Bottom is Sand and Mud, and you lay Landlock'd. Near this Place branches out two Arms or Rivers, one called the South and the other the East; in the East River is 3 Fathom Water a good way up, but the other is Shoal; in these Rivers are plenty of Salmon; and their Banks are stored with various Sorts of Wood. Between

the

[9]

the S.W. Point of the Bay, and Weſt Point of the Harbour is a Cove, wherein are ſunken Rocks, which ſtretcheth off a little without the Line of the two Points; in the open Bay is 7, 8, and 9 Fathom Water, but no ſafe Anchorage, becauſe of the N.W. and W. Winds, which blow right in, and cauſe a very great Sea.

About 1 League to the S.W. of the Bay of *St. Barbe* lies the Bay *St. Gene-* Bay St. Ge-*veive*; in and before this Bay lie ſeveral ſmall Iſlands, two only of which are of neveive. any conſiderable extent; the Northermoſt of theſe two which is the largeſt, called *Current-Iſland*, is of a moderate height, and when you are to the N.E. of it, the Weſt Point will appear bluff, but is not high; if to the Weſtward it will appear flat, and white like Stone Beach; near half a Mile S.W. by S. from this Point is a Shoal, upon which is 3 Fathom Water; the other Iſland (called the *Gooſeberry-Iſland*) lying to the Southward and within *Current-Iſland*, hath a Croſs on the S.W. Point of it, from which Point ſtretches out a Ledge of Rocks, near half a Mile to the Southward; on the South Point of this Ledge is a Rock that juſt covers at High water; the beſt Channel into the Bay is to the Southward of theſe Iſlands, between the Rocks above-mentioned and a ſmall Iſland lying South from it, (which Iſland lies near the South Shore) this Channel is very narrow, and hath not leſs than 5 Fathom at Low-water in it, the Courſe in is E. by N. before you come the Length of the afore-mentioned Rock, you muſt be careful not to approach too near the S.W. end of *Gooſeberry-Iſland*, nor yet to the Main, but keep nearly in the Middle between both; if you get out of the Channel on either Side, you will immediately fall into 3 and 2 Fathom Water; as ſoon as you are within the ſmall Iſland above-mentioned, you muſt haul to the Southward, and bring *St. Geneveive-Head* (which is the S.W. Point of the Bay) between the ſmall Iſland and the Main, in Order to avoid the middle Bank, you may either Anchor behind the ſmall Iſland, in 5 and 6 Fathom Water, or ſteer over with the ſaid Mark into the Middle of the Bay, and Anchor with the S.W. Arm open in 7 and 8 Fathom Water; it is very good Anchoring in moſt Parts of the Bay, and pretty Convenient for Wooding and Watering; the ſnuggeſt Place is in the S.W. Arm, the Channel going into which is narrow, and 4 Fathom deep. There is a Channel into the Bay between *Current-Iſland* and *Gooſeberry-Iſland*, wherein is not leſs than 3 Fathom Water, it is but narrow and lies cloſe to the N.E. end of *Gooſeberry-Iſland*; there alſo is a Channel for Boats to the Eaſtward of all the Iſlands. The middle Bank is a Shoal lying in the Middle of the Bay, that nearly dries at Low-water, it is pretty large and hath not leſs than 4 Fathom Water all round it.

Four Miles to the Weſtward of the Bay of *St. Geneveive* is the Harbour of *Old Ferolle*, which is a very good and ſafe Harbour, formed by an Iſland called Old Ferolle. *Ferolle-Iſland*, lying parallel with the Shore. The beſt Paſſage into this Harbour is at the S.W. end of the Iſland, paſſing to the Southward of a ſmall Iſland in the Entrance, which Iſland is very bold too: When you are within this Iſland you muſt haul up N.E. and anchor behind the S.W. end of *Ferolle-Iſland* in 8 and 9 Fathom Water, where you lie Land-lock'd in good Groun ; you may alſo anchor any where along the Inſide of the ſaid Iſland, and find a

B   good

good Channel up to the N.E. end thereof, where there is an exceeding good Place for Fishing Ships to lie in like a Bason, in 5 and 6 Fathom Water, form'd by three Iflands lying at the N.E. end of *Ferolle-Ifland*; there is also a narrow Channel into this Place from the Sea of 2 Fathom at Low-water, between the Northermost of thefe Iflands and the Main; here is convenient Places for many Fishing Ships, and plenty of Wood and Water; on the outfide of thefe Iflands are fome Ledges of Rocks a fmall Distance off.

Dog-Ifland. From the S.W. end of *Ferolle-Ifland* to *Dog-Ifland* is W.S.W. between 4 and 5 Miles; *Dog-Ifland* is only divided from the Main at High-water, is much higher than any Land near it, which makes it appear when you are a good way to the Eastward to be some Diftance from the Main.

Bay of St. Margaret. From *Dog-Ifland* to *Point Ferolle* is W.S.W. 3 Miles; between them is the Bay of *St. Margaret*, which is large and fpacious, with feveral Arms and Iflands in the Bottom of it, abounding with great Plenty of Timber of the Spruce and Fir kind, and watered by fmall Rivers; it affords good Anchorage in many Parts of it, particularly on the Weft-fide which is the beft Place, as being the cleareft of Danger, and moft convenient for Wood and Water.

New Ferolle. Between *St. Margaret's Bay* and Point *Ferolle*, is a fmall Bay called *New Ferolle*, which lies in S.S.W. about 1 Mile. and is quite flat all over, having not quite 3 Fathom in any Part of it, and in fome Places not more than 2, and open to the N.E. Winds; there is a Stage on each Side of the Bay, and Room for as many more.

Point Ferolle. Point *Ferolle* is fituated in Latitude 51° 02′ North, is 2 Miles in Length, of a moderate Height, and join to the Main by a low Neck of Land, which divides *New Ferolle* Bay from the Bay of *St. John's*, which makes it appear like an Ifland at a Diftance; all the North-fide of the Point is very bold too, having 20 Fathom Water very near it; but from the S.W. Part ftretches out a Ledge of Rocks into the Bay of *St. John's*.

This Part of the Coaft may be eafily known by a long Table-Mountain, in the Country above the Bay of *St. John's*; the Weft-end of this Mountain, from the Middle of the Point *Ferolle* bears S. by E. and the Eaft-end S. 59° 30′ E.

Remarks between Green Ifland and Point Ferolle. In turning between *Green-Ifland* and Point *Ferolle*, you ought not to ftand nearer the Shore (until you are to the Weftward of *Flower Ledge*) than half a League, unlefs well acquainted; you will have for the moft Part at that Diftance off 20 and 24 Fathom Water; after you are above the Ledges, that is, to the Weftward of them, the Shore is much bolder, but the Soundings not quite fo regular; you will have in fome Places 15 and 16 Fathom Water clofe to the Shore, and in others not above that Depth 2 Miles off; the Land between *Green-Ifland* and *St. Barbe*, next the Sea, is very low and in fome Places woody. The Land between the Bay of *St. Barbe* and Point *Ferolle*, is higher and hilly, the moft Part covered with Wood, and watered with Numbers of Ponds and fmall Rivers.

In

[11]

In the Harbour of *Griguet*, *Quirpon*, and *Noddy Harbour*, it flows Full and Of the Tides. Change about E. by N. in the Bay of *Piftolet*, and Places adjacent E. by S.

In all which Places it flows up and down, or upon a Perpendicular; Spring-Tides 5 Feet, and Nip-Tides 3 Feet.

At *Green-Ifland* S.E. Bay *St. Barbe*, and Bay *St. Geneveive* S.S.E. *Old* and *New Ferolle* about S. by E.

In all which Places it flows up and down, or upon a Perpendicular; Spring-Tides 7 Feet, and Nip-Tides 4 Feet.

Before *Quirpon* in settled Weather, the Tide or Current sets to the Southward nine Hours out of twelve, and stronger than the other Stream; in the *Streights* the Flood in the Offing sets to the Westward two Hours after it is high Water by the Shore, but this Stream is subject to Alterations in blowing Weather.

On the Coast of *Labradore*, a little way in-land from *Labradore* Harbour, or Bay *Phillipeaux*, is a very remarkable Mountain, forming at the Top three round Hills called our *Ladies Bubbies*. This Mountain bears from the Bay of Our Ladies *St. Barbe* N.W. a quarter N. from the Bay of *St. Geneveive* N. 30° W. and Bubbies. from *Dog-Ifland* N. 14° 45′ West.

Bell-Isle which lies at the Entrance of the *Streights*, to which it gives Name, is about 7 Leagues in circuit and pretty high; on the N.W. Side of it is a Bell-Ifle. very small Harbour fit for small Craft, called *Lark-Harbour*, within a little Island that lies close to the Shore; and at the East Point of the Island is a small Cove, that will only admit Fishing-Shallops; 2 Miles N. by E. from this Point lies a Ledge of Rocks, part of which appears above Water, and on which the Sea always breaks very high, you will have 20 Fathom close to this Ledge, and 55 Fathom between it and the Island; all about this Island is irregular Soundings, but you will not find less than 20 Fathom home to the Island, excepting on a small Bank lying N.W. 4 Miles from the N.E. end, whereon its said is only 5 Fathom.

Red-Bay on the Coast of *Labradore*, about 8 Leagues to the Westward of R d Bay. *Chateaux* is an exceeding good Harbour, with excellent Conveniencies for the Fishery.

York or *Chateaux* Bay on the Coast of *Labradore*, lies W.N.W. a quarter W. York or Cha-5 Leagues and a half from the West-end of *Bell-Isle*, and N.W. half N. teaux Bay on 8 Leagues and a half from the Island of *Quirpon*. In crossing the Streights the Coast of from *Quirpon* to *Chateaux* Bay, it is advisable to fall in with the Coast, a little Labradore. to the W.ward of the Bay, unless the Wind be E.erly and clear Weather, as there is not the least Danger to the W.ward, but to the E.ward are several low rocky Islands. This Bay may be known by two very remarkable rocky Hills on *Caftle* and *Henley* Islands, which Islands lay in the Mouth of the Bay, those Hills are flat at top, and the steep Cliffs round them have something the Resemblance of Castle Walls; but as these Hills are not distinguishable at a

B 2 Resemblance

Diſtance, becauſe of the high Land on the Main within them; the beſt Marks for knowing the Bay, when in the Offing, is as follows; all the Land to the Weſtward of it is high of a uniform even Figure, terminating at the Weſt-ſide of the Bay with a conſpicuous Nob, or Hillcock; about *Chateaux* Bay, and to the Eaſtward of it is hilly, broken Land, with many Iſlands along Shore, but there is no Iſlands to the Weſtward of it; to ſail into the Bay you leave both the Iſlands, on which ſtand the two Caſtle Hills on the Starboard-ſide; and for large Ships to keep clear of all Danger, they muſt keep Point *Grenville* (which Point is known by a Bacon upon it) on with the Weſt Point of *Henley* Iſland, which Point is a ſmooth black Rock, and may be known by a ſmall black Rock juſt above Water, about a Cable's Length without it) until you are abreaſt of the Eaſt Point of *Whale* Iſland; then to avoid the middle Rock, on which is only 9 Feet, and which lies nearly in the Middle between the Eaſt Point of *Whale* Iſland, and the ſaid black Point of *Henley* Iſland; you muſt haul over either cloſe to the little black Rock, lying off the ſaid Point of *Henley* Iſland, or elſe borrow on the *Whale* Iſland, but not too near it, it being flat a little way off; when you are ſo far in as to open the narrow Paſſage into *Temple* Bay, in order to ſail up into *Pitt's* Harbour, haul to the Weſtward, until you bring the outer Point of *Caſtle* Iſland a little open with *Whale* Iſland; that Mark will lead you up into *Pitt's* Harbour, which is large and ſpacious, with a good Bottom in every Part of it, and covered from all Winds; you lie in 10 or 14 Fathom; here is excellent Conveniencies for the Fiſhery, and Plenty of Timber at Hand; formerly Ships from *France* carried on a moſt valuable Fiſhery at this Place for Whale, Cod and Seals. There is a good, though narrow Paſſage into the Northward of *Henley* Iſland, though which you carry 3 Fathom and a half Water; 1 Mile to the Eaſtward of *Henley* Iſlands lies *Seal* Iſlands, from them to *Duck* Iſland is 3 Miles and a half; between *Seal* Iſlands and *Duck* Iſland is *Bad* Bay which is open to the Eaſterly Winds, and full of Rocks, ſome above and ſome under Water.

Bad Bay.

Soundings. Croſſing the *Streights* from *Quirpon* to *Chateaux*, you will meet irregular Soundings from 20 to 30 Fathom on the *Newfoundland* Side, and in Places near the Shore, you will have 30 to 40 Fathom; in the Middle of the *Streights* in the Stream of *Bell-Iſle*, is from 20 to 30 Fathom, and between that and *Chateaux* Bay from 45 to 80 Fathom; within a Mile of the Coaſt of *Labradore*, to the Weſtward of *Chateaux* Bay, you will have 25, 30, and 35 Fathom; further up the *Streights*, as far as Cape *Norman* and *Green* Iſland, you will have 40 and 45 Fathom in the Middle, leſs towards *Newfoundland*, and more towards the Coaſt of *Labradore*.

St. Peters. About 7 Miles to the Eaſtward of *Seal* Iſlands is *St. Peter*'s Iſlands, a Parcel of ſmall barren Rocks; within them is *St. Peter*'s Bay, which is a good Bay open only to the S.E. Winds.

Cape Charles. Cape *Charles* makes with a high Hill ſteep towards the Sea, and ſloping inland, ſo that when you are to the Weſtward of *Chateaux*, Cape *Charles* will make like an Iſland.

From

[13]

From *St. Peter's* Iflands to Cape *Charles* Ifland the Courfe is N.E. half N. Diftance near 4 Leagues; between them lies *Niger* Sound, which is an Inlet 2 Leagues deep, before which lies feveral Iflands. You may pafs to the Northward or Southward of any of thofe Iflands into the Sound; the Courfe in is N.W. the beft Anchorage is on the North fide in 9 Fathom Water.

Niger Sound.

From Cape *Charles* to the *Battle* Iflands (which are the outermoft of the *Caribou* Iflands) the Courfe is N. by E. half E. 4 Miles, and from the Northermoft of the *Battle* Iflands to Point *Lewis* is N.N.W. ¼ W. 5 Miles; between the *Battle* Iflands and the great *Caribou* Ifland is a good Harbour for fmall Veffels; the South entrance is very narrow and hath only three Fathom Water; this Entrance is not eafily diftinguifhed by reafon of a fmall Ifland before it; the North Entrance is much wider paffing to the Weftward of the three fmall Northermoft of the *Battle* Iflands; you may anchor from 5 to 10 Fathom Water. This Place is much reforted to by the Savages, and is by them named *Ca-tuc-to*. And Cape *Charles* they call *Ikkegaucheacleuc*.

Caribou and Battle Iflands.

Between the *Caribou* Iflands and Cape *Lewis* lies *St. Lewis's* Bay, in which are many Iflands and Inlets which have not yet been examined.

St. Lewis Bay.

From the North part of Cape *Lewis* at a quarter of a Mile from the Shore are two flat Rocks, and alfo feveral funken Rocks, all which are within that Diftance from the Shore; round this Point is the Entrance of a fmall Cove running in S.S.W. half a Mile, named *Deep Water* Creek, but very narrow and hath from 20 to 40 Fathom Water in it.

Deep Water Creek.

From the North Part of Point *Lewis* to the South Head of *Petty Harbour* Bay, the Courfe is North 1 Mile and a half; it is a high bold Shore; from the South Head to the North Head of this Bay the Courfe is N. ¼ E. 1 Mile and half; this Bay runs up W.N.W. 1 Mile; in it is 20 to 40 Fathom Water. At the Bottom of it is *Petty* Harbour; the Entrance is to the Northward of a low Point of Land which fhuts the Harbour in from this Sea, fo as not to be feen till very near it; the Entrance is very narrow, it is not above 50 Fathom broad, there is 5 Fathom in the Middle, and 3 Fathom clofe to the Sides; the narrow Part is but fhort, and after you are within the Entrance the Harbour becomes wide, running up W. by N. a Mile and half, and a third of a Mile broad, wherein Ships may anchor in any Part from 12 to 7 Fathom, and lie intirely Land-lock'd. From the North Head of *Petty Harbour* Bay to Point *Spear* the Courfe is N. half E. 2 ¼ Miles; betwixt them is *Barren* Bay and *Spear* Harbour; *Barren* Bay is to the Northward of the North Head of *Petty Harbour* Bay, in it is no Shelter.

Petty Harbour.

Spear Harbour is to the Southward of *Spear* Point, this is a very good Harbour; coming from the Northward about Point *Spear*, you will open two Iflands in the Bottom of a fmall Bay; the beft Paffage in, is betwixt the two Iflands, and to keep the North Ifland clofe on Board, there is 4 Fathom along fide of it, after you are half a Cable's Length within the Iflands fteer for the Middle of the Harbour, and anchor in 7 or 8 Fathom, there is good Room to moor; fmall Veffels may go on either Side of the Iflands; there is 2 Fathom

Spear Harbour.

at

[14]

at low Water; but obferve in coming from the Southward, you will only diftinguifh one Ifland, for the Northermoft Ifland will be fhut in under the Land fo as not to be difcerned till you get within the Heads.

Three Harbours.   From Point *Spear* to the Entrance of the *Three Harbours* the Courfe is W.N.W. about 3 Miles between them there are feveral fmall high Iflands laying within half a Mile of the Shore called *Spear* Iflands; they are all bold too, and there is 20 Fathom within them, N.N.E. E. from the S.E. Head of the Entrance of the 3 Harbours, lies two fmall Iflands clofe together, called *Double* Ifland, about as high as they are broad; and about half a Cable's Length to the Eaftward of them Iflands are 2 funken Rocks, on which the Sea breaks in bad Weather. Nearly in the Middle of the Entrance of the *Three Harbours* lies 2 Iflands clofe together, which moftly appear as one Ifland by being fo clofe together; they are fteep too; Ships may pafs on either fide of them in 12 and 14 Fathom, and anchor within them in *Queen Road* in 16 Fathom; by the S.E. end of the Iflands is the wideft Paffage, and room for Ships to work in or out.

Sophia Harbour.   The firft and Southermoft Harbour within *Queen Road* is *Sophia* Harbour; it runs up S. by E. 1 Mile and half, and has from 15 to 10 Fathom Water for that Diftance; then it tends away round a low Point to the Eaftward, and becomes a Mile broad; but thence is very fhoal Water, and only fit for fmall Veffels.

Port Charlotte.   Port *Charlotte* is the middle Harbour, and a very good one for any Ships; there is a low flat Ifland on the Starboard-fide of the Entrance, and from this Ifland runs a Reef of Rocks a third of the Channel over to the South fide, to avoid which keep the South fide neareft on board, for it is fteep too, having 9 Fathom clofe to the Shore; therefore keep the South fide neareft till you are a quarter of a Mile within the Entrance, then you may anchor in any Part of the Harbour betwixt 12 and 17 Fathom, only giving the Starboard-fide a Birth of half a Cable's Length to avoid a fmall Reef that lays along that Side.

Mecklenburg Harbour.   *Mecklinburg* Harbour is the Northermoft of the three, and lies up N.W. half W. and W.N.W. 2 Miles; in the lower Part of this Harbour is 20 Fathom, but in the upper Part is no more than 12 Fathom room for Ships to moor; to fail up to the Head keep the Larboard-fide neareft, to avoid the Ledge of Rocks that lay along the Starboard-fide about 30 Fathom from the Shore. Thefe Rocks lay within the narroweft Part of the Harbour, and above the low Point on the Starboard-fide; the beft Anchorage is at the Head of the Harbour.

St. Frances or Alexes River.   From the Iflands at the Entrance of the *Three Harbours* to Cape *St. Francis*, the Courfe is N. half E. about 5 Miles; between them is the Entrance into *St. Francis* or *Alexes* River, betwixt 2 low Points about a Mile acrofs; this River runs up about 10 Leagues, where the Water is frefh and a very ftrong Tide; in it are many Bays, Harbours and Iflands; the firft Part of this River runs up W.N.W. 3 Miles and a half. There are 4 Iflands within the Entrance, 2 of which are on the Larboard-fide, and further up 2 on the Starboard-fide; the outermoft Ifland on the Larboard-fide, which is about a Mile within the Entrance, is a high round Ifland in the Shape of a Sugar-Loaf with
the

the top Part cut off, and is a very good Mark to fail in by; there is a Ledge of Rocks about half a Cable's Length from the S.E. Point of the Entrance; and E.S.E. half a Mile from the said Point there is a flat Rock always above Water, with a Ledge of funken Rocks half a Cable's Length to the N.E. from it; and half a Mile without this flat Rock, on the same Line with the Point, there is another flat Island, with a Ledge of funken Rocks a Cable Length to the N.E. from it; in failing into this River, to avoid thefe Ledges, keep to the Northward of the flat Iflands till you bring the *Sugar-Loaf* Ifland, which is within the River, a third of the Channel over from the S E. Point; that Mark will keep you clear of the Ledges; and to the Northward of them, you may either fail or work in, taking Care not to fhut the *Sugar-Loaf* Ifland in with the N.W. Point, and bring it no nearer the S E. Point than a third of the Breadth of the Channel; after being within the Points, there is no Danger but what is to be feen; there is Anchorage within the 2 Iflands on the Larboard-fide in 12 and 14 Fathom, but you will lay open to the N.E. the beft Place to anchor within the firft Part of the River, is in *Ship's* Harbour, which Ship Harbour. is on the Larbeard-fide about 2 Miles and a half from the Entrance where the Courfe into it is S.S.W. 1 Mile and a half; at the Entrance it is ¾ of a Mile broad, at the Head it is broader; there is 12 and 15 Fathom Water, and good Anchorage in fecurity againft all Winds; at 3 Miles and a half from the Entrance the Courfe of the River is W. by S. 7 Miles, in the Middle of it are feveral great and fmall Iflands: Sailing up along the South fide of the Iflands there is no Danger, and not lefs than 40 or 50 Fathom Water, but on the Starboard or North fide of the Iflands there is much lefs Water, and Anchorage all the Way up in 12 and 17 Fathom. The Courfe up the third Part of the River is W.S.W. 4 Miles; here is only two Iflands, on the Larboard or South fide of which is very good Anchoring in 12 Fathom; on the North fide is 30 Fathom Water; the Land about here is very high and well covered with Wood; here the Water is frefh, and 7 Miles further up is a Barr, on which there is not above 3 Feet at low Water, the River above that Barr runs W. and W.N.W. 6 Miles, but the Head of it is not yet known; by the rapid Stream probably it comes from great Lakes afar off.

One Mile to the Northward of *St. Frances* River there is a Harbour called *Merchant-men's* Harbour; betwixt the River and this Harbour there are 2 or 3 Merchant-funken Rocks laying a Cable's Length off from the fecond Point from the Ri- mens Har-ver; there is no Danger in failing into this Harbour; it runs in firft W.N.W. bour. and then W. about a Mile, it is 2 Cable Lengths wide at the Entrance, and 3 at the Head of it, where Ships may anchor in 12 Fathom Water.

To the Northward of this Harbour, round a fmall Point, there is an Inlet which runs up W.N.W. 5 Miles, where it turns to the Southward into *St. Frances* River; it is about one third of a Mile broad at the Entrance, and continues the fame breadth about 2 Miles up, and then becomes very broad, with an Ifland in the Middle fhaped not unlike a Leg; there is no Danger in this Inlet but what appears above Water; along the South fide of *Leg* Ifland there is Anchorage in 12 or 13 Fathom. At about 3 Miles and a half within the Entrance, the lower Part of *Leg* Ifland forms 3 very good Harbours, with 7 and 12 Fathom Water in them: on the North fide of *Leg* ifland there
is a

[16]

Gilbert's River. is a large Space about a Mile broad and 2 Miles long, in it is from 60 to 80 Fathom Water; from which to the N.W. is a Paſſage into *Gilbert*'s River, which runs up from thence W.N.W. 6 Miles, and is about half a Mile broad, and from 50 to 60 Fathom Water in it; then *Gilbert*'s River divides into two Branches, one to the W.N.W. 7 or 8 Miles, the other S.S.W. 6 Miles, the Head of which is within a Mile of *St. Frances* River; both theſe Branches are full of ſmall Iſlands, Rocks and Shoals on each Side, but in the Middle is good Anchorage all the way up from 10 to 20 Fathom; this River has alſo a Paſſage out to Sea to the Northward of Cape *St. Francis*, between *Hare* Iſland and

Hare Iſland. *Fiſhing* Iſlands; from *St. Frances* Iſland to the North end of *Hare* Iſland is W.N.W. 2 Miles and a half; within *Hare* Iſland there is a ſmall Harbour, to ſail into it you muſt paſs round the North end of *Hare* Iſland, there is from 12 to 5 Fathom Water within this Harbour, and no Shoals in it; but the beſt

Fiſhing-Ships Harbour. Harbour hereabouts is *Fiſhing Ship* Harbour, which is formed by 3 Iſlands laying along the Shore a Mile to the Northward of *Hare* Iſland; the beſt Paſſage into it is betwixt the 2 Weſtermoſt Iſlands, that Entrance bears from *Hare* Iſland N.W. There is no Danger in this Paſſage; Ships may ſail right in N.W. up to the Head of the Harbour, and anchor in 12 Fathom; there is good Room for any Ships to moor; there are two other Paſſages to this Harbour, one to the Weſtward from the Entrance of *Gilbert*'s River, the other to the Eaſtward paſſing to the Northward of all the *Fiſhing* Iſlands, and hath 7 Fathom through, but this is a very narrow Paſſage and difficult for thoſe not acquainted. From the Northermoſt *Fiſhing* Iſland to Cape *St. Michael* the Courſe is N. by W. ½ W. Diſtance 6 Miles; this Part of the Coaſt is bold too and very high Land.

Occaſional Harbour. Two Miles to the Southward of Cape *St. Michael* lies *Occaſional* Harbour, which may be eaſily known by two large Rocks called *Twin* Rock, which lies about two thirds of a Mile without the Entrance, they lay cloſe together, Ships may paſs on either Side of them; the Entrance to this Harbour is betwixt 2 high Lands, and runs up S.W. about 2 Miles, then W.N.W. there is no Danger in this Harbour, both Sides are ſteep too; and about 2 Miles up there is good Anchorage in 7 and 10 Fathom; the Winds betwixt the high Land at the Entrance always ſets right into the Harbour or right out.

St. Michael's Bay. From Cape *St. Michael*'s to Cape *Bluff* the Courſe is N. by W. 4 Leagues; theſe 2 Capes forms the great Bay of *St. Michael*, which contains a great Number of Iſlands, Inlets, Rivers, &c. which are not yet known. Cape *Bluff* is

Cape Bluff. a high bluff Land, and may be ſeen 15 or 16 Leagues; the beſt Place yet known for large Ships to anchor within *St. Michael*'s Bay, is on the South ſide, that is, firſt keep Cape *St. Michael* Shore on board, then keep along the South ſide of the firſt Iſland you meet with, which is called *Long* Iſland, till you come near as far as the Weſt end of it, and there anchor from 12 to 20 Fathom; you will there lay Land-lock'd, and may work out again to Sea on either Side of *Long* Iſland. At the Entrance of this Bay is a large ſquare Iſland, within which are many ſmall Iſlands which form ſeveral Harbours.

The Land from Cape *Bluff* to the Northward lies N.N.E. 5 or 6 Leagues, and makes in ſeveral high Points.

F I N I S.

DESCRIPTION

OF PART OF THE

COAST OF LABRADORE,

FROM

Grand Point of *Great Mecatina* to *Shecatica*.

N. B. All Bearings and Courses hereafter-mentioned, are the true Bearings and Courses, and not by Compass; the Variation being 26d. 00m. W. this present Year, 1768.

FROM *Grand Point* to outer Rocks off the *Islands* of *Entrance*, the Course is S. E. by E. ¼ E. 2 ¼ Miles.
From the Outer Rocks off the *Islands* of *Entrance*, to the *Murr Rocks*, the Course is E. by S. ¼ E. 3 ¾ Miles.
From *Murr Rocks* to *Flat Island*, the Course is N. E. ¼ E. Distance 5 Miles.
From *Flat Island* to *Treble Hill Island*, the Course is N. by E. 5 ¼ Miles.
From *Treble Hill Island* to *Fox Islands* (which is a Cluster of Islands, lying S. S. E. ¼ E. from *Eagle Harbour*) the Course is N. ¾ E. 3 Leagues.
From *Fox Islands* to the Rocks off the Entrance of the Port of *St. Augustine*, called *St. Augustine's Chain*, the Course is N. E. by E. 5 Leagues.
From the Rocks called *St. Augustine's Chain* to *Shag Island*, the Course is N. E. ¼ E. 2 ¼ Leagues.
From *St. Augustine's Chain* to the Rocks without *Shag Island*, called *Shag Rocks*, the Course is N. E. by E. Distance 3 Leagues.
From the *Shag Rocks* to the Rocks off the East End of the *Island* of *Shecatica*, the Course is N. E. ¼ E. 3 Leagues.
From the outer Rocks off the *Islands* of *Entrance* to the *Bay de Portage*, the Course is N. W. by N. ¼ W. 4 Miles.
From the outer Rocks off the *Islands* of *Entrance* to outer Point of *Mecatina Island*, the Course is N. by W ¼ W. 4 Miles.
From the outer Point off *Mecatina Island* to *Gull Island*, the Course is N. E. by E. 1 Mile.

Courses and Distances from Island to Island along the Coast, between Grand Point and Shecatica, which Courses carry you without all other Islands and Rocks.

Courses and Distances along shore passing within the Great Mecatina.

From

From *Gull Island* to *Green Island*, at the Entrance of *Red Bay*, the Courſe is N. N. E. ¼ E. 1 League. This Courſe will carry you clear of the *Shag Rocks*, as far as you paſs without *Gull Island*.

From *Gull Island* to *La Boule Rock*, off the N. W. End of *Great Mecatina Island*, the Courſe is N. E. by N. ¼ E. 4 Miles.

From *La Boule Rock* to *Green Iſland*, the Courſe is W. by S, ¼ League.

From *La Boule Rock* to *Duck Iſland*, the Courſe is N. N. W. ¾ W. 1 League.

From *Duck Iſland* to *Round Iſland*, at the Entrance of *Ha Ha Bay*, the Courſe is N. by E. ½ E. 1 ¼ Mile.

From *Round Iſland* into the Harbour of *Little Fiſh*, the Courſe is S. W. by W. ½ W. ¼ League.

From *Round Iſland* into the Bay of *Ha Ha*, the Courſe is N. N. E. ¼ E. ½ League, leaving all Iſlands on the Starboard Side.

From *La Boule Rock* to *Loon Iſlands*, the Courſe is N. ¼ E. 1 League.

From *La Boule Rock* to *Gooſe Iſland*, the Courſe is N. E. 5 ¼ Miles.

From *Gooſe Iſlands* to *Fox Iſlands*, the Courſe is N. E. by N. 2 Leagues.

Grand Point and Entrance Iſlands. The *Grand Point* of *Great Mecatina* lieth in the Latitude of 50d. 41m. N. and is the extream Point of a Promontory which ſtretches off from the Main. The Extream of this Point is low: from thence it riſeth gradually to a moderate Height, and may be eaſily known from ſeveral adjacent Iſlands and Rocks, which lie off S. E. by E. ¼ E. from it; the neareſt of which is a ſmall low Rock, and is within ½ Cable's Length from the Point. Two of theſe Iſlands are much larger and higher than the others; the Outermoſt are ſmall low rocky Iſlands, and lie 2 ¼ Miles from the *Grand Point*.

Murr Iſlands and Rocks. From *Grand Point*, E. by S. 5 ¼ Miles, lie the two *Murr Iſlands*, which are the Southermoſt Iſlands on this Part of the Coaſt. The Northermoſt *Murr Iſland* lieth from the other N. N. W. ¼ W. about ½ Mile. Theſe Iſlands are very remarkable, being two flat barren Rocks of a moderate Height, and ſteep Clifts all round. About ½ Mile to the S. E. of the Southermoſt *Murr Iſland* lie the two *Murr Rocks*, which are above Water. And E. N. E. ¼ E. 1 ¼ Mile from the Southermoſt *Murr Iſland*, lieth a Ledge of Rocks under Water, on which the Sea generally breaks.

Bay de Portage. From *Murr Iſlands*, N. W. by W. 2 Leagues lieth the *Bay de Portage*: the Land over this Bay maketh in a Valley, each Side being high; at the Entrance lieth an Iſland of a moderate Height, which forms the Harbour. You may ſail into this Harbour on either Side of the Iſland, but the Eaſtern Paſſage is only fit for ſmall Veſſels, there being only 2 Fathom Water in the Entrance at low Water. The Weſtern Paſſage is ſufficiently large and ſafe for any Veſſel to turn in, there being in it from 6 to 8 Fathom Water at low Water. Large Veſſels bound for this Harbour muſt be careful to avoid two ſunken Rocks, on which there is 2 ¼ Fathom Water at low Water. The Northermoſt of theſe Rocks lies from *Mutton Iſland*, S. by E. 1 ¼ Mile, and the

the Southermoſt lies from the *Seal Rocks*, N. by E. ¼ E. ½ Mile. Veſſels may borrow within 1 Cable's Length of *Mutton Iſland*, or *Seal Rocks*.

The Harbour of *Great Mecatina* lieth N. W. ½ W. 2 Leagues from *Murr Iſlands*, and N. by E. 2 ¼ Miles from *Grand Point*. This Harbour is formed by *Mecatina Iſland* and the Main, and is a ſafe, but ſmall Harbour, yet will admit Ships of Burthen, there being not leſs than 3 Fathom Water in either Paſſage at low Water; but they muſt moor Head and Stern, not being Room to moor otherwiſe. To ſail into this Harbour through the Weſtern Paſſage, there is not the leaſt Danger. To ſail in through the Eaſtern Paſſage, obſerve the following Directions : From the Eaſtern Point of the Iſland, run N. N. W. for the Main, and keep the Main cloſe on Board, till you bring the Weſtern Point of the Iſland on with the Point of *Dead Cove* (this is a ſmall Cove on the Main, which lays open to the Eaſtward; the Land which forms it is very low, with ſome Bruſh Wood on it), and ſail in that Direction till you are above a ſtony Point, which is the N. Point of the ſaid Cove, or till you bring the North Point of *Gull Iſland* (which is a ſmall Iſland lying N. E. by E. 1 Mile from *Mecatina Iſland*) on with the N. E. Point of *Mecatina Iſland*, you will then be within a Spit of Rocks, which ſtretches off from *Mecatina Iſland*, and muſt then haul directly over for *Mecatina Iſland*, in order to avoid a Ledge which ſtretches off from the South Point of *Dead Cove*, and may anchor, when you bring the Weſtern Paſſage open in 6 or 7 Fathom Water, in great Safety. Veſſels coming from the Eaſtward. and bound for the Harbour of *Mecatina*, and would paſs to the Northward of *Gull Iſland*, muſt be careful either to keep *Gull Iſland*, or the Main, cloſe on Board, in order to avoid a ſunken Rock that lays near half way between *Gull Iſland* and the Main; on one Part of which there is not above 3 Feet Water at low Water.

Harbour of Great Mecatina;

Gull Iſland.

The higheſt Part of the Land, between *Grant Point* and *Ha Ha Bay*, is directly over the Harbour of *Mecatina*.

The *Great Iſland* of *Mecatina* lies 3 Miles from the Main, and is in Length, from North to South, 3 ¼ Miles, and in breadth, from Eaſt to Weſt, 3 Miles, is high Land, but much higher in the Middle than either End. The N. E. Point of this Iſland maketh in a remarkable Bluff Head, which is in the Latitude 50d. 46m. N. Round this Head to the Northward, and within a Cluſter of ſmall Iſlands (on either Side of which is a good Paſſage), lieth a Cove, which runs in S. by W. ¼ W. about 1 ¼ Mile from the ſaid Iſlands; Veſſels may anchor in this Cove, in great ſafety, from 14 to 20 Fathom Water, good Ground. Here is Wood and Water to be had.

Great Iſland of Mecatina.

The *Great Iſland* of *Mecatina* being the moſt remarkable Land about this Part of the Coaſt from whence Veſſels may beſt ſhape a Courſe for other Places, I will here give the Bearings and Diſtances of the moſt remarkable Points, Headlands, Rocks; and Harbours from it,

From

Courses and Distances from Great Island of Mecatina to other Places.
: From the *Round Head* of the *Great Island* of *Mecatina* to *Mecatina Island*, the Course is W. by S. ¼ W. 3 ¼ Miles.
From *Round Head* to the outer Rocks off the *Islands* of *Entrance*, the Course is S. S. W. ½ W. 5 Miles.
From *Round Head* to *Murr Islands*, the Course is S. ¼ E. 5 Miles, nearly.
From the *Bluff Head* of the *Great Island* of *Mecatina* to *Flat Island*, the Course is S. E. by S. 5 Miles.
From *Bluff Head* to *Loon Islands*, the Course is N. by W. ¼ W. 4 Miles.
From *Bluff Head* to *Round Island*, at the Entrance of *Ha Ha Bay*, the Course is N. W. by N. ¼ W. 6 ¼ Miles. This Course leaves *Loon Islands* on the Starboard Side, and *Duck Island* on the Larboard Side.
From *Bluff Head* to *Treble Hill Island*, the Course is E. N. E. ½ E. 3 ½ Miles.
From *Bluff Head* to *Double Hill Island*, the Course is North 5 ¼ Miles.
From *Bluff Head* to *Goose Islands*, the Course is N. by E. ¾ E. 5 ¼ Miles.
From *Bluff Head* to the *Fox Islands*, the Course is N. N. E. ¼ E. 11 Miles.
From *Bluff Head* to *St. Augustine's Chain*, the Course is N. E. 25 Miles.
From *Bluff Head* to *Shag Island*, the Course is N. E. 10 ¼ Leagues.
From *Bluff Head* to *Shecatica*, the Course is N. E. ¼ E. 13 Leagues 2 Miles.

Little Fish Harbour.
: The Harbour of *Little Fish* lies in East and West, is but small, and is formed by an Island covered with Wood. You may sail into this Harbour on either Side of the Island, but to the Northward is the best Passage. In the Bay to the Southward of the Island, lies a Ledge of Rocks, Part of which is always to be seen. E. by S. ¼ Mile from the East Point of *Wood Island*, lieth a Rock, on which there is only 2 Fathom Water at low Water. You may anchor in this Harbour at the back of the Island in 7 or 8 Fathom Water, good Bottom, and have Room sufficient to moor. Here is both Wood and Water to be had. Off the Northern Point of the Entrance into this Harbour, called *Seal Point*, lie 2 small Islands, and a Sandy Cove, where there is a Seal Fishery carried on.

Between the Harbour of *Little Fish*, and the Bay of *Ha Ha*, is a remarkable high round Hill, which maketh in a Peek, and may serve as a good Mark for knowing either of those Places by.

Ha Ha Bay.
: The Bay of *Ha Ha* lieth from *La Boule Point* N. N. W. ¼ W. 5 ¼ Miles, in the Mouth of which there are several Islands, which form several Passages; but the best is between *Seal Point* and *Round Island*, leaving all the Islands on the Starboard Side: this is a wide and safe Passage, there being no Danger but what appears above Water. This Bay runs up North 7 Miles, at the Head of which, on the Starboard Side, are several Islands; within these Islands, to the Eastward, are many good Anchoring-Places, from 9 to 20 Fathom Water. Vessels may occasionally anchor all along the Eastern Shore within

within this Bay, in 12 and 14 Fathom Water, Mud Ground: On the Western Side it is deep Water. N. ¼ W. 2 Miles from the Entrance on the W. Side, is a high bluff Head; round this Head, W. by N. ¼ W. ½ Mile, is a small but safe Harbour for small Vessels, in which you have 12 Fathom, good Bottom. This Harbour is formed by an Island, on either Side of which there is a safe but narrow Passage.

After you leave the Bay of *Ha Ha*, proceeding to the Eastward, you lose Sight of the Main Land (till you come to the Bay of *Shecatica*), which is hid from you by the Number of great and small Islands of different Heights, so numerous, and so near each other, that they are scarce to be distinguished as Islands till you get in amongst them.

Amongst these Islands are a great many good Roads and Harbours; some of the best and the easiest of Access are as follow:

Eagle Harbour lies near the West End of *Long Island*, and is formed by a Cluster of Islands, on which a *French* Ship of War, of that Name, was lost. This Harbour is capable of holding a Number of Shipping with great Security, having in it from 10 to 20 Fathom Water, good Bottom; but it is not easily to be distinguished by Strangers: the best Way to find it, is to shape a Course as afore directed, from the *Great Island* of *Mecatina*, to *Fox Islands*, which lie from the Westernmost Entrance of the Harbour, S. E. by S. ½ E. 1¼ Miles. It is also to be known by a large deep Bay, which forms to the Eastward of it, without any Islands in it, but to the Westward is a vast Number. If you intend for the East Passage into this Harbour, you must first steer from *Fox Islands*, N. ¼ E. 2½ Miles into the Bay, when you will observe, to the N. W. of you, a remarkable high Island, round which, to the Northward, is a safe Passage of 3 Fathom into the Harbour, where you may anchor in great Safety from all Winds. In the Western Passage into this Harbour, is 2½ Fathom Water, fit only for small Vessels, being a narrow Passage, between many Islands. This Part of the Coast is very dangerous for a Vessel to fall in with in thick Weather, by reason of the infinite Number of small and low Islands, and some Rocks under Water.

Eagle Harbour.

From the *Bluff-Head* of *Great Mecatina Island*, to *St. Augustine's Chain*, the Course is N. E. 8 Leagues and 1 Mile. The West Island of *St. Augustine* is of a moderate Height, the West Part being highest and quite low in the Middle, but is not easily to be distinguished at a Distance, by reason of the Islands within being much higher. ¼ Mile to the Eastward of this Island is the East Island, something larger, but not quite so high, and is even at Top. Between these two Islands, after passing between the *Chain* and *Square Islands*, is a safe Passage for small Vessels into this Port; they may anchor between the *West Island* and *Round Island*, or they may run to the Northward past *Round Island*, and anchor in 6 or 7 Fathom Water, where they

Port of St. Augustine.

will

(6)

will have good Room to moor. S. by W. ¼ W. about ½ League from the West *St. Augustine's Island*, runs a Chain of small Islands, called *St. Augustine's Chain*, the Outermost of which is a remarkable round smooth Rock. ¼ Mile to the West of this Island lay Rocks under Water, which always break, and shew above Water at ½ Ebb. About ¼ Mile to the S. W. of these Rocks is a high black Rock above Water; between these two is the best Passage for large Vessels into the Port of *St. Augustine*. You must steer, from this black Rock, for a remarkable low Point, which will bear N. ¼ W. till you open the Port of *St. Augustine*, and then haul in and anchor as before; or you may steer up the Passage between this Point and *Round Island*, and anchor as before directed.

River St. Augustine.   The Entrance of the River *St. Augustine* lays, from the Port of *St. Augustine*, 4½ Leagues to the N. W. with several large and small Islands between them: the River is not navigable for any Thing but Boats, by reason of a Bar across the Entrance, which drys at low Water. This River, at two Miles up, branches into two Arms, both tending to the N. W. 14 or 16 Leagues. There is Plenty of Wood to be had in this River.

Shag Island.   From *St. Augustine's Chain* to *Shag Island* the Course is N. E. ½ E. 2½ Leagues. This Island is very remarkable, being small, high, and in the Middle is a round peeked Hill. From this Island to the Eastward is a Number of small Rocks above Water, the Outermost lies E. by S. ½ E. 1½ Mile from *Shag Island*. N. W. by W. 2½ Mile from *Shag Island*, lieth the

Bay and Harbour of Sandy Island.   Bay and Harbour of *Sandy Island*, which is a very safe Harbour. To sail into this Harbour you must pass to the Eastward of *Murr Rocks*, and keep the Starboard Point of the Bay on Board, you will then see a small Rock above Water to the N. W. which lays off the Entrance of the Harbour; you may pass on either Side of this Rock, and then steer in N. ½ W. for the Harbour, there being no Danger but what appears. In this Harbour there is good Room to moor in 5 and 6 Fathom Water, and a good Bottom: there is not any Wood to be had, but Plenty of Water.

Cumberland Harbour.   *Cumberland Harbour* lies N. ½ W. 1 League from the Outer *Shag Rocks*, and is to be known by a remarkable high Hill on the Main, which is the highest hereabouts, and makes at the Top like a Castle, being steep Clifts appearing like Walls. This Hill lies N. W. by N. about 3½ Leagues from the Entrance of the Harbour. The Outer Islands, named *Duke and Cumberland Islands*, which form the Harbour, are of a moderate Height, the Easternmost making in two round Hills. To sail into this Harbour there is no Danger but what appears above Water, except a small Rock, which lays S. S. E. ½ Mile from the West Head, the Entrance is ½ Mile wide, and ½ Mile long; from the East Head, steer for the Inner Point on the West Side; after you are the Length of that Point, you may haul to the Eastward, and anchor where you please, from 20 to 7 Fathom Water, in good Ground, and an excellent roomy Harbour fit for any Ships, and is the best Harbour and the easiest of

Access

Accefs on this Coaft. Here is good Water, but for Wood you muft go up *Shecatica Bay*.

The Bay of *Shecatica* lies 2¼ Miles to the N. E. from the Entrance of *Cumberland* Harbour, and runs many Miles up the Country to the Northward, in feveral Branches and narrow crooked Paffages, with many Iflands, which form feveral good Harbours; the Paffages are too narrow for Veffels to attempt without being very well acquainted. *Bay of Shecatica.*

To the Eaftward of the Bay of *Shecatica*, and N. N. E. ½ E. 2¼ Leagues from the Outer *Shag Rocks*, lies the Ifland of *Miftanogue*; within it to the Northward, and before the Mouth of the Bay of the fame Name, is very good Anchorage, from 20 to 15 Fathom Water, good Ground, and fufficient Room to moor: to go into the Road, you may pafs round the Weft End of the Ifland, which is bold too, or round the Eaft End betwixt it and the Ifland of *Shecatica*, but this laft Paffage is only for fmall Veffels. There is good Anchorage quite to the Head of the Bay of *Miftanogue*, which is long and narrow. This Ifland and the Main Land here is high and barren, but there is both Wood and Water to be had in the Bay of *Miftanogue*. A little to the Eaftward lieth the Ifland of *Shecatica*, between it and the Main is a good Paffage for fmall Veffels, where there is a confiderable Seal Fifhery carried on. Three Miles to the N. E. of the Ifland of *Shecatica* lieth the Bay of *Pettit Pene*, which runs up N. 5 Miles, but is not fit for Veffels to anchor in, being deep Water, narrow, bad Ground, and entirely expofed to the Southerly Winds. *Ifland and Road of Miftanogue.* *Ifland of Shecatica.* *Bay of Pettit Pene.*

N. B. All the Iflands along the Coaft are quite barren, the Outer ones being fmall and low rocky Iflands, the Inner ones are large and high, covered moftly with green Mofs.

No Wood to be got but at fuch Places as are mentioned in the foregoing Directions.

The Courfe and the Flowing of the Tides along this Coaft are very irregular, no certain Account can be given thereof; they depend much upon the Winds, but in fettled moderate Weather I have found it high Water at *Shecatica*, on the Full and Change, at 11 o'Clock, and at *Mecatina* at half paft 2 o'Clock, and rifes and falls upon a Perpendicular about 7 Feet.

F I N I S.

The following SEA-CHARTS *are Sold by* R. SAYER *and* J. BENNETT, Map, Chart, and Print Sellers, (No. 53.) *Fleet-Street.*

1. CHANNEL, Six Sheets, 10s. 6d.
2. Ditto, One Sheet, 2s.
3. Atlantic Ocean, Four Sheets.
4. Ditto, One Sheet, 2s.
5. Açores, One Sheet, 2s.
6. Madeiras, One Sheet, 2s.
7. Cape de Verd, One Sheet, 2s.
8. Bermudas, One Sheet, 2s.
9. Newfoundland, 2s.
10. The Banks of Ditto, 2s.
11. S. E. Coaſt of Ditto, 2s.
12. S. Coaſt of Ditto, 5s.
13. W. Coaſt of Ditto, 5s.
14. Straights of Belle-Iſle, 4s.
15. Labradore, Part I. 2s.
16. Ditto, Part II. 2s.
17. River St. Laurence, Twelve Sheets, 12s.
18. Gulf of St. Laurence, One Sheet, 2s. 6d.
19. Sable Iſland, 1s.
20. Halifax and Nova Scotia, 2s.
21. Gut of Canſa, 1s.
22. Magdalene Iſlands, 1s.
23. Chaleur Bay, 1s.
24. Riſtagouch Harbour, 1s.
25. Finland, 2s.
26. Mediterranean, Three Sheets, 3s. 6d.
27. Straights of Magellan, 3s. 6d.
28. Boſton Harbour, 2s. 6d.

DIRECTIONS

FOR

NAVIGATING ON THAT PART

OF THE

COAST of LABRADORE,

FROM

Shecatica to *Chateaux*, in the Straits of *Belle-Ifle*.

Note, All Bearings and Courfes hereafter-mentioned, are the true Bearings and Courfes, and not by Compafs; the Variation being 26 Degrees W. this prefent Year, 1769.

*B*OWL *Ifland* lieth E. by N. 2 Leagues from the Ifland of *Shecatica*, and Bowl Ifland. 1 Mile from the Main; is a remarkable round Ifland of a moderate Height.
About this Ifland, and between it and *Shecatica*, are a number of fmall Iflands and funken Rocks; which renders this part of the Coaft dangerous, unlefs there is a Frefh of Wind, and then the Sea breaks on the Rocks.
From *Bowl Ifland* to the Entrance of the *Bay D'omar* the Courfe is N. E. by N. ½ E. Bay D'omar Diftance 2 Miles. This Bay runneth up N. by E. nearly 3 Miles, with high Land on both Sides; is about 2 Cables Length, wide all the Way up. Off the Coves it is wider. The Weftern Shore is the higheft. Without the Eaft Point lie 2 fmall Iflands about 1 Cable's Length off Shore. In this Bay there is very good Anchorage, the beft being at about 2 Miles within the Entrance, oppofite a Woody Cove, on the W. Side, where you may lie fecure from all Winds in 14 or 16 Fathom Water, and be very handy for Wooding and Watering. About 1 Mile within the Entrance on the Weft Side lyeth a remarkable green Cove, off which it is fhoal a fmall Diftance from the Shore;

one

Little Bay. One Mile to the Eastward of *Bay D'omar* lyeth *Little Bay*, in which is tolerable good Anchorage for small Vessels. E. N. E. ½ E. distant 3 Leagues from *Bowl Island*, begins a Chain of Island and Rocks, lying E. N. E. 3 Leagues,
Dog, Old Fort, and Esquimaux Island. and from 3 to 5 Miles distant from the Main, the Eastermost of which are called *Outer*, or *Esquimaux Islands*; the middle Part are called *Old Fort Islands*; and the Westermost are called *Dog Islands*. Within these Islands on the Main are several good Bays, and Harbours, but are too difficult to attempt, unless very well acquainted, the Passages being very narrow, and a Number of Sunken Rocks.

Anchorage. N. ½ W. 4 Miles from the W Side of the outer *Esquimaux Islands* is very good Anchorage for small Vessels, between two high Islands. Within these Islands lieth the River *Esquimaux*.

Point Belles Amour. From outer *Esquimaux Island* to *Point Belles Amour*, the Course is N. 59 ° E. distant 13 Miles. This Point is low and green, but about 1 Mile inland is high. Round this Point to the Eastward is a Cove, in which is Anchorage for small Vessels in 7 Fathom Water, but open to Easterly Winds.

Bradore Harbour. From *Point Belles Amour* to the Entrance of the Harbour of *Bradore* the Course is E. by N. 2 Leagues nearly. This Harbour is to be known by the Land between it and *Point Belles Amour*, being high Table Land, the Land on the East side of it being low near the Sea, and tending to the Southward, or by our Lady's Bubbies, which are three remarkable round Hills, seen all along this Coast, lying N. by E. ¼ E. 2 Leagues from the Island of *Ledges*, which
Our Ladies Bubbies. formeth this Harbour. This Island is of a moderate Height, having a great Number of small Islands and Rocks about it. On the East Side of this Island is a Cove, called *Blubber Cove*, wherein is Anchorage, in 2 ¼ Fathom Water, for small Vessels. There are Two Passages into the Harbour of *Bra-*
Island of Ledges. *dore*; but that to the Northward of the Island of *Ledges*, is by no means safe, there being a Number of sunken Rocks in that Passage: The Eastern Passage is safe, taking care to avoid a small Rock, which lies S. 3 ½ W. ½ Mile from the Low Point on the Main where the Houses stand. On this Rock the Sea mostly breaks, and shews above Water, at ¼ Ebb. On the East Side, within the Rock, is a small Cove, called *Shallop Cove*. From the Point above the Cove, called *Shallop Cove Head*, stretches off a Shoal, one Cable's Length from the Shore, and continues near the same Distance, quite to the Head of the Harbour.

Green Island. From the Island of *Ledges* to *Green Island*, the Course is S. 30 W. distant 5 Miles. On the East side of this Island is a Cove, wherein a Fishery is carried on. Between this Island and the Main, and between it and the Island *Bois*, is a clear safe Passage.

Island Bois. The Island *Bois* lyeth 2 Miles to the Eastward of *Green Island*, and is of a moderate Height, and a safe Passage all round it. To the Northward of this Island, lyeth *Blance Sablon*, in which is Anchorage, but the Ground is not very good, being a loose Sand.

Forteaux Bay. From the South Point of the *Isle au Bois*, to the West Point of *Forteaux Bay*, the Course is N. 70 E. distant 8 ¼ Miles. This Bay is 3 Miles broad, and nearly the same Depth. At the Head of which, on the West Side, is good Anchorage, from 10 to 16 Fathom Water, but is open to the Southward. Off the East Point of this Bay is a Rock, which maketh, in the Form of a

Shallop

(3)

Shallop under Sail, either coming from the Eastward, or the Westward: On the West Side of the Bay is a Fall of Water, which may be seen in coming from the Eastward.

L'Ance a Loup lyeth 1 League to the Eastward of *Forteaux Bay*. The Land between these Bays, being rather low near the Shore, at the Head of this Cove is tolerable good Anchorage in 12 Fathom: On the West Side lyeth *Schooner Cove*, in which is very good Anchorage for small Vessels in 7 Fathom Water, sandy Bottom. The two Points that form the Entrance of this Cove, bear N. N. E. ½ E. and S. S. W. ½ W. distant 2 Miles. The East Point is high Table Land, with steep Clifts to the Sea stretching N. E. 2 Miles nearly, and called the *Red Clifts*.

Wolf Cove, or L'Ance a Loup.

Red Clifts.

From the *Red Clifts* to the West Point of *St. Modeste Bay*, the Course is N. 38 E. distant 7 Miles, then N. by E. ½ E. 1 Mile to *St. Modeste Island*, which is a small low island, within which a small Craft may anchor, but is a bad Place.

St. Modeste.

Ship Head lieth 1 ½ Mile to the N. by E. from *St. Modeste Island*. Round this Head to the Northward, is *Black Bay*; in which there is tolerable good Anchorage in 10 Fathom Water.

Black Bay.

From the West End of *Red Clifts*, to the West Point of *Red Bay*, the Course is North 47 ° E. distant 6 Leagues. This is an excellent Harbour, and may be known by *Saddle Island*, which lies at the Entrance of this Bay, and is high at each End, and low in the Middle; and by a remarkable round Hill on the W. Side of the Bay, opposite the West End of *Saddle Island*; the Land on the West Side the Bay is high, and on the East Side rather low. At the Head of this Bay, it is high and woody. There is no Danger in sailing into this Bay, passing to the Westward of *Saddle Island*, and taking care to avoid a small Rock that lies near the W. Point on the Main, (this Rock shews above Water at ¼ Ebb) and a Shoal which stretches off about a Cable's Length from the inner Side of *Saddle Island*. The *Western Bay* lies in to the Northward of the West Point, in which is very good Anchorage from the Westerly Winds; but open to the Eastward. There is no Passage, except for Boats, to the Eastward of *Saddle Island*. In coming from the Eastward, Care must be taken to avoid a small Rock, which lies 1 Mile from the *Twin Islands*, (which are Two small black rocky Islands, lying off the East end of *Saddle Island*) and near 1 Mile off Shore. The aforementioned high round Hill on the West Side of the Bay, on with the Saddle on *Saddle Island*, will carry you on this Rock; the Sea generally breaks on it.

Red Bay.

Twin Islands.

Two Leagues and a half to the Eastward of *Red Bay*, lies *Green Bay*, in which is tolerable good Anchorage for small Vessels, in 12 Fathom Water, but open to the S. E. Winds. From *Saddle Island* to *Barge Point*, the Course is E. N. E. distant 10 Miles, and from thence to the Entrance of *Chateaux Bay*, is N. E. by E. distant 5 ¼ Leagues.

For Directions about *Chateaux Bay*, *Belle-Isle*, &c. See *Mr. Cook's Account*.

At

At *Red Bay*, the Tide flows, Full and Change, at half paſt Nine o'Clock.

At *Forteaux Bay*, at Eleven.

At *Bradore*, at Half paſt Eleven.

In all which Places it flows up and down, or upon a perpendicular Spring Tide, 7 Feet; and Neap Tides, 4 Feet.

F I N I S.

DESCRIPTION

OF THE

COAST of LABRADORE,

FROM

CAPE CHARLES

TO

CAPE LEWIS.

Note, *The Bearings hereafter mentioned are the true Bearings, and not by Compafs, the Variation being* 27 *Degrees* W. *this prefent Year,* 1770.

C*APE Charles Ifland* lieth Eaft, Diftance 1 ¼ Mile, from *Cape Charles,* and is of a moderate Heighth, with feveral fmall Rocks to the Eaftward and Weftward of it.

From the North Point of *Cape Charles Ifland* into *Alexis Harbour* the Courfe is W. N. W. 4 Miles. This Ifland is very fmall, and rather low. Within this Ifland is an excellent Harbour, formed by feveral high Iflands and the Main; in this Harbour is very good Anchorage from 17

to

to 22 Fathoms Water, muddy. You may fail into it on either Side of Center *Island*, but to the Northward of it is the beft Paffage.

Battle Iflands. From *Cape Charles Ifland* to the *Battle Iflands* the Courfe is N. N. E. 5 ¼ Miles. This Courfe will carry you to the Eaftward of the Rocks, which lieth 1 Mile to the Eaftward of the Northermoft *Battle Ifland*. This Ifland is high and round at Top.

River Iflands. From the Northermoft *Battle Ifland* to the *River Iflands* the Courfe is N. 76° W. Diftance 7 ¼ Miles. To the Weftward of the Eaftermoft *River Ifland* is Anchorage for Veffels in 30 or 35 Fathom Water, muddy Bottom. Veffels may pafs to the Southward of thefe Iflands up the River *St. Lewis*.

Cutter Harbour. From the South Point of the Eaftermoft *River Ifland* to *Cutter Harbour* the Courfe is S. 50° W. Diftance 1 Mile. In this Harbour there is tolerable good Anchorage for fmall Veffels.

River St. Lewis. From the Northermoft *Battle Ifland* to the Entrance of the River *St. Lewis* the Courfe is N. 61° W. 7 ¼ Miles; from thence the Courfe up the River is W. by N. 5 Miles; then N. 58° W. 8 Miles to *Woody Ifland*. (The North Point of the River is low Land for about 2 Miles up, then the Land is rather high on both Sides and woody; at the Head of the River is very fine Wood of different Kinds, fuch as Birch, Fir, Juniper, and Spruce; this River feems to be well ftored with Salmon.) At about 4 Miles up the River is very good Anchorage, and continues fo till you come up as high as *Woody Ifland*; but above this Ifland there are feveral Shoals.

St. Lewis's Sound. One Mile to the Northward of the North Point of *St. Lewis* River lieth the Entrance of *St. Lewis's* Sound, which runneth up W. by N. 1 League, at the Head of which is very good Anchorage, in taking Care to avoid a Shoal which ftretches off from a fandy Beach on the larboard Side at about 2 Miles within the Entrance.

Dear Harbour. From the Northermoft *Battle Ifland* to the Entrance of *Dear Harbour* the Courfe is N. 51° W. Diftance 3 Leagues. This is a very good Harbour in which you anchor from 18 to 10 Fathom Water, fecure from all winds. To fail into this Harbour there is not the leaft Danger, and the beft Anchorage is at the Back of *Dear Ifland*.

From the Northermoſt *Battle Iſland* to *Cape St. Lewis* the Courſe is N. N. W. ¼ W. 5 Miles. This Cape is high ragged Land; 1 ¼ Mile to the N. W. of the Cape lieth *Fox Harbour*, which is but ſmall, and only fit for ſmall Veſſels, but ſeems to be very convenient for a Fiſhery.

Cape St. Lewis.
Fox Harbour.

MICH. LANE.

DESCRIPTION

OF THE

COAST of LABRADORE,

FROM

CAPE St. MICHAEL

TO

SPOTTED ISLAND.

Note, *The Bearings hereafter mentioned are the true Bearings, and not by Compass, the Variation being* 32° W. *this present Year,* 1770.

CAPE St. Michael lieth in the Latitude of 52° 46′ N. is high Land and steep towards the Sea, and is to be known by a large Bay which forms to the Northward of it, having a Number of large and small Islands in it; the largest of these Islands, called *Square Island*, lieth in the Mouth of the Bay, and is 3 Miles long, and very high Land.

The best Anchorage for large Vessels in *St. Michael's Bay* is on the South Side; that is, keep *Cape St. Michael's* Shore on board, then keep along the South Side of the first Island you meet with, which is called *Long Island*, till you come near as far as the West End of it, and there anchor from 12 to 20 Fathom; you will there lay land-locked, and may work out again to Sea on either Side of *Long Island*. From Mr. Gilbert's Directions.

From *Cape St. Michael's* to the Entrance of *Square Island* Harbour, the Course N. 63° 30′ W. Distance 3¼ Miles, in the Entrance lieth a small

Island

(2)

Island of a moderate Height; the best Passage is to the Westward of this Island, there being only 2 Fathom Water in the Eastern Passage.

The N. E. Point of *Square Island* is a high round Hill, and maketh (in coming from the Southward) like a separate Island, being only joined by a low narrow Neck of Land, N. 54° W. Distance 1 League. From this Point lieth the Entrance into *Dead Island* Harbour, which is only fit for small Vessels, and is formed by a Number of Islands; there is a Passage out to Sea between these Islands and the Land of *Cape Bluff*.

Cape Bluff.   *Cape Bluff* lieth N. by W. Distance 8 Miles from *Cape St. Michael's*, and is very high Land, ragged at Top, and steep towards the Sea. These Capes form the Bay of *St. Michael*, in which are several Arms well stored with Wood.

Cape Bluff Harbour.   *Cape Bluff* Harbour is a small Harbour, fit only for small Vessels. To sail into it keep *Cape Bluff* Shore on board till you come to a small Island, and then pass to the Westward of it and anchor.

Barren Island.   From *Cape Bluff* to *Barren Island* the Course is N. ¼ E. Distance 1 League. From the South Point of this Island to *Snug* Harbour the

Snug Harbour.   Course is W. Distance 1¼ Mile. This Harbour is small, but in it there is very good Anchorage; is 26 Fathom Water, and no Danger sailing into it.

Stoney Island.   One Mile to the Northward of *Barren Island* lieth *Stoney Island*. On the Main within these Islands lieth *Martin* and *Otter* Bays, in the Northermost of which is very good Anchorage, with Plenty of Wood, and no Danger but what shews itself.

On the West Side of *Stoney Island* is a very good Harbour for small Vessels, called *Duck* Harbour. Large Vessels may anchor between the West Point of *Stoney Island* and *Double Island* in 20 or 24 Fathoms Water, and may sail out to Sea again on either Side of *Stoney Island* in great Safety.

Hawke Island lieth 1 Mile to the Northward of *Stoney Island*. Within *Hawke Island* lieth *Hawke Bay*, which runneth to the Westward 2 Leagues, and then brancheth into two Arms, one running to the S. W. 2 Leagues, and the other West 5 Miles; these Arms are well stored with Wood. After you are within *Pigeon Island*, there is very good Anchorage quite to the Head of both Arms.

On the South Side of *Hawke Island* lieth *Eagle Cove*; wherein is very good Anchorage for large Vessels in 30 or 40 Fathoms Water: Small Vessels may anchor at the Head in 7 or 8 Fathoms.

On the Main within *Hawke Island*, about 5 Miles to the N. E. of *Hawke Bay*, lieth *Caplin Bay*. Here is very good Anchorage in this Bay, and Plenty of Wood at the Head.

Partridge Bay lieth 5 Miles to the Northward of *Hawke Island*. In it is very good Anchorage, but difficult of Access, unless acquainted, by reason of a Number of small Islands and Rocks which lieth before the Mouth of it. The Land hereabouts may be easily known. The South

Point

Point of the Bay, a remarkable high Table Hill and barren; all the Land between this Hill and *Cape St. Michael* being high, the Land to the Northward of it low.

From *Cape St. Michael* to *Seal Iflands* the Courfe is N. ¼ E. Diftance 9 Leagues.

From *Seal Iflands* to *Round Hill Ifland* the Courfe is N. ¼ Eaft. Diftance 13 Miles. This Ifland is the Eaftermoft Land on this Part the Coaft, and may be known by a remarkable high round Hill on the Weft Part of it.

From *Round Hill Ifland* to *Spotted Ifland* the Courfe is N. 36° W. Diftance 2 Leagues. From *Spotted Ifland* the Land tends away to the N. W. and appears to be feveral large Iflands.

From *Seal Iflands* to *White Rock* the Courfe is N. by W. ¼ W. Diftance 2 Leagues. From this Rock the Courfe into *Shallow Bay* is S. W. Diftance 2 Miles. Here is tolerable good Anchorage in this Bay, and no Danger except a fmall Rock which lieth off a Cove on the larboard Hand, and about ¼ of the Bay over; this Rock fheweth above Water at Low-water. There is very little Wood in this Bay.

From *White Rock* to *Porcupine Ifland* the Courfe is N. 52° W. Dif- Porcupine tance 2 Leagues. This Ifland is high and barren. You may pafs on Bay. either Side of this Ifland into *Porcupine Bay*, where is very good Anchorage, but no Wood.

Sandy Bay lieth on the S. E. Part of the Ifland of *Ponds*, and N. W. Sandy Bay. by N. ¼ W. Diftance 5 Miles from *White Rock*. In it is very good Anchorage in 10 Fathoms Water, Sandy Bottom, and feems very handy for a Fifhery, except the Want of Wood. Between this Bay and *Spotted Ifland* are a great Number of Iflands and Rocks, which makes this Part of the Coaft dangerous.

MICH. LANE.

REMARKS

MADE BETWEEN

The ISLAND of GROIAS

AND

CAPE BONAVISTA,

1768.

THE Ifland *Groias* lies 2 Leagues from the Main, is about 5 Leagues Ifland Groias. round. The North End of it lies in the Lat. 51 Deg. 0 Min. N. off from which, at 1 ¼ Miles Diftance, are feveral Rocks, high above Water, alfo off from the N. W. Part; otherwife this Ifland is bold too all round. Between it and the Main is from 20 to 40 Fathom Water.

The Harbours of *Great* and *Little St. Julien's* and *Grandfway* lie within Great St. Julien's. the Ifland of *St. Julien*, which bears N. W. ¼ N. diftant 8 ½ Miles from the North End of *Groias*. The S.W. End of it is but very little feparated from the Main, and is not to be diftinguifhed as an Ifland, till you are near it. There is no Paffage at the S. W. End but for Boats. To fail into thefe Harbours, you may keep clofe to the N. E. End of the Ifland, as you pafs which the Harbours will appear open to you. There is no Danger in the Way to *Great St. Julien's*, which is the Eaftermoft Harbour, until you are within the Entrance, then the Starboard Side is fhoal near one third over; when you are paffed the firft Stages, you may anchor from 8 to 4 Fathom Water: To fail into *Little St. Julien's*, you muft (to avoid a funken Rock, which lies Little St. Julien's. directly before the Mouth of the Harbour,) firft fteer to directly for *Great St. Julien's*, till you are abreaft of the Entrance of *Grandfway*; then you may fteer directly into *Little St. Julien's*, and anchor in 4 or 5 Fathom Water. Ships in both thofe Harbours commonly moor Head and Stern.

Grandfway is not a Harbour for Ships; but very convenient for Fifhing Grandfway. Craft.

Croque Harbour lies 4 Miles to the Southward of *St. Julien's* Ifland, and Croque. has been defcribed in Mr. *Cook's* Direction.

Four Miles and a Half to the Southward of *Groias* lies *Bell-Ifle*, which is Bell-Ifle off above 20 Miles round; there is a little Harbour at the South Part of this Newfoundland. Ifland

A

Island fit for Fishing-craft; but it is too difficult for Shipping. There are some other Coves about this Island, where Shallops may shelter occasionally.

Carouge Harbour. S. S. W. 7 Miles from *Creque Harbour* lies *Carouge Harbour*, which bears W. ¼ N. from the South End of the Island *Groias*. Immediately within the Entrance of this Harbour it divides into two Arms, one to the N. W. the other to the S. W. Directly in the Middle of the S. W. Arm is a Shoal, on which is only 7 or 8 Feet Water at Low Water; you may pass on either Side of it, and anchor from 20 to 8 Fathom Water, in good holding Ground: There is also good anchoring in the N. W. Arm; but, in general, is not so good as in the S. W. Arm.

Conch Harbour. S. S. W. 3 Miles from the South Point of *Carouge Harbour* lies *Fox Head*, round which, to the N. W. lies *Conch Harbour*, in which is good Anchorage, well up to the Head of it, in good holding ground, in 11 Fathom Water. It is open to the S. S. E.

Hilliard's Harbour. About 2 Leagues to the S. W. from *Conch*, is *Hilliard's Harbour*, by the French called *Botitot*; this is but a very indifferent Place for Shipping, but convenient for Fishing-craft.

Englée. Four Miles and a half further to the S. S. W. is the Harbour of *Englée*. This Harbour is situated on the North Side of *Canada Bay*. To sail into this Place, you must pass a remarkable low White Point, on *Englée Island*, which forms the North Entrance of *Canada Bay*; then keep near the Shore until you are abreast of the next Point, which makes the Harbour; then haul round it to the S. E. taking Care not to borrow too near the Point, it being shoal a Cable's Length off; and you may anchor from 15 to 7 Fathom, very good holding Ground; but this is well up in the Cove, which is too small to lie in, unless moored Head and Stern. In *Bide's Arm*, which runs up North from *Englée*, near 2 Leagues, there is no good Anchorage, it being very deep Water: Within the South End of *Englée Island* there is a good Harbour for Shallops; but there is no Passage even for Boats, from thence to the Place where the Ships lie, except at High Water, or, at least, Half Tide.

Canada Bay. *Canada Bay* lies up N. N. W. from *Point Canada*, (which is the South Point that forms the Entrance of *Canada Bay*,) upwards of 4 Leagues and a Half. This Bay cannot be of any Use for Shipping, otherwise than as a Place of Shelter in Case of Necessity. On being catched near the Shore in a hard Gale of easterly Wind, Ships may, with the greatest Safety, run up, and anchor in this Bay free from all Danger. In such Case, when you are above two small Rock Isles, which lie near *Bide's Head*, called the *Cross Islands*, you will observe a low White Point, and another low Black one a little above it. Off the latter a sunken Rock lies about two Cables Lengths; therefore keep the Middle of the Bay, and you will meet with no danger, except a Rock above Water, which lies a Mile below the Point of the Narrows; leave this
Rock

Rock on the Larboard Hand, keeping the Middle of the Water, and you will carry 18 Fathom through the narrowest Part; soon after you are above which, the Bay widens to upwards of a Mile a-cross; and you may anchor in 18 and 20 Fathom Water, good holding Ground, and secure from all Winds.

Three Miles South from *Canada Point* is *Canada Head*. It is pretty high, Canada Head. and very distinguishable, either to the Northward or Southward; but when you are directly to the Eastward of it, it is rather hid by the high Lands in the Country called the *Clouds*.

Upwards of 4 Miles to the S. W. from *Canada Head* is *Hooping Harbour*, Hooping by the *French* called *Sansfond*. This Place has two Arms, or rather Bays, Harbour. the one lying up the Northward, and the other to the Westward. There is very deep Water in the North Arm, until you approach near the Head; it is a loose sandy Bottom, intirely open to Southerly Winds, and not a Place of Safety for Shipping. In the Westward Arm a Ship may safely anchor in a moderate Depth of Water.

About 4 Miles to the Southward of *Hooping Harbour* is *Fouchée*. There Fouchée. is no Anchorage in this Place until you approach near the Head, where there is a Cove on the North Side. The Land is extremely high on both Sides, and deep Water close to the Shore. This Cove is about 2 or 3 Miles from the Entrance, in which there is Anchorage in 18 Fathom Water, but so small that a Ship must moor Head and Stern. There is another Arm, which runs near 2 Miles above this; it is extremely narrow, and so deep Water, that it is never used by Shipping.

Three Leagues to the S. W. from *Fouchée*, is *Great Harbour Deep*, by the Orange Bay, *French* called *Bay Orange*: It may be known from any other Place, by the or Great Harbour Deep. Land at its Entrance being much lower than any Land on the North Side of *White's Bay*, and bears N. W. ¼ N. from *Partridge Point*. This is a large Bay. A little within the Entrance there is a small Cove on each Side, generally used by the Fishing Ships, tho' very dangerous for a Ship to lie in: They always moor Head and Stern; notwithstanding, if a Gale of Wind happens to the Eastward, they are in the greatest Danger. Near 3 Miles within the Entrance of this Bay, it branches out in three Arms: In the North Arm, which is much the largest, there is so deep Water, you will have no Anchorage until you approach near the Head; the middle Arm is the best Place for Ships to anchor in 7 Fathom Water, and a good Bottom.

From *Orange Bay*, 2 Leagues to the S. W. is *Grandfather's Cove*, by the Grandfather's Cove, *French* called *L'Ance L'Union*. This is an Inlet of about 2 Miles, directly open and Little to the S. E. Winds; it may be known, when near the Shore, by the North Harbour Point of it appearing like an Island, and bears N.W. by W. ¼ W. from *Partridge Point*. It is but an indifferent Harbour for Shipping. Scarcely 2 Miles further, is another Inlet, called *Little Harbour Deep*, by the *French La Vache*.

A 2 This

This is also directly open to the S. E. Winds; off the North Point of this Inlet, are some Rocks, ¼ a Mile from the Shore, which always shew above Water, about which is good Fishing-Ground; the Water is not very deep in any Part of this Inlet, and when you are half Way from the Entrance to the Head, it becomes quite shoal.

Great and Little Cat Arms. About 2 Leagues further to the S. W. is *Little Cat Arm*, which is an Inlet that lies up W. 2 Miles. This Inlet is about 2 Miles from *Great Cat Arm*. Off the North Head there are some Rocks, which shew above Water; to avoid which, in sailing in, keep nearest to the South Side; but you will find no Anchorage till you approach near the Head of this Arm, where you will be securely land-locked.

Great and Little Cony Arms. Upwards of 3 Leagues to the S. S. W. from *Great Cat Arm*, is *Cony Arm Head*. This is the most remarkable Land on the West Side of *White Bay*; it bears W. S. W. Distance 8 leagues from *Partridge Point*. The Land, all the Way, runs nearly straight, until you come to this Head, which projects out nearly 1 Mile and ¼, forming a deep Bight, which is called *Great Cony Arm*. There is no Kind of Shelter for Shipping at this Place. N. W. from the Head, is *Little Cony Arm*, which is a convenient little Place for Fishing Craft, but at the Entrance it is too shallow for a Ship.

Frenchman's Cove. From *Cony Head*, about 4 Miles further up the Bay, is a Cove called *Frenchman's Cove*, in which a Ship might safely anchor.

Jackson's Arm. From *Frenchman's Cove*, about a League further to the South, round a low ragged Point, is *Jackson's Arm*, in which is pretty deep Water, except in a small Cove on the Starboard Hand, where a Ship may moor Head and Stern. This Place affords the largest Timber in *White's Bay*.

Sop's Arms. From *Jackson's Arm*, 4 Miles further to the Southward, is the North End of *Sop's Island*, which bears S. W. ¼ W. Distance about 10 ¼ Miles from *Partridge Point*. This Island is 11 Miles in Circuit, by which, and *Goat Island*, is formed a long Passage, or Arm, called *Sop's Arm*; in the North of which a Ship may safely anchor, just within the North End of *Sop's Island*. The best Passage into this Arm, is by the North Side of *Sop's Island*. There is also Anchorage between *Sop's Island* and the Main, before you come the Length of *Goat Island*, but the Water is deep; there is a Cove at the North End of this Island, called *Sop's Coves*, and two other small Coves opposite on the Main, called *Hart's Cove*, in all of which a Fishery is carried on, but Ships generally anchor in the upper Part of the Arm, within *Goat Island*.

River Head. From the North End of *Sop's Island*, to the River at the Head of the Bay, the Distance is upwards of 6 Leagues. This Place is called *Gold Cove*. Here the River branches out into several small Streams of Water.

Near

(5)

Near 5 Leagues down from the River Head, and nearest the S. E. Side of the Bay, lies *Granby's Island*, by some called *Mid-Bay Island*. This Island affords no Cove nor Shelter for Boats. On the S. E. Part of it, about 2 Cables Lengths off, there is a Shoal, whereon is not above 1½ Fathom Water. Nearly abreast, or rather below this Island, on the S. E. Side of the *White Bay*, is *Purwick Cove*, in which Shipping may safely anchor, and good Conveniencies for the Fishery. About 5 Miles to the N. E. of this Cove, and W. by S. ½ S. from the North End of *Sop's Island*, lies *Westward Arm*. This Westward Arm lies up about S. E. 4 Miles, in which Ships may safely anchor, in about 18 Fathom Water: There is a Cove on each Side of this Arm, at its Entrance; that on the N. E. Side, called *Bear Cove*, is much the best, where small Ships may securely moor, sheltered from all Winds, in 12 Fathom Water; the other Cove, which is called *Wild Cove*, is but an indifferent Place, being open to the N. W. Winds, and a foul rocky Bottom; the Point on the N. E. Side of *Western Arm*, is called *Hauling Point*.

Two Leagues to the N. E. of *Hauling Point*, is another Arm, lying up about S. E. by S. 3 or 4 Miles, called *Middle Arm*. At the Entrance of this Arm is a rocky Island, from which, quite home to both Shores, is a Shoal, whereon is from 1 to 2, and, in some Places, 3 Fathom Water. The best Passage into this Arm is, to keep the Larboard Shore on board; but this is not proper for large Shipping. Between this Arm and *Hauling Point* lies the *Pigeon Islands*, about which is good Fishing-ground.

About 1 Mile and ¼ to the N. E. from *Middle Arm*, is another, called *Southward Arm*, in which a Ship may safely anchor in 17 Fathom Water, entirely land-locked; here she will be nearly 3 Miles within the Heads, but there is good Anchorage in any Part below, from 20 to 25 Fathom, before you are near so far up. A little above the inner Point, on the North Side, is a Mussel Bank entirely across the Arm, which is nearly dry at low Water; and above this Bank you will again have 11 and 12 Fathom, and continues deep to the River Head. This Arm is nearly 5 Leagues above *Partridge Point*, and may be known, when sailing up the S. E. Side of the *White Bay*, by its being the first Inlet, and bears W. by S. from *Cony Arm Head*, which lies on the other Side of the Bay, and which Head is always very conspicuous.

Near a League from *Southward Arm*, towards *Partridge Point*, is *Lobster Harbour*. This is a small round Harbour, with a shoal narrow Entrance; at low Water, at some Places in the Entrance, there is not above 8 or 9 Feet Water; but, after you are in, you will have 12 and 13 Fathom all over the Harbour. Small Ships may enter at proper Times of Tide.

It flows, on Full and Change Days, nearest E. by S. and W. by N. in all Places in *White Bay*. From *Canada Head* the Current generally sets up the *White Bay*, on the N. W. Side, and down the Bay on the other Side; and between

(6)

between *Partridge Point* and *Cape John*, it generally runs about S. E. by E. It is obferved, that the Flood, or Ebb, fcarce ever makes any Alteration in the Courfe of the Current.

From *Canada Head* to *Fleur de Lys*, the Courfe is S. nearly 10 Leagues. This Harbour is fituated about 4 Miles to the S. E. from *Partridge Point*, and bears S. W. by W. ¼ W. Diftance about 10 Miles from the Weft End of the Weftermoft of the *Horfe Iflands*. The Entrance of this Harbour is not diftinguifhable, until you come pretty near the Shore; but it may be known at a Diftance, by a Mountain over it appearing fomething like the Top of a Fleur de Lys. *Fleur de Lys*, from which it takes its Name. There is no Danger in failing into this Harbour, until you come within 2 Cables Length of the Harbour Ifland, which is on the South Side, at which Diftance there lies a Rock, whereon there is not above 6 Feet at low Water: it is fhoal from this Rock home to the Ifland; to avoid which, keep the Starboard or North Shore on board, and you may come to in any Part of this Harbour above the faid Ifland, in 4½ and 5 Fathom Water, fheltered from all Winds.

Horfe Iflands. The two *Horfe Iflands* are fituated between *Partridge Point* and *Cape John*. The Weft End of the Weftermoft *Horfe Island* bears E. ¼ N. Diftance 10 or 11 Miles from *Partridge Point*; and the S. E. Part of the Eaftermoft Ifland bears N. W. by W. from *Cape John*, Diftance near 5 Leagues. Thefe Iflands are about 6 Leagues in Circuit, and tolerable high; there are three Rocks above Water lying to the Northward of the Eaftermoft, and on the Eaft Side of the faid Ifland are funken Rocks, at fome Places, near a Mile from the Shore. There is a fmall Harbour, fit for Shallops, at the S. E. Part of this Ifland.

Bays of Verte, *Bay Verte* and *Mynx* lie to the S. E. from *Fleur de Lys*, are fmall Places not and Pine, or fit for Shipping. At *Mynx* it is impoffible for more than one Ship to lie, Mynx. which is between a fmall Rock Ifland and the Main, moored Head and Stern. Between thefe Places is *Bay of Verte*, or *Little Bay*, which runs up S. E. full 3 Leagues; and towards the Head there is Plenty of good Timber. *Bay of Pine*, or *Mynx*, is an Inlet of about 5 Miles, affords no Anchorage, except at *Mynx*, which is at the Entrance, as before mentioned.

Pacquet Har- Near 5 Leagues to the S. E. from *Fleur de Lys*, is the Harbour of *Pacquet*, bour. at ½ a Mile within the Entrance. This Harbour divides into two Arms, the one extending to the N. W. and the other to the S. W. The N. W. Arm is a very good Place for Shipping to lie in entirely land-locked; the S. W. Arm is a Mile long, but narrow, yet is a fafe fnug Harbour. This Harbour is not very diftinguifhable until you approach pretty near; it bears S. ¼ W. from the Paffage between the *Horfe Iflands*, and may be known by the South Head, it being a high Rock Mountain; the North Point is rather low, off

which

(7)

which lie three Rock Isles; both Shores are bold too. Steer directly in, and anchor in the N. W. Arm, in about 14 Fathom Water.

About 2 Leagues from *Pacquet*, to the S. E. is *Great Round Harbour*. This is a convenient little Harbour for Fishing-ships; there is no Danger in sailing into it; both Shores being bold too, you may anchor within the two inner Points in 4 and 5 Fathom, entirely land-locked. *Little Round Harbour*, which is about 1 Mile ½ round a Point to the N. E. from this, is not fit for Shipping; it is only a Cove, wherein is but 2 Fathom, and a loose sandy Bottom. Great Round Harbour.
Little Round Harbour.

About 4 Miles to the S. W. from *Cape John* is the small Harbour of *La Cey*. This Place is open to the N. N. W. There is no Danger in sailing in; you may anchor in any Depth you please from 8 to 3 Fathom Water. La Cey Cey.

Cape John is a lofty ragged Point of Land. It lies in the Latitude of 50 d. 06 m. N. and may be known by the *Gull Isle*, which is a small, high, round Island, bearing nearly E. about 4 Miles from the Pitch of the Cape. Cape John.
Gull Isle.

From *Cape John* to the *Bay of Twilingate*, the Course is S. E. by E. Distance 11 or 12 Leagues. This is but an indifferent Place for Shipping, it being directly open to the N. E. Winds, which heave in a very great Sea. N. ½ W. about 4 Miles from the Entrance of this Bay, there is a Bank, on which, in the Winter, the Sea has been seen to break, between which and the Shore there is from 50 to 80 Fathom Water. Bay of Twilingate.

Wire Cape Cove, which lies on the West Side of the Westermost *Twilingate Island*, that makes *Twilingate Bay*, is a Place for Fishing-craft only. Wire Cape Cove.

From *Cape John* to *Fogo Head*, the Course is E. by S. ½ S. Distance 17 or 18 Leagues. Immediately to the Eastward of this Head is *Fogo Harbour*. This is a pretty good Harbour for Fishing-ships, &c. but the Entrance is intricate and dangerous. To sail into this Harbour with a Westerly Wind, and coming from the Westward, keep close on board of *Fogo Head*; it is very bold too, and nothing to fear, until you open a narrow Entrance, scarcely half a Cable's Length wide. Steer directly in, in keeping right in the Middle, and you will carry from 8 to 4 Fathom Water through. When you are through this Passage, which is commonly called the *West Tickle*, if you intend to anchor in the Westward Bight, steer to the S. E. till you bring the Point between the Bights to bear W. by N. to avoid the Harbour Rock, which is a funken Rock, that scarcely ever shews but at dead low Water, Spring Tides; then you may haul up to the Westward, and anchor from 6 to 5 Fathom, good holding Ground, and sheltered from all Winds. Fogo Harbour.

N. B. Coming from the Westward, you must not be afraid to make bold with *Fogo Head*, otherwise you will miss the *West Tickle*; and as there is generally (more particularly with a Westerly Wind,) a strong Current running to the Eastward, Ships making that Mistake, seldom can work up again:

Coming

Coming from the Eastward, and bound into *Fogo*, to avoid *Dean's Rock*, (which is a sunken Rock, in the Track between *Joe Batt's Point* and *Fogo Harbour*,) when abreast of *Joe Batt's Point*, you must steer W. N. W. (by Compass,) until a remarkable round Hill, called *Brimstone-hill*, appears in the Hollow of the Harbour. Then you may steer directly for the *East Tickle*, which may be known by the Lanthorn on the Top of *Sim's Isle*, which makes the West Side of the *Tickle*; as you approach, you will discover the Entrance. Give Birth to the Point on the Starboard Hand, which is that on *Sim's Isle*, and steer directly up the Harbour, keeping nearest the South Side, and you will carry from 5 to 3 Fathom Water through; immediately when you are round the Point, steer S. S. W. to avoid the Harbour Rock, and follow the above Directions for anchoring. As there are two Entrances to this Harbour, and both narrow, you may chuse according to the Wind. The *Middle Tickle* is only fit, and even intricate, for Shallops, though it appears the widest.

Little Fogo Island.   About 7 Miles to the N. E. from the Entrance of *Fogo Harbour* lies *Little Fogo Island*; from which, above 2 Leagues Distance, to the Northward, Eastward, and Westward, lie a great Number of small Rocks, above and under Water, which makes this Part of the Coast exceeding dangerous, especially in foggy Weather.

Bacaleau.   Between the Bay of *Twilingate* and *Fogo Head*, nearly Midway, lies the Isle of *Bacaleau*. To the S. W. from this Island, near 3 Miles, is the Harbour of
Herring Neck.   *Herring Neck*, which is a fine Harbour, sufficient for any Ships.

Wadham's Isles.   From the round Head of *Fogo*, which is the N. E. Part of the Island, to the outermost *Wadham's Island*, the Course is S. E. by E. Distance 14 or 15 Miles. There is a very good Passage between these Islands, often used by Shipping. This Passage is above a Mile wide, and is between the second and third Island; that is, you are to leave two of the Islands without, or to the Northward of you. Those Islands are about 5 Leagues in Circuit, and lie near 2 Leagues from the Main Land.

Cape Freels.   From the outermost of *Wadham's Islands*, that is, the N. E. Isle, to the *Gull Isle* off *Cape Freels*, the Course is S. E. Distance 10 Leagues. *Gull Isle* is a
Gull Isle.   small Rock Island, and lies about a Mile and a Half from the Pitch of *Cape Freels*, which is a low Point of Land; between this Cape and *Green's Pond Island* are several small Islands and sunken Rocks along Shore. There is no Passage from the Cape towards *Green's Pond* for Shipping within the *Stinking Isles*, without being very well acquainted.

Stinking Islands.   The *Stinking Islands* lie S. S. E. 2 Leagues from *Gull Island*, and N. N. W. 13 Leagues from *Cape Bonavista*.

N. ½ E. from *Cape Bonavista*, and N. 27 d. 00 m. E. about 10 Leagues from
Funk Island.   *Cape Freels*, lies *Funk Island*. This Island lies in the Latitude of 49. 52. N. it is
but

but fmall and low, not to be feen above 4 or 5 Leagues in clear Weather. There are two fmall Ifles, or rather Rocks, at a fmall Diftance from the N. W. Part. This Ifland is much frequented by Sea Birds of various Kinds.

About W. N. W. Diftance 7 Leagues from *Funk Ifland*, lie the dangerous Rocks, called *Durel's Ledge*, upon which the Sea almoft always breaks. Durel's Ledge.

Green's Pond Harbour is fituated on the Weft Side of *Bonavifta Bay*. It bears from the *Stinking Ifles*, S. 63 W. Diftance upwards of 4 Leagues. It may be known by the *Copper Iflands*, which lie to the Southward of the Harbour, and are pretty high, and Sugar Loaf topped. This Harbour is formed by feveral Iflands, that are detached about half a Mile from the main Land; the largeft of which is called *Pond Ifle*, and makes the North Side of the Harbour. This Ifland is tolerably high, and near 5 Miles in Circuit. The other Iflands, making the South Side, are but fmall. This is but a fmall Harbour. Towards the upper Part two Ships can fcarcely lie a-breaft. There is no Danger in failing into this Harbour, until you approach its Entrance, where you muft be careful of a Shoal; it is of but very fmall Extent, whereon is not above 6 or 7 Feet at Low Water; you may pafs on either Side of this Shoal; but the North Side is the wideft, and beft Paffage. Green's Pond.

S. 70 d. W. about 4 Miles from the *Copper Ifland* is *Shoe Cove Point*. About 2 Miles to the Northward of this Point lies *New Harbour*; in which Ships may fafely anchor, though it is but a fmall Harbour. New Harbour.

Indian Bay runs up Weft about 4 Leagues above this Harbour; at the Head of which there is Plenty of good Timber. Indian Bay.

From *Copper Ifland* to the *Gull Ifle* off *Cape Bonavifta*, the Courfe is S.E. ¼ S. Diftance 10 ¼ Leagues; and S. 20 d. W. Diftance 2 Leagues from *Gull Ifland*, lies *Port Bonavifta*. It is a very unfafe Place for Ships to ride in, being directly open to the Winds between the N. and W. and a loofe fandy Bottom. Port Bonavifta.

Barrow Harbour bears W. ¼ N. 8 Leagues from *Port Bonavifta*. This is a very good Harbour. Barrow Harbour.

From *Port Bonavifta*, W. ¼ S. about 10 Miles, lies the little Harbour of *Keels*, which is only fit for fifhing Craft. Keels.

B DIREC-

DIRECTIONS
FOR NAVIGATING
From Cape RACE to Cape BONAVISTA,
Made by CAPTAIN SOUTHWOOD;
With his REMARKS upon the FISHING BANKS.

Cape Race. FROM Cape *Race* to Cape *Ballard* is N. N. E. about 3 ¼ or 4 Leagues,
Glam Cove. between which, about half way, is *Glam Cove*, which is only for Boats;
Chain Cove. and near to Cape *Ballard* is another Cove, called *Chain Cove*, where are several Rocks lying before it, (but there is no Harbour, or Bay, for Ships to ride in,) and fish between the two Capes.

Cape Ballard. But to the Northward of Cape *Ballard* is another Cove for Boats; and about 4 Miles from the Cape is *Freshwater* Bay, near half way between Cape
Renowes. *Ballard* and *Renowes*, *Renowes* being the Southermost Harbour the *English* have in *Newfoundland*.

From Cape *Ballard* to the S. Point of *Renowes* the Course is N.N.E. about 2 Leagues. *Renowes* is but a bad Harbour, by Reason of sunken Rocks going in lying in the Fairway, besides other Rocks on each Side, but it is a good Place for Fishing.

They who go in there should be very well acquainted; when you are in, where Ships usually ride, you have not above 15 Feet Water, and but small Drift, by Reason of Shoals about you, and a S. S. E. Wind brings in a great Sea, so that it is very bad riding, and only used in Summer-time : The Harbour lies N. W. about a League in; but you must keep the South-side going in, for that is the clearest.

Renowes Rock. Off the S. Point of the Entrance of the Harbour is an Island, a small Distance from the Shore; and off the said S. Point of the Harbour, S.E. by E. about half a League is a great Rock high above Water, called *Renowes* Rock, which you may see at least 3 Leagues off in fair Weather, but the Rock is bold to go on either Side.

From *Renowes* Point to *Fermowes* is a League and a half N. E. by N. N. N. E. and N. tending about, but being a little without *Renowes*, the Course will be N. N. E. till you come open of the Harbour of *Fermowes*. Between
Bears Cove. the said two Harbours is a Cove, called *Bears* Cove; a Place only for Boats to stop at if the Wind be contrary, but no Inhabitants.

Fermowes. *Fermowes* is a very good Harbour, and bold going in, no Danger but the Shore itself; it lies in N.W. and N.W. by W. Being past the Entrance, there are

(11)

are several Coves on each Side in the Harbour, where Ships may and often do ride; the first Cove on the Starboard-Side (going in), or North Side, is called *Clears* Cove, where Ships seldom (but may) ride: the next within it, Clears Cove. a little Distance on the North Side, is the Admiral's Cove (where lives a Planter); in this Cove you lie land-locked from all Winds, and ride in 7 or 8 Fathom, good Ground.

The Vice-Admiral's Cove (so called) is on the S. Side, farther in, or more Westerly, and is a very good Place to ride in for many Ships, good Ground; and above the said Cove, on the S. Side, farther in, is another Arm or Cove, where also yon lie secure. You have about 20 Fathom Water in the Entrance of the Harbour; but within you have from 14 to 12, 10, 9, 8, 7, and 6 Fathom, as you please, and the Head runs up at least 4 Miles and a Half.

From *Fermowes* to *Agua Fort* the Course is N. by E. about a League, be- Agua Fort. tween which are two Heads, or Points of Land, about a Mile from each other, the Southermost, or next to *Fermowes*, is called *Bald-head*, about a Mile from Bald-head. the Harbour's Mouth of *Fermowes*; between which is a pretty deep Bay, but all full of Rocks, and no Safety for Boats to come on Shore at in a Storm; it is but a Mile from the Harbour, which is safe for Ships or Boats, and not above 2 Miles to the entering of *Agua Fort*.

The next Head to the Northward of *Bald head* is *Black-head*, lying N. and Black-head. S. one from the other about a Mile asunder; and from *Black-head* to the Point of *Agua Fort* Harbour is NW. by N. a Mile, which Harbour is very good, and safe for Ships; it lies in WNW. There is a great Rock above Water going in on the South Side, which is bold too; you run up about 2 Miles within the Harbour's Mouth, and ride on the North Side, and lie land-locked, as it were Pond, like to *Ferryland-pool*, but larger, where, with a Piece of Timber, you may make a Stage from your Ship to your Stage on Shore, being an excellent Harbour, and Water deep enough.

From *Agua Fort* to *Ferryland-head* (the South Part of the Head), the Course is E. about 3 Miles. *Crow* Island, being about a Mile from *Agua Fort*, Crow Island. lies ENE. from the Harbour's Mouth, and from the SE. End of *Crow* Island lies a Shoal about a Cable's Length.

From the N. Part of *Ferryland-head* to *Ferryland*, the Course is W. by N. Ferryland-about 2 Miles; to go into *Ferryland* Port, or Harbour, you must sail between Head. the N.Part of *Ferryland-head* and *Buoy* Island; it is not very broad, but there is Buoy Island. Water enough, and clean Ground; being within the said *Buoy* Island, you may Port of Ferrun in and anchor where you please, it being of a good handsome Breadth; ryland. or you may go into the *Pool*, which is a Place on the Larboard Side (going The Pool. in), with a Point of *Beach*, where you ride in 12 Feet Water at low Water, and there the Admiral's Ships generally ride (the Stages being near, several Planters Inhabitants live in this Place). From *Buoy* Island, almost into the Land to the Westward, are small Islands and Rocks, which make *Ferryland*

B 2 Harbour

(12)

Harbour or Port, and divide it from *Coplins* Bay; between the said Rocks in some Places is a Passage for Boats, and the Water rises hereabouts three and a half, four, and sometimes five Feet, and sometimes three Feet, and so it does generally in all the Harbours of this Land.

From *Ferryland-head* to Cape *Broyle-head*, is N. by E. almost 4 Miles; between which are three Islands, which lie before *Coplins* Bay; there are Channels to sail between them to *Caplins* Bay, that is, between *Buoy* Island, which is to the sternmost and greatest, and *Goose* Island, which is the middle-most, and is the second in Bigness next to *Buoy* Island; also you may sail thro' between *Goose* Island, which is the middlemost, and *Stone* Island, which is the Northermost; but these Passages are large enough for Ships to sail or turn in or out; but between *Stone* Island and the North-shore, (that is Cape *Broyle*,) there is no Passage for a Ship, only for Boats, there being a great Rock between *Stone* Island, and the North Shore.

Buoy Island,
Goose Island,
Stone Island.

Caplins Bay. *Caplins* Bay is large and good, and runs in a great Way WNW. at least 6 Miles within the said Islands, where many Ships may ride in good Ground, and where sometimes meet the *Newfoundland* Ships that are bound with Convoy to the *Streights*, but generally rendezvous at the Bay of *Bulls*.

Cape Broyle. From Cape *Broyle-head*, (the North-part of it,) which lies in the Bay or Harbour of Cape *Broyle*, WNW. and NW by W. about 7 Miles and a half, and from the South Point of the Entrance to the North Point or Head, is about 2 Miles broad, and lies N. by W. and S. by E. one from the other.

Cape *Broyle* is the most remarkable Land on all the S. Coast of *Newfoundland*, for coming out of the Sea either from the Southward or Northward, it makes a Swamp in the Middle, and appears like a Saddle. ESE. from the North Point of Cape *Broyle*, about half or three-quarters of a Mile, lies a sunken Rock, called *Old Harry*, on which is but 18 Feet Water; the Sea breaks upon it in bad Weather, but between the Shore and it is Water enough of 12 and 13 Fathom, and without it is a Ledge of about the same Depth, where they use to fish, but off the Ledge is deep Water of 40 or 50 Fathom and deeper. In very bad Weather the Sea breaks home almost to the Shore from *Old Harry*, by Reason of the Current that sets strong generally to the Southward.

Old Harry.

Brigus by South. From Cape *Broyle* to *Brigus* by South, (so called to distinguish it from another *Brigus* in the Bay of *Conception*,) is a League, but from the North-head of Cape *Broyle* Bay to *Brigus*, is but little more than a Mile, and lies in NW. and NW. by W. *Brigus* is a Place only for small Ships of not above 7, or 8 Feet Draught of Water to ride in the Cove, which is not altogether safe neither; it is a Place for Fishing, where live two planters; there is an Island so called where they build their Stage, and make their Fish upon, who come there Fishing, but the Water comes not quite round, unless in a great Storm or Rage: It is a place of little consequence.

From

From Cape *Broyle* to Cape *Neddick*, the Courſe is North by Eaſt N[...]
ly, 5 Leagues; and from *Brigus* Point to Cape *Neddick* is N E. Alm ſt [...]
and a half between which is *Freſh-water* Bay, but of no Note. Cape
dick is a high Point, flat at Top, and ſtrait down to the Water.

From Cape *Neddick* to *Baline-head* is about half a League N E. by E. between which is *Lamanche*. *Lamanche* is only a Cove in the Bay, where is Lamanche.
no ſafe riding for any ſhip.

From *Baline-head* to *Baline* Cove is more than half a Mile, near three- Baline-head.
quarters; it is a Place where Ships uſe to keep two or three Boats with a Stage
for Fiſhing, where one Planter lives; the Place is not for Ships, only ſmall
Veſſels may come in to lade, and lie within the Rock called the *Whales-back*, Whales-
which Rock breaks off any Sea, and there are two Rocks above Water, one back.
on each Side going in, and the *Whales-back* in the Middle, but without the
ſaid Rocks that are above Water.

Againſt *Baline* Cove lies *Gooſe* Iſland, about a Mile or half a League to Gooſe Iſland.
the Seaward of *Baline*. *Gooſe* Iſland is a pretty large Iſland, three-quarters
or near a Mile long.

From *Baline-head* to *Iſle de Spear* is NNE. a Mile within the greateſt of Iſle de Spear.
the ſaid Iſlands, which is the Northermoſt. Ships every Year fiſh there; on
this Iſland is a Stage on the Inſide, that is, on the Weſt-ſide, and good
riding in Summer Seaſon, the Iſland being pretty large, but the Northermoſt Iſland is only a round Hill fit for no uſe.

The next to the *Iſle de Spear* is *Toads* Cove, where a Planter lives, a Toads Cove.
Place for Boats to fiſh, but not for Ships to ride.

A little without *Toads* Cove (or to the Eaſtward) is *Boxes* Iſland, between Foxes Iſland.
which and it is no Paſſage, but only for Boats to go through at High-water.

From *Baline-head* to the *Momables* Bay is N. by E. about 4 Miles, and lies Momables
N.W. near 2 Miles; it lies open to the Sea, yet is a good Place for Fiſhing. Bay.

From *Baline-head* to the North Point of *Momables* Bay, (which is the South-
point of *Whitleſs* Bay,) the Courſe is N.N.E. Northerly, 4 Miles off, which
Point is a Shoal of Rocks that lie a great Way off, ſo that Men muſt be well
acquainted to go with Ships between the ſaid Point and *Green* Iſland, which is Green Iſland.
a ſmall Iſland right off againſt the ſaid Point, a little more than a Mile; for
if you intend to come through between them, then it is beſt to keep the
Iſland-ſide, which is cleareſt.

From the ſaid Shoal Point, or South-point of *Whitleſs* Bay, the Land on Whitleſs Bay.
the South-ſide of the Bay lies in, firſt Part N.N.W. and after more Weſterly.

From

From the South Point of *Whitlefs* Bay to the North Point of the faid Bay is NE. by N. about a League, fo that it is a large going into the Bay, and Gull Ifland. about a League within *Gull* Ifland to the Head of the Bay, there is turning in or out, but about half Way into the Bay on the North Side (where the Planters live and the Admiral's Stage is), there is a Ledge of Rocks which you muft avoid; the moft Part of them may be feen above Water; you may lie but little without the outermoft, which appears dry. This is a far better Bay than *Momables*, by reafon of the *Gull* and *Green* Ifland laying without before it; you may fail between the Iflands, or between *Gull* Ifland and the South Point of Bay *Bulls*, yet Ships, after the Beginning of *September*, will not care to ride in *Whitlefs* Bay, but rather come to Bay *Bulls*, which is but a League and a Half by Sea to it, and not above two Miles and a Half over Land.

Bay Bulls. From Cape *Broyle* to Bay *Bulls* is NNE. half Eafterly 5 Leagues, from the South Head of Bay *Bulls* to the North Head, called *Bull-head*, the Courfe is NE. Northerly a Mile and a Quarter, or thereabouts, between which two Heads go in the Bay *Bulls*, lying WNW. for at leaft two Miles, and after that NW. for about a Mile, to the River-Head. In this Bay is good Riding, from 20 Fathom at the firft Entrance between the Heads, to 18, 16, &c. Bread and after you are fhot within *Bread and Cheefe Point*, which is a Point half the CheefePoint. Bay in, on the North Side, where there is a Cove, in which the Admirals keep their Stage. You muft give this Point a little Birth, for a funken Rock that lies off that Point not half a Cable's Length, elfe all the Bay is bold too, and nothing to hurt you but what you fee. Being paft that Point, run up and anchor (or turn up) againft the high Hills called *Joan Clays Hill* (bring it NE.), in 13 or 14 Fathom, which you will have there almoft from Side to Side, but Merchantmen run farther in, and anchor fome in 10, 9, or 8 Fathom, not above a Point open, and others not above half a Point. Men of War ride not three Points open. Here generally the Fleet is made up; that is, here they meet ready to fail (commonly for the *Streights*), by the 15th or 20th of *September*. It is from Side to Side againft *Joan Clays Hill* as aforefaid, 430 Fathom, fo that it wants but 10 Fathom of half an *Englifh* Mile broad.

From Bay *Bulls* to *Petty* Harbour the Courfe is NE. by N. three and a half or four Leagues (between which is nothing remarkable of Bays or Coves, but a fteep dead Shore only). About Mid-way is a Place called The Spout. the *Spout*, being a hollow Place which the Sea runs into, and, having a Vent on the Top of the Land, near the Water-Side, fpouts up the Water in fuch a Manner that you may fee it a great Way off, efpecially if there be any Sea, which caufes the greater Violence.

Petty Harbour. *Petty* Harbour, the Entrance of it is a large Bay, for from the South Point to the North Point is a League Diftance, NNE. and SSW. and it is a League in, where the Ships ride that fifh there, being but a little Cove. It lies in WNW.

Cape Spear. From the North Point of *Petty* Harbour to Cape *Spear*, the Courfe is NE. by N. two Miles, or thereabouts, and from thence the Land tends into the NW. to *Black-head*, and fo to the Harbour of St. *John's*.

From

(15)

From Cape *Spear* to the Harbour of St. *John's* is NW. by N. four Miles; Cape Bay. between which are three Bays, the firſt is from Cape *Spear* to *Black-head*, and Deadman's is called Cape *Bay*; the ſecond is from *Black-head* to *Low-point*, and that is Bay. called *Deadman's* Bay, ſeveral Men and Boats being formerly loſt in that Freſhwater Bay; the third is from *Low-point* to St. *John's* Harbour, and that is called Bay. *Freſh-water* Bay.

The Harbour of St. *John's* is an excellent good Harbour, (tho' narrow in St. John's. the Entrance,) and the chief in *Newfoundland*, for the Number of Ships uſed and employed in Fiſhing, and for Smacks; as alſo for the Number of the Inhabitants here dwelling and remaining all the year; it is narrow going in, not above 160 Fathom broad from the South-point to the North-point, but bold to the very Rocks, or Shore itſelf, and you have 16 or 17 Fathoms, the deepeſt between the two Heads; it lies NNW. but it is yet more narrow after the firſt Entrance, by Reaſon of two Rocks lying within, on each Side, but above Water, between which you are to fail, it being juſt 95 Fathom broad between them. But being paſt them you may run in boldly, (it being then wider by a great deal,) and can take no Hurt but from the Shore, only within the foreſaid Rock, on the South-ſide of it, a Point within *Ring-Noon*, (which Ring Noon. is a ſmall Bay,) there lies a ſunken Rock about 30 Fathom off the Shore, which has not above 8 Feet Water on it. Being in the Harbour you may anchor in 8, 7, 6, 5, or 4 Fathom, as you pleaſe, and lie landlocked from all Winds, for it lies up WSW. You muſt obſerve that you cannot expect to ſail in, unleſs the Wind be at SW. or to the Southward of it, and then the Wind caſts in between the two Hills till you are quite within the Narrow, and there you have Room enough. But if it be a WSW, or a more Weſterly, the Wind will caſt out, and you muſt warp in.

But be ſure, if unacquainted, that you miſtake not the Harbour of St. Caution. *John's*, for a Place called (*Quiddy Viddy* or) *Kitty Vitty*, which is within a Kitty Vitty, Mile of it, and ſhews an Opening like a good Harbour, as St. *John's*, but it or Quiddy Viddy. is not ſo, being a Place only for Boats to go in; it is narrow and dangerous, even for Boats, at low Water; you may know it by a round bare Hill (Head like) in the Form of a Haycock, which is called *Cuckold's Head*, and is juſt at the South Part of the Entrance of this *Kitty Vitty*, and to the Northward of St. *John's* ¼ of a Mile or more; but beſides this, your Courſe from Cape *Spear* will guide you.

From St. *John's* to *Torbay* the Courſe is between N. by E. (being at a little Diſtance without the Harbour) and N. About 2 Leagues and a half between St. *John's* and *Torbay*, are ſeveral Points which have Names given them, that is from St. *John's* to *Cuckold's Head* going into *Kitty Vitty*; the next is *Small-Point*, which lies NE. by N. about 2 Miles from St. *John's*; the third is *Sugar Loaf Point*, and lies N. by E. from *Small Point* half a League; the fourth is *Red-Head*, and lies N. from *Sugar Loaf*; about 2 Miles, between which, that is, *Sugar Loaf* and *Red-Head*, is a Bay, called *Logy* Bay. And the fifth

(16)

Torbay. fifth Point is the South Point of *Torbay*, and lies N. by W. half a Point Westerly from *Redhead*, about 2 Miles. This said Point of *Torbay* is lower than all the rest. From the said South Point of *Torbay* to the Anchoring-place where Ships usually ride, the Course is W. by N. 2 Miles and more, where you anchor in 14 Fathom against *Green* Cove. But if you are open of the Bay, the Course is WSW. for the Bay is large, and at least a League from the South Point to the North Point, which North Point is called *Flat*
Flat Rock. *Rock:* So that if you come from the Northward by *Flat Rock*, (which is a low Black Point with a flat Rock lying off it, and breaks on it,) your Course then into *Torbay* is S. W. a League. There live two Planters at *Torbay*. It is a bad Place for Ships to ride in with the Wind out at Sea; for being open to the Ocean there falls in a great Sea.

Red head. From the North Point of *Torbay* (called *Flat Rock*) to *Red-head* by N. the
Black-head. Course is N. by W. about half a League; but from *Flat Rock* to *Black-head* by N. the Course is N. by W. ¼ W. 2 Leagues.

Cape St. From *Black-head* to Cape St. *Francis* is N.W. 5 Miles; Cape St. *Francis*
Francis. is a whitish Point, and low in Comparison to the other Land, but at Sea the high Land over it is taken for the Cape. Within the Point of the Cape to
Shoe Cove. the Southward of it is a Cove, called *Shoe* Cove, where Boats used to come a tilting, (using the Fishermens Expression,) that is, to split and salt the Fish they catch, when blowing hard and is bad Weather, cannot get the Places they belong to in Time. In this Cove you may haul up a Boat to save her if the Wind be out; for which Northerly, Westerly, and Southerly Winds you will lie safe. There is a good Place off it to catch Fish.

Sunken About half a League off, triangular-ways, lie sunken Rocks; the outer-
Rocks off the most lie E.N.E. from the Cape, about a Mile and three-quarters: There are
Cape. also great Rocks above Water, like small Islands, the outermost of which lies about three-quarters of a Mile E. from the Cape; and the innermost not half a Mile off Shore; between which Rocks (or Island) and the sunken Rocks you may go (as I have done) with Boats, and find Water enough for any Ship: But men are unwilling to venture, there being no Advantage in the Case. These great Rocks make the aforesaid *Shoe* Cove the better and more safe.

There is also another Cove to the Northward of the Point of the Cape for Boats when the Wind is off the Shore, but else not safe.

Bell-Isle. From Cape St. *Francis* to *Bell-Isle* is S. W. and S.W. by S. 5, or 5 and a half Leagues, being a large Island, not above a League from the Shore, against
Portugal which Island on the Main is a Cove, called *Portugal* Cove, where they used to
Cove. catch and cure Fish in Summer-time, and lies to Eastward. *Bell-Isle* is about 2 Leagues in Length, and about 3 Miles broad, and the Ships that fish there lie in a little Cove on the South-side of the Island, which will contain 5 or 6 Ships, according to the Rate as they lie in Bay *Verds*. This Description of *Bell-Isle*, (besides my own setting it from several Places,) I had from Mr. *John Guy,*

Guy of *Carbonera*, and Mr. *Bennet* of St. *John's*, in *August*, 1675, and the same confirmed by Mr. *Spark*, in Bay *Bulls*, on *September* 8, 1675, who had been fishing and made Voyages at *Bell-Isle* and *Portugal* Cove.

From Cape St. *Francis* to the Island *Bacalieu*, is N. by E. about 10 Leagues. *Bacalieu* is an Island 2 Leagues long, and above half a League broad, about which Boats used to fish: There are no Inhabitants on it, but Abundance of Fowls of several Sorts, which breed there in the Summer-time. Between this Island and the Main, is about a League, where you may sail through with Ships, if you please. Bay of *Verd's-head* and the S.W. End of *Bacalieu* lie E. by N. and W. by S. one from the other about a League and a half. Island Baca-lieu.

From Cape St. *Francis* to the Bay of *Verds-head*, is the N. about 8 Leagues and a half. And from the Head to the Bay, or Cove, where Ships ride, is about three-quarters of a Mile, to the Westward of the Head; the Place where Ships ride is not above a Cable's Length from one Point to the other; which lie North and South one from the other; you lay your Anchors in 10 Fathom, and your Ships lie in 5 Fathom, with a Cable out; your Stem then is not above half a Cable's Length from the Stages. The Ships that ride there, are forced to seize their Cables one to another, and you cannot ride above 7 or 8 Ships at most: It is a bad Place, and hazardous for Ships to ride, except in the Summer-time, by reason of the great Plenty of Fish, and they being so near them, make Fishing-ships desire that Place the more, altho' there are several Inconveniences in it, as being a very bad Place for Wood and Water, &c. Bay Verds.

The Ships lie open to the S.W. into the Bay of *Consumption*. Now there is a Cove also on the East-Side of the Bay *Verd's-head*, about a Musquet-shot over from Bay *Verds* itself, called the *Black Cove*, where Stages are, and Boats kept to catch Fish. Black Cove.

Bay *Verds* is easy to be known by the Island *Bacalieu*, and also by another Head within *Bacalieu* shooting out, called *Split Point*; and also Bay *Verd's-head* itself, which is the Westermost; these three Heads shew very bluff, and very like one another, when you come from the Southward; there is no Danger in going into Bay *Verds* but what you see. Here dwell several Planters.

From Bay *Verds-head* to *Split Point*, which is against *Bacalieu* Island, the Course is E.N.E. about half a League. Split Point.

From Bay *Verd's-head* to *Flamborough-head*, is S.W. by W. about 2 Leagues: *Flamborough-head* is a black steep Point, but no Place of Shelter for a Boat, but when the Wind is off the Shore; neither is there any Safety between Bay *Verds* and *Carbonera*, (which is about 10 Leagues and a half, and lies S.W. and by S.) only two Places for Boats, the one in the S.W. Cove of *Green-bay*, which is but an indifferent Place, and lies S.W. about 4 Leagues and a half from Bay *Verds*; the other in *Salmon* Cove, which is about 3 Leagues to the Northward of *Carbonera*. Flamborough Head.

(18)

Green Bay. From Bay *Verds-head* to *Green-bay*, is S.W. about 4 Leagues and a half. This Bay is above a League over, but has nothing confiderable in it, only the aforefaid S.W. Cove, and a Place in the Bottom of the Bay, where the *Indians* come every Year to dig Oaker to oaker themfelves.

Black-head. From the South Point of *Green-bay* to *Black-head* is S.W. a League ; and **SalmonCove.** from *Black-head* to *Salmon* Cove, is S.W. by W. 4 Miles : It is a Place of Shelter for Boats, an Ifland lying in the Middle; a River in the faid Cove runs up, in which are Store of Salmon.

From *Black-head* to *Carbonera*, is S.W. ½ S. between 4 and 5 Leagues.

Carbonera. From *Salmon* Cove to *Carbonera*, the Courfe is S.W. about 3 Leagues. The South End of *Carbonera* Ifland is low, upon which is a Fort of 20 Guns, which the Merchant-men made for their Defence. The Harbour of *Carbonera* is very bold on both Sides, fo is the Ifland, between which and the Main are Rocks, which are juft under Water. This is a good Place for Ships to ride in, and for catching and curing of Fifh, having feveral Inhabitants, with good Pafturage, and above 100 Head of Cattle, which afford good Milk and Butter in the Summer-time. There is very good anchoring in clear Ground, fair turning in or out, being a Mile broad, and 3 Miles in the River, riding in 5, 6, 7, and 8 Fathoms, or deeper Water, if you pleafe. But to the Northward of this Point of *Carbonera* are two Coves where Planters live, and keep Boats **Clown Cove.** for fifhing ; the Northermoft of thefe two Coves is called *Clown* Cove, not good for Ships, but for Boats, being about 2 Miles from *Carbonera* ; the **Crocketts** other is called *Crocketts* Cove, where live two Families, and is but a little to **Cove.** the Northward of the Entrance of *Carbonera* Bay or Port.

If you are bound or intend for *Carbonera*, you may go on which Side of the Ifland you pleafe, which lies without the Bay (or Entrance) about a Mile from the Shore; but if you go to the Southward of the Ifland, you muft keep the Middle between the Point of the Ifland, and the South Point of *Carbonera*, becaufe it is foul off the S.W. End of the Ifland, and off the South Point of the Main, therefore your beft going in is to the Northward of *Car-* **Carbonera** *bonera* Ifland, and fo is the going into Harbour *Grace*, to the Northward of **Ifland.** Harbour *Grace* Ifland; *Carbonera* lies in W.S.W. 2 ¼ or 3 Miles, and from *Carbonera* to Harbour *Grace* S.S.E a League or more.

Carbonera and Harbour *Grace* lie N.N.W. and S.S.E. one from the other above a League ; but Harbour *Grace* lies from the Entrance W.S.W. at leaft 8 Miles, and is a Mile broad. But between *Carbonera* and Harbour *Grace* is **Mufketa** *Mufketa* Cove, where Ships may ride, but feldom ufe it. Here live two **Cove.** Planters ; it is not fo convenient for Fifhing-fhips as other Places, although clean Ground, Water enough, and large.

Harbour Grace, You may turn into *Harbour Grace*, all the Bay over from Side to Side, and come off which Side you pleafe of the Rock called *Salvages*, which is almoft in

the

the Middle of the Channel. But there is another Rock on the North-fide called *Long Harry*, fomething without *Salvages*, near the North-fhore, where you go between the Main and it with Boats, but needlefs for Ships, although Water enough. Both the Rocks are a great Height above Water. Being within, or to the Weftward of the Rock *Salvages*, you may turn from Side to Side by your Lead, till you draw towards a Mile off the Point of the Beach (within which the Ships ride); you may then keep the North-fhore, becaufe there is a Bar or Ledge fhoots over from the South-fide, almoft to the North-fhore.

To know when you are near the faid Bar, or Ledge, obferve this Mark; you will fee two White Rocks on the Land by the Water-fide, in a Bank on the North-fide, which fhews whiter than any Place elfe, and is about a Mile below, or to the Eaftward of the Beach, which is good to be known, being a low Point, nothing but Beach for a pretty diftance; keep the faid North-fhore pretty near, where you will have 3 Fathom and a half on the Bar, and prefently after 4, 5, 6, and 7 Fathom; but if you ftand over to the South-ward till you are got within the faid Bar, or Ledge, you fhall not have above 7, 8, and 9 Feet Water: This Sand tends S E. from thwart the aforefaid two White Rocks, and runs over clofe to the South-fide. But being paft that as aforefaid, you may turn from Side to Side till within the Beach, and ride landlocked in 4, 5, or 6 Fathom, or higher up in 7, 8, 9, or 10 Fathom, as you pleafe. The Harbour, or River, runs up S W. by W. at leaft two Leagues above the Beach, navigable.

Marks of the Bar, or Ledge.

Being bound for *Harbour Grace*, be fure to go to the Northward of the *Harbour Grace* Iflands, which lie before the Harbour above a Mile off: For the Southward of the Iflands between it and the South-fhore of the Harbour, is foul Ground: The Harbour lies in W S W.

Harbour Grace Iflands.

From *Harbour Grace* to Cape St. *Francis*, is Eaft Northerly 7 Leagues and a half.

From *Harbour Grace* to *Bryant's* Cove, is S W. about half a League, but is no Place where Ships ufe: One Planter lives there, it being a good Place for catching of Fifh. In the Entrance of this Cove lies a Rock in the Middle, but above Water. You may go in on either Side with a Ship, and have 4 or 5 Fathom, and anchor within it in clean Ground.

Bryant's Cove.

From *Harbour Grace* to *Spaniards* Bay, is SSW. about three Leagues. This Bay is deep and large, almoft like Bay *Roberts*; but there are no Inha-bitants, neither do Men ufe this Place for Fifhing, but there is good anchor-ing all over the Bay: it is but a fmall Neck of Land over Bay *Roberts*.

Spaniards Bay.

From *Spaniards* Bay to Bay *Roberts*, is S E. by E. Southerly about two Miles. This Bay is about two Miles and a half broad, from the North Point to the South Point, which lie N W. and S E. one from the other; there is very

Bay Roberts.

(20)

very good turning into the Bay, and no danger but what you see. You may borrow on either Side, and go close to the Island which lies on the Starboard-side going in. The Bay is at least three Leagues long from the first Entrance; it runs up with two Arms, after you are a League in; the one lies up WNW. and is the deepest, and the other SW. Being past the Island, or to the Westward of it, which is bold too, you may run up about a Mile, and lie landlocked in 9 or 10 Fathom within the Island.

Sheeps Cove. From Bay *Roberts* to Port *Grave*, is 3 or 4 Miles about the Point; this Bay is large, deep, and very bold, as the other Bays are; there is a Cove on the Starboard-side going into this Bay, called *Sheeps* Cove, where you may moor your Ship by Head and Stern, and ride in 4 and a half, and 5 Fathom, but your Anchor, to the SW. lies in 22 Fathom, about a Cable and a quarter's Length from your Ship.

Port Grave. From *Sheeps* Cove to Port *Grave*, is West by South a Mile, or somewhat more, but Ships ride not within the small Islands which are by Port *Grave*, it being shoal Water within them, but ride off without them.

Cupids Cove. From *Sheeps* Cove to *Cupids* Cove, the Course is SSW. about 4 Miles It is a good Place for a Ship or two to ride in 4, 5, or 6 Fathom, and not above a Point open; the Cove lies in SW. and the South-side of the Bay to *Burnt-head* lies NE. by E. and SW. by W. one from the other about a League; for *Sheeps* Cove and *Cupids* Cove are in the same Bay of Port *Grave*; but *Cupids* Cove is on the South-side, and the other on the North-side; the Bay runs up WSW. and is about three Leagues long.

Burnt-head. *Burnt-head*, which is the South Point of the Bay, and Port *Grave*, lie SE. by E. and NW. by W. two and a half or three Miles. *Burnt-head* is so called by reason the Trees that were on it are burnt down.

Brigus. From *Burnt-head* to *Brigus*, is S. by W. a League. The South Point of *Brigus* is a high ragged Point, which is good to know it by: The Bay of *Brigus* is not above half the Breadth of Port *Grave* Bay, and you run up SW. by W. and WSW. about half a League, and anchor on the North-side, where two Planters live in a small Bay. Only small Ships use this Place, it being so far up the Bay of *Conception*.

Colliers Bay. From *Brigus* to *Colliers* Bay, is SSW. two and a half or three Miles; it is a Place now not inhabited. And from *Colliers* Bay to *Salmon* Cove, is S. about two Miles and a half, but no Place considerable, and without Inhabitants. It is sometimes called *Salmon* Pool.

Harbour Main. From *Salmon* Cove to *Harbour* Main, the Course is SSE. about two Miles. In this Place lives a Planter; it is a good Place for Fishing, but Ships seldom go so high up in the Bay.

From

From *Burnt-head* to *Harbour* Main is about three Leagues and a half.
And from *Harbour* Main to *Holyroad* is SE. by S. about two Miles; then Holyroad.
the Land tends about to the Eaſtward towards *Bell-Iſle*. *Holyroad* has 11
Fathom Water, good Ground.

From Bay *Verds-head* to *Split-point*, the Courſe is ENE. half a League. Split-point.

From *Split-point* to the Point of the *Grates*, NNW. two Leagues. Grates.

From the Point of the *Grates* to the NW. or North End of the Iſland *Ba-* Bacalieu.
calieu, the Courſe is E. by S. four and a half or five Miles.

From the *Grates* to *Break-heart-point*, NNW. WNW. and W. tending Break-heart-
about two Points; between the *Grates* and this Point is a Bay where Boats point.
may lie with a Wind off the Land of *Break heart-point*; there is a Ledge of
Rocks, but above Water.

From *Break-heart-point* to *Sherwick-point*, going into *Old Perlican*, the
Courſe is SW. by S. 5 or 6 Miles. To the Southward of *Break-heart-point*
is a ſmall Iſland ſome little Diſtance off the Shore, called *Scurvy* Iſland; be- Scurvy Iſland.
tween the ſaid Iſland and *Sherwick-point*, runs in a pretty deep Bay, and lies
in SE. from *Sherwick-point* about three Quarters of a Mile.

Sherwick-point is bold, off which is a Rock above Water; this Point is the Sherwick-
North Point of *Old Perlican*. They who are bound to *Old Perlican*, cannot point.
go with a Ship to the Northward of the Iſland, that is, between the Iſland and
Sherwick-point; although it ſeems a fair Paſſage, yet it is altogether foul
Ground, and a Shoal of Rocks from the Main to the Iſland (which Iſland is
about a Mile and a Quarter round, and about Half a Mile in Length); therefore, whoever intends for *Old Perlican* with a Ship, muſt go to the Southward Old Perlican.
of the Iſland, between that and the Main, and run in within the Iſland, and
anchor in 4 or 5 Fathom. But there is a Rock juſt even with the Water, and
ſome under Water, that lie about the Middle of the Bay, within the Iſland,
or rather neareſt to the Main. *Old Perlican* is but an indifferent Road; if
the Wind comes out at WNW. you are forced to buoy your Cables for the
Badneſs of Ground, and the Boats go a great Way to catch Fiſh, about five
or ſix Miles, unleſs it be in the very Middle of Summer. In this Place live
ſeveral Planters.

From *Old Perlican* to *Sille* Cove is WSW. Southerly, about 7 Leagues; Sille Cove.
Sille Cove is but an indifferent Place for Ships, ſuch as Bay *Verds*.

From *Old Perlican* to *New Perlican*, the Courſe is WSW. 8 Leagues. This New Perli-
is a very good Harbour, where you may lie landlocked in 5, 6, 7, 8, 9, or can.
10 Fathom. It is very bold and large going in, ſo that if you can ſee the
Point before Night, you may ſafely run in, nothing to hurt you but the Shore
itſelf; the Eaſtermoſt Point going in is called *Smutty-noſe* Point, and the
Weſter-

(22)

Weſtermoſt *Gorlob* Point, between which Point is the Entrance, which is almoſt two Miles broad, and has about 20 Fathom Water; and as you ſail in it grows narrower and ſhoaler, lying in firſt WSW. after runs up to the Weſtward in a Bight, where you lie landlocked, and above Half a Mile broad, ſo that you may turn in and out, and anchor in what Depth you pleaſe, from 12, 10, 8, 6, 5, or 4 Fathom, very good Ground. The Deſcription of this Harbour I had from Mr. *John Edward*, who fiſhed there formerly, all the reſt being of my own Experience. From *New Perlican* it is about 5 Leagues over to *Random-head*, and they lie neareſt NW. and SE. one from the other. In

Random. the River or Bay of *Random* are ſeveral Arms and Harbours; for *Random* and *Smith's* Sound come all into one, but it is 9 or 10 Leagues under the Head of each where they meet, and there is a little Iſland at the Head, where is 4 and 5 Fathom; only at the Iſland going through you have not above 12 Feet Water, and it is not a Mile broad there, as I was informed by Planters at *Bonaventure*, who uſually go a Furring there in the Winter: *Smith's* Sound runs in WSW. as far as I could ſee off *Bonaventure*. I was alſo informed that it is but 15 Leagues from *Bonaventure* to *Tickle* Harbour, the Bottom of *Trinity* Bay; but there is a Bay called Bay *Bulls*, which runs in three or four Leagues, and is not over from thence to *Placentia* Bay (the Back or Weſt Side of the Land) above two Miles: and that the Iſlands of *Placentia* Bay are about 9 or 10 Leagues long each, and five Miles broad, on which are many Deer; they lie NW. and SE.

Ireland's Eye. From *Bonaventure* to *Ireland's* Eye is SW. 2, or 2 Leagues and a Half.

Port Bonaventure. From *Bonaventure-head* to *Bonaventure*, the Courſe is NW. Half a Point Weſterly, about two Miles or more, but being got a Mile from the Head, then the Harbour lies NW. by N. about a Mile to the Admiral's Stage. The Port *Bonaventure* lies within two ſmall Iſlands, between which you ſail in, but you may go on either Side of the Iſland between that and the Main, if you have a leading Wind, no Danger, and ſhall have 4 or 5 Fathom at leaſt, and run within the ſaid Iſlands, and anchor in that Depth, in good Ground. You have there a very ſecure Place for Boats in bad Weather, running in within a Point behind, or to the Northward of the Admiral's Stages, like a great Pond, leaving the Planter's Houſe on the Larboard Side; this Place will contain above 100 Boats in Security.

Gull Iſland. There is an Iſland which lies off the W. Point of the Harbour, called *Gull* Iſland, off which they uſed to fiſh; from the ſaid Iſland the Harbour lies in N. about a Mile. There are ſeveral Iſlands which are without, off *Bonaventure*,

Green Iſland. the one is from the Port SSW. 5 or 6 Miles, called *Green* Iſland, which is a pretty big Iſland, and you ſee it as ſoon as you come out of *Trinity* Harbour in fair Weather; another Iſland lies SW. by S. 3 Miles, and another Iſland without that about 4 or 5 Miles from *Bonaventure*; the Courſe is SW. by S.

Horſechops. From the *Bonaventure-head* to the *Horſechops* is ENE. 3½ Leagues.

But

(23)

But from *Bonaventure-head* to *Trinity* Harbour, is N E. by N. about 3 Leagues; between which are some Bays, but not for Ships to ride in, unless the Wind off the Shore.

The *Horsechops* and *Sherwick-point* (being the North Point of *Trinity* Harbour) lie WNW. and E S E. one from the other 2 Leagues; between the *Horsechops* and *Trinity* Harbour are two Places where Ships used to fish; the one is *English* Harbour, and is WNW. from the *Horsechops* 2 Miles, and after you are about a Point, tends ENE. again; it is a clean Bay, and you ride in 4 or 5 Fathom Water; a Planter or two live here. English Harbour.

From *English* Harbour to *Salmon* Cove, the Courſe is NW. by W. Westerly about half a League; it is a Place for Fishing, and there is a River which runs up about 2 Miles to the Northward. Salmon Cove.

Without *Salmon* Cove is a Headland, called *Foxes* Iſland, yet joins to the Main by the Neck of Beach. To the Northward of the ſaid Iſland, or Headland, between it and *Sherwick-point*, runs in a Bay, called *Robin Hood's*; and in the ſaid Bay, behind a Point which lies out, ſmall Ships ride, and fiſh there. Foxes Iſland.

From the *Horsechops* to *Trinity* Harbour, the Courſe is WNW. about 2 Leagues. *Trinity* Harbour is the beſt and largeſt Harbour in all the Land, having ſeveral Arms and Coves where many hundred Ships may all ride landlocked: It is a Place which you may turn in or out, being bold too on each Side, neither is there any danger but what you ſee, only going into the S W. Arm, where the Admiral's Stage uſually is, lies a Shoal, called the *Muſchel-Bank*, which ſhoots off from the Point within the ſmall Iſland on the Larboard-ſide going in, and lies over NW. about a third of the Breadth of that Arm, which you muſt avoid: Being within that Bank, which will diſcover itſelf by the Colour of the Water, you may edge over cloſe to the South Shore, if you pleaſe, or keep your Lead to avoid the *Muſchel-Bank*, giving it a little Diſtance: You may anchor in 14, 12, or 10 Fathom, and you may come ſo near to the Stage on Shore as to make a Stage with Topmaſts to your Stage on Shore, to lade or unlade your Ship. It is a moſt excellent Harbour; for after you are in this SW. Arm, there is another runs up WNW. near 2 Miles; and near the Head of that another runs up SSW. but there is a Bar, or Ledge, at the Entrance of this SSW. Arm, but the former WNW. is a large Place, and good Anchoring for 500 Sail of Ships. You have beſides theſe forementioned Arms, the Main Harbour (turning or) lying up NNW. and being within the Harbour's Mouth, you may ride in a Cove, large and good on the Starboard or Eaſt-ſide, and landlocked in good Ground, where Planters live; and over-againſt that Cove, on the Larboard or Weſt-ſide, are two other Coves; the Northermoſt of them is called the *Vice Admiral's* Cove, for the Conveniency of curing Fiſh: And above, or to the Northward of that, is a large Cove, or Arm, called *God Almighty's* Cove, where there is Room enough for 3 or 400 Sail of Ships to ride, all in clear Ground, neither Winds nor Sea can hurt you, nor any Tide; in which Place Ships may lie Trinity Harbour.

undiſ-

undiscovered till you run up so far as to bring it open. Several other Places there are in this excellent Harbour, in good clean Ground, tough Clay in all the Arms and Coves of *Trinity*, and have 4 and 5 Fathom Water within two Boats Length off the Shore any where, and 6, 7, 8, 9, 10, 12, and 14 Fathom, and some Places more, in the Middle of the Arms and Channels, as you please; you may turn in or out, as aforesaid, observing your Tide, which rises there about 4 Feet, sometimes more. For not only *Sherwick-point* is bold, which is the Northermost, but also *Salvages*, which is the Southermost.

Green-bay.

From the *Horsechops* to the South Head of *Catalina* Bay is NE. by N. and NE. 5 Leagues. About a League to the Northward of the *Horsechops* is *Green-bay*, which runs pretty deep in, but no Place where Ships use to ride or fish. Being past *Green-bay*, there is no Place or Cove for Boats till you come to *Ragged* Harbour, or *Catalina*.

South Head of the Bay of Catalina to the North Head.

From the South Head of *Catalina* Bay to the North Head is NNE. 3 Leagues; between which two Heads is *Ragged* Harbour and *Catalina* Harbour. *Catalina* Harbour lies from the South Head N. by E. Northerly about 2 Miles.

Ragged Harbour.

Ragged Harbour is so called by reason of the Abundance of ragged and craggy Rocks which lie before and within the Harbour; there is no going into the Southward with Ships, but only for Boats, and that you must be well acquainted with, for there are very many Rocks above and under Water.

They who intend for *Ragged* Harbour with a Ship must go to the Northward of all the aforesaid ragged Rocks or Islands that lie before it (which make the Harbour), and run so far to the Northward till they bring *Ragged* Harbour open; then sail in between a round Island which lies close to the Main, and a great black Rock which lies off the North End of all the *Ragged* Islands; sail in till they are about the Middle of the aforesaid Islands, which will be to seaward of them, and anchor there. There is a River of fresh Water at the Head of the Harbour, but no Inhabitants.

Catalina Harbour.

Two Miles to the Northward of *Ragged* Harbour is the Harbour of *Catalina*. which is a very good and safe Harbour, and good Ground, not above 8 Fathom, from 3 to 4, 5, 6, 7, or 8 Fathom, as you please. You may, with a leading Wind, sail between the small Island which is a little to the Southward of the Harbour, and have 4 or 5 Fathom at the least going through, but it is not above a Cable's Length broad; or you may go without the said Island to the Eastward of it, giving the Island a small Birth, and so sail in with the Middle of the Harbour; for about a Mile Distance from the South Point of the Harbour, ENE. is a Shoal, upon which if there be ever so small a Sea, it breaks; but you may sail between the Island and the Shoal, or you may go to the Northward of it, between the Shoal and the North-shore, and borrow off the North-side of the Main off *Little Catalina*, a Bay which lies in.

Being

(25)

Being off *Little Cattalina*, all the Way to the Harbour you have not above 10 Fathom, and from 10 to 8 and 7 Fathom, then 8 and 9 Fathom again. It is reported there is a Rock which lies about three quarters of a Cable's Length from the South Point of the entering into the Harbour, which has but 9 or 10 Feet Water on it, but by all the Endeavours I made by Sounding I could not find it, putting in three Times in a Shallop. However, it is eafily avoided, if any fuch, by keeping fomething nearer to the North Shore, till you are fhut within the faid Point, for all the Harbour over is good Sounding. Clofe to the Shore, within the Harbour, you may anchor in 5 Fathom, land-locked. In the SW. Arm the Harbour lies in WSW. or you may anchor in 3 Fathom and a Half within to the Southward of the little fmall *Green* Ifland within the faid Harbour, or run up two Miles towards the River-head, where frefh Water runs down. In this Harbour you may anchor in 7, 6, 5, or 4 Fathom. There is a Kind of a Boar rifes in this Place very often, that will caufe the Water to rife 3 Feet prefently, and then down again; and you have it two or three Times in three or four Hours at certain Seafons. It is a very good Harbour, and Abundance of Herb *Alexander* grows on that fmall Ifland in the Harbour. Here is Store of Salmon to be caught at the Head of the Harbour, if you have Nets. Here are no Inhabitants. And near a fmall Cove in the WNW. within the fmall Ifland, is a Fire Stone of a glittering Colour, a Kind of Mineral, excellent good Wheel-locks growing in the Rocks.

Cattalina Harbour.

From *Cattalina* Harbour to *Little Cattalina* is NNE. about half a League; it feems to be a good fandy Bay, but I went not into it.

Little Cattalina.

From *Cattalina* Harbour to the North-head of the Bay is NE. Eafterly, a League and a half.

From the North-head of *Cattalina* Bay to *Flower's* Point, the Courfe is N. by E. a League and a half; off which Point are funken Rocks, called *Flower's* Rocks; the Sea breaks upon them in a fwelling (or great) Sea, and they dif-cover themfelves plain; they lie about half a League off Shore, which are the utmoft I could perceive with all the Curiofity I had to take Notice of them, by paffing by them twice in the Day-time; you may go between the Point of the *Flower's* (which has fome Rocks lying off it) and the faid funken Rocks; you have a Mark if in the Day-time to go without them, which is to keep Cape *Larjan* open to *Bira's* Ifland, and that will carry you clear without to the Eaftward of them with any Ship. Some would perfuade us that the *Flower's* Rocks lie 2 or 3 Leagues off, but I am not of that Opinion, knowing to the contrary.

North-head of the Bay of Cattalina. Flower's Point. Sunken Rocks. Mark to go clear off the faid Rocks.

From *Flower's* Point to *Bird's* Ifland the Courfe is N. by W. about three Miles and a half. Within the faid *Bird's* Ifland is a large Bay, one Arm within the South Point of the Land, which runs up WSW. a good Diftance, where Ships may ride: There is another Arm alfo runs up within fome Rocks, which are above Water; but I went not into that Arm, for the Bay runs to Cape *Larjan*;

Bird's Ifland. Cape Larjan.

D

(26)

Larjan; *Birds* Island abounds with Willocks, Gannots, Pigeons, Gulls, &c. which breed there in Summer.

From *Birds* Island to Cape *Larjan*, the Course is North Easterly, between two and three Miles.

From *Flower's* Point to Cape *Larjan* is N. half a Point Westerly; Cape *Larjan* is but a low Point, off which lies a great Rock above Water.

Spiller.Point. From Cape *Larjan* to *Spillers* Point is NNW. a small League; between which Cape and *Spillers* Point runs in a pretty deep Bay, over which Point, between that and Cape *Larjan*, you will see the high Land of Port *Bonavista* when you are a good Distance off at Sea, being high Land. *Spillers* Point is indifferent high, steep up, and bold too.

Cape Bona- From *Spillers* Point to Cape *Bonavista*, the Course is NNW. about a
vista. League, between which is a very great and deep Bay, so that Men unacquainted would judge that there went in the Harbour of *Bonavista*. It is but a small Distance of about two Miles and a half over, from the Bottom of the Bay to Port *Bonavista*, by Land, and is but a mere Neck of Land; from *Redhead* Bay to this Bay is not above half a Musket-shot. The Head of Cape *Bonavista* appears at a Distance of a Sky-colour. About three quarters of a
Gull Island. Mile N. by W. from the Cape, is a small Island called *Gull* Island, easy to be known, being indifferent high, and highest in the Middle, and makes somewhat like the Form of a *Fleur-de-lys*, or a Hat with great Brims; you may see it 4 or 5 Leagues off in clear Weather. And N.E. about a League from Cape *Bonavista*, is a Ledge of about 10 Fathom Water on it, where Boats use to fish. Cape *Bonavista* lies in Latitude 49 Degrees 10 Minutes.

From Cape *Bonavista* to Port *Bonavista*, the Course is SW. about five Miles. If you come from the Southward, and intend for *Bonavista*, you may sail between *Gull* Island and the Cape, they being both bold too, and about three quarters of a Mile asunder, but you must leave *Green* Island to your Larboard Side going to *Bonavista*, for between it and the Main is but narrow, and some Places shoal Rocks, not safe for Ships to pass through; but you may
Green Island. sail between the said *Green* Island and the *Stone* Island, with any Ship without
Stone Island. Danger, being safe and bold; or you may go the Westward of *Stone* Island, and run to the Southward till you open the Bay or Harbour of *Bonavista*, and
Moses Point. are past *Moses* Point, and so to the Southward of the Rocks, called the *Sweeres*,
Sweeres. which are high Rocks, within which you ride (for there is no Passage to the Northward of them) and lie in 11, 10, 9, 8, 7, 6, or 5 Fathom, as you please, and must always have a good Anchor in the SW. and another fast in the *Sweeres*, or anchor in the NW. for Westerly Winds blow right into the Road.
Port Bona- It flows generally to the Northward about *Bonavista*, and the Places adjacent
vista. WNW. that is a WNW. Moon makes the highest Water, which most Masters of Ships using these Parts have observed.

With

With small Vessels you may go between *Green* Island and the Main (but not with great Ships), and so to *Red-head*; but the Bay between the Points (over-against *Green* Island) and *Red-head* is all foul Ground to anchor in. A little Distance, about a Cable's Length from the Shore, is a sunken Rock, but with Boats you may go between the Shore and it; the Sea breaks on it. Being past *Red head*, you sail SW. to *Moses* Point; between which two Points is a large Bay or Cove, called *Baylies* Cove, where you may anchor on Occasion. There is a Stage kept generally for Fishing every Year, on the Larboard or North Side of the Bay.

From the East Part of the Grand Bank of *Newfoundland*, in the Latitude 45 D. 06 M. to the East Part of the Bank *Queco*, in 44 D. 16 M. I made 120 Leagues Distance. The North Part of the Bank *Queco* in Latitude 45 D. 06 M. the SW. of *Queco* in 44 D. 16 M. and the Isle of *Sabes*, in the Latitude 44 D. 16 M. and about 14 Leagues to the Westward of Bank *Queco*; the North Part of *Queco* on a West Course is about 18 Leagues in Length; from the NW. Part of *Queco* to the Harbour of *Caufo* is NW. by W. half W. 39 Leagues, after you have lost Sounding of *Queco*, on which is commonly about 35 Fathom, unless on the SE. Part, where (and on a certain Spot near the Middle, as the Fishermen inform us,) there is but 18 Fathom after you are to the Westward of *Queco*, and also before you have 100 and 95 Fathom, black Mud; there is a small narrow Bank, about 2 Leagues to the NW. of the Middle of *Queco*, but it reaches not so far to the Northward as the North Part of *Queco*; about 20 Leagues WNW. from the NW. Point of *Queco*, you will strike Ground on *Frenchman*'s Bank, which is a narrow Bank that stretches ESE. and WNW. thwart the Harbour of *Caufo*, about nine Leagues off; you must keep your Lead going when you reckon yourself nigh this Bank, or else on a NW. Course you will soon be over it, being not past 3 Leagues broad, and when over it you will have 100, and 95 Fathom Water, black Mud; it is the best Way to fall to the Westward of *Caufo*, because on the *French* Coast you have no Soundings, as I have heard the Fishermen say, and the Winds in the Summer are generally SW. and WSW. and very often foggy.

Note. The Ground to the Westward of *Caufo* rises very sudden from 100, 95, 70, to 40 Fathom, hard Ground; then you are not past 2 or 3 Miles off the Land: be careful of sailing in with *Caufo* in foggy Weather, for SE. and ESE. from it lie sunken Rocks, which in fair Weather seldom appear at High Water.

The Course and Distance of the Coast of Newfoundland, *between* Cape Race *and* Cape Spear.

By Captain HENRY SOUTHWOOD.

These Courses set by a Meridian Compass with Allowance of Variation.

	Course.	Leagues.	Miles.
FIRST from Cape *Race* to Cape *Ballard*	NNE.	3 ½ or 4	or 11
From Cape *Ballard* to the South Point of *Renowes*	NNE.	2	6
From Cape *Ballard* to *Renowes* Rock, which is high above Water	NE. ½ N.erly	2	6
From Cape *Ballard* to *Ferryland-head*	NE. by N. ½ N.	5	15
From *Renowes* Point to *Fermowes* N.E. by N. and NNE. and N.	NNE. ½ E.	1 ½	5
From *Renowes* to *Ferryland-head*	NE. by N. ½ N.	3 ½	or 11
From *Fermowes* to *Bald-head*	NNE.	½	1 ½
From *Bald-head* to *Ferryland-head*	NE.byN.½ N.erly	1 ½	5
From *Bald-head* to *Black-head*	N.	½	or 1 ½
From *Black-head* to *Ferryland-head*	NE. by E.	1	3
From *Black-head* to *Agua Fort*	NW. by N.	1 ½	or 4
From *Agua Fort* to *Ferryland-head*, the South Part of the Head	East Northerly.	2	6
From *Agua Fort* to *Crow Island*	E. and NE. by E.	1 ⅓	4
From *Crow Island* to *Ferryland-head*	E. by S.	½	or 1 ½
From *Ferryland head* to Cape *Broyle-head*	N. by E.	1 ¼	4
From the East End of *Buoy Island* to Cape *Broyle-head*	NNE.	1	3
From *Ferryland-head* to the S. of *Gull Island*, which is off of *Whitless-bay*	NNE.	5 ⅔	16
From *Ferryland-head* to Cape *Spear*	NNE. ½ E.	11	33
From Cape *Broyle-head*, the Bay or Harbour Cape *Broyle* lies in	WNW.	2 ½	7
From C. *Broyle-head* to the N. Head of C. *Broyle* Harbour, or *Brigus* Point	N. by W.	⅔	2
From the said North Point of Cape *Broyle* Harbour into *Brigus*, is	NW. ½ W.	⅓	1
From Cape *Broyle-head* to Cape *Neddick*	N. by E. N.erly	1 ⅔	or 5
From Cape *Neddick* to *Baline-head*	NE. by N.	⅓	1
From Cape *Broyle* to *Baline-head*	NNE. ½ N.erly	2 ⅙	7
From *Baline-head* to *Baline*, is NW. and NW. by W. 3-4ths of a Mile	NW. by W.	⅓	1
From *Baline-head* to *Isles De Spear*, the Body of them	NNE.	¼	or ¾
From *Baline-head* to the SE. End of *Spear Island*	NE.	⅔	2
From *Baline-head* to the SE. End of *Goose Island*	E. by N.	⅓	1
From *Baline-head* to *Green Island*	NE. ½ Northerly	1 ½	or 5
From *Baline-head* to *Gull Island*	NE. by N.	2	or 6
From *Baline-head* to *Fay Bull's-head*	NE. by N.	3 ½	or 10
From *Baline-head* to the N. Point of *Momables-bay*, or S. Point of *Whitless bay*	NNE. ½ N.erly	1 ¾	5
From the North Point of *Momables-bay*, or South Point of *Whitless-bay*, to Bay *Bulls* South Point	N.E. by **N.**	1	3
From the said Point of *Momables* to *Green Island*	SE.	½	or 1 ¼
From the said Point of *Momables* to the NW. End of *Gull Island*	NE.	⅔	2
From the said Point to the South End of *Gull Island*	ENE.	½	or 1 ½
From the South Point of Bay *Bulls* to the North Point of Bay *Bulls*	NE. Northerly	⅓	or 1 ⅛
From Bay *Bulls* to the South Point of *Petty-harbour*, the Spout between	NE. by N.	3 ½	10
From the South Point of *Petty-harbour* to the North Point of *Petty-harbour*	NNE.	1	3
From the North Point of *Petty harbour* to Cape *Spear*	NE. by N.	1	2 ½
From Cape *De Spear* to St. *John's* Harbour	NW. by N.	1 ⅓	or 4

The

The Courſes and Diſtances of the Coaſt of Newfoundland, *from* Cape Spear *to* Bay Verds, Bacalieu, *and ſeveral Ports and Headlands in the Bay of* Conſumption, *or* Conception.

	Courſe.	Leagues.	Miles.
From Cape *Spear* to Cape St. *Francis* N. and N. by W. and NW. by N.	N. by W.	7 ½	or 22
From Cape *Spear* to St. *John's* ——	NW. by N.	1 ⅓	4
From Cape *Spear* to *Sugar Loaf* ——	N.	2 ⅓	7
From Cape *Spear* to *Red-head* ——	N.	2 ½	8
From St. *John's* to *Small Point* ——	NE. by N.	⅔	or 2
From *Small Point* to *Sugar Loaf* ——	N. by E.	½	or 1 ½
From *Sugar Loaf* to *Red-head* ——	N.	⅔	2
From *Red-head* to the South Point of *Torbay* ——	N. by W. ½ W.ly	½	2
From the South Point of *Torbay* to *Green Cove*, or Anchoring-Place ——	W. by N.	1	3
From the South Point of *Torbay* to the North Point, called *Flat Rock*	NE.	1	3
From the North Point of *Torbay*, or *Flat Rock*, to *Red-head* ——	N. by W.	⅓	2
From *Flat Rock* to *Black head* (by North) ——	N. by W. ½ W.ly	2	or 6
From *Black-head* to Cape St. *Francis* ——	NW.	1 ⅔	or 5 ½
From Cape St. *Francis* to Bay *Verds-head* ——	N.	8 ¾ or 9	26
From Cape St. *Francis* to the Iſland *Bacalieu* ——	N. by E.	9	27
From Cape St. *Francis* to *Bell-Iſle* in the Bay of *Conſumption*, SW. and	SW. by S.	5 ¼	17
From Cape St. *Francis* to *Green-bay* in the Bay of *Conſumption* ——	NW. ½ N.	6 ⅔	20
From Cape St. *Francis* to *Black-head* in the Bay of *Conſumption* ——	NW.	6	18
From Cape St. *Francis* to the North Point of *Carbonera* ——	W. ½ N.	7	21
From Cape St. *Francis* to *Spaniard's-bay* ——	WSW. ½ S.	9	27
From Cape St. *Francis* to Port *Grove* ——	SW. by W.	9 ¾ or 10	30
From Cape St. *Francis* to *Holyhead*, which is the Bottom of *Conſumption-bay*	SW. by S.	12 ½ or 13	38
From *Holy Road* to *Harbour Main* ——	NW. by W.	⅔	2
From *Harbour Main* to *Salmon Cove* ——	NW.	⅔	2
From *Salmon Cove* to *Collier's* Bay ——	N.	¾	2
From *Collier's* Bay to *Brigus* (by North) ——	NNE.	⅔	or 2 ½
From *Brigus* to *Burnt-head* (which is the South Point of *Porto Grove* Bay)	N. by W.	1	3
From *Harbour Main* to *Burnt-head* ——	N. ¼ E.	3 ¼ or 4	or 12
From *Burnt-head* to the South Part of *Great Bell-Iſle* ——	E. by N.	3	10
From *Burnt-head* to the North Part of *Great Bell-Iſle* ——	NE. by E. ½ E.	4	15
From *Burnt-head* to Cape St. *Francis* ——	NE. by E. N.ly	10	30
From *Burnt-head* to the South Point of Bay *Roberts* ——	N. by E.	1 ⅓	or 4
From *Burnt-head* to *Cupid's Cove* ——	WSW.	1	3
From the South Point of Bay *Roberts* to the North Point of Bay *Roberts*	NW.	¾	or 2
From the South Point of Bay *Roberts* to the South Point of *Bell-Iſle* ——	ESE. Eaſterly	4	12
From the North Point of Bay *Roberts* to the North Point of *Spaniards* Bay	N. by W. N.erly	3	2 ¼
From *Spaniards* Bay to the South Point of *Harbour Grace* ——	NNE.	1	9
From the North Point of *Harbour Grace* to *Carbonera* ——	N. by E.	1 ¼	4
From *Carbonera* to Bay *Verds*, NE. by N. and NE. ——	NE. Northerly	10 ½	31
From *Carbonera* to *Black-head* (NE. Northerly) ——	NE. Northerly	4 ½	13
From Bay *Verds* to *Flamborough-head* ——	SW. by W.	2	6
From Bay *Verds-head* to the South Weſt End of *Bacalieu* ——	E. by N.	1 ⅓	4
From Bay *Verds head* to *Split Point*, which is againſt *Bacalieu* Iſland ——	ENE.	½	or 1 ½

Courſes

Courses and Distances from Split Point, *which is a Mile and a Half from* Bay Verd's-head *in* Newfoundland, *to several Places in the Bay of* Trinity.

	Course.	Leagues.	Miles.
From *Split Point* to the *Grates* — — —	NNW.	2	or 7
From the Point of *Grates* to the NW. or N. End of *Bacalieu* — —	E. by S.	1 ¾	5
From the *Grates* to *Break-heart Point* N. by W. and W. by N. —	NW. by W. Nly	1 ⅓	4
From *Break-heart Point* to *Sherwick Point* near *Old Perlican* —	SW. by S.	1 ½	or 4
From *Sherwick Point* is about a Mile or more into the Road, but no Passage for a Ship to the Northward of the Island — —	SSW.	½	2
From the *Grates* to the South Head of *Cattalina* Bay — —	N. by E.	10	30
From the *Grates* to the *Horsechops* — — —	NW. by N.	9	28
From the *Grates* to *Bonaventure* Harbour is NW. by W. half Westerly, and	SE. by E. ½ E.ly	11 or 12	34
From the North End of *Bacalieu* to *Cattalina* Harbour NNW. Northerly	NNW. ½ N.ly -	13	40
From *Sherwick Point* at *Old Perlican* to the South Head at *Cattalina* —	N. a little Easterly	12	37
From *Sherwick Point* to the Middle of the high Land of *Green* Bay —	N. by W. W.ly	9 ½	28
From *Sherwick Point* to the high Land of the *Horsechops* — —	NNW. N.erly	9	27
From *Sherwick* to *Bonaventure-head* (the high Land of it) — —	NW. Northerly	9 ½	29
From *Sherwick* to *Salvages* Point — — —	W. by S.	3 ½	9
From *Sherwick* or *Old Perlican* to *New Perlican* — —	WSW.	8	25
From *Old Perlican* to *Silly Cove* — — —	WSW. S.erly	7	22
From *Silly Cove* to *Random-head* — — —	NW.	5 ½ or 6	17
From *Silly Cove* to *Bonaventure-head* — — —	N. by E.	9	27
From *Bonaventure-head* to *Bonaventure* NW. by W. and NW. by N. —	N. by W.	1	4
From *Bonaventure-head* to *Ireland's Eye* — — —	WSW.	2	or 7
From *Bonaventure-head* to *Trinity* Harbour — —	NNE.	2 ½	5
From *Bonaventure-head* to the *Horsechops* — —	ENE.	3 ½	10
From the *Horsechops* to *Sherwick Point* being the N. Point of *Trinity* Harbour	W. by N.	2 ½	7
From the *Horsechops* to the South Head ---- — —	NW. by N.	4	16
From the South Head of *Cattalina* Bay to the Northward — —	NNE.	2 ½	7
From the South Head of *Cattalina* Bay to *Cattalina* Harbour —	NNE.	1 ½	or 5
From the North Head of *Cattalina* Bay to *Flower's Point* — —	N. by E.N.erly	1 ½	or 5
The *Flower's* Rocks sunken are about a Mile and a half off from Shore	E.	½	1 ½
From *Flower's Point* to *Bird's Island* — — —	N. by W.	1 ½	4
From *Flower's Point* to Cape *Larjan* — — —	N. ½ Westerly	2	
From Cape *Larjan* to *Spillers Point* — — —	NNW.	1	
From Cape *Larjan* to Cape *Bonavista* — — —	NNW. ½ Nly	2	
From Cape *Bonavista* to *Moses Point*, entering Port *Bonavista* —	SW.	1 ⅔	or 5
From Cape *Bonavista* to *Gull Island* — — —	N. by W.	⅓	or 1
From Cape *Bonavista* to Cape *Freels* — — —	NNW.	10 or 12	
From Cape *Bonavista* to *Salvages* — — —	WNW.	9	
From Cape *Bonavista* to *Stone* Island, over the North End of *Green* Island	W.		
From Port *Bonavista* to *Keel's* Point W. 5 Leagues, *Salvages* lying to the Northward of *Keels* about 3 Leagues — — —			

Depth

(31)

Depth of Water on the Bank, and off the South Part of the Coaſt of Newfoundland, *ſounded as we ſailed in and out in his Majeſty's Ship the* S W A N : *By Captain* HENRY SOUTHWOOD.

		Fathom.
Cape *Race* Weſt, and	Cape *Race* Weſt 43 Leagues, and Cape *Spear* NW.	40 rough FiſhingGround.
Cape*Spear*NW.byW.	by W. little Weſterly, 39 Leagues you have - -	ſmallStones,Sands&Shells
*Renowes*andCape*Spear*	*Renowes* W. by N. 68 Leagues, and Cape *Spear* WNW. Northerly 65 Leagues, you have then 95 Fathom on the outer Edge of this main Bank - -	95 Fine whitiſh Sand, with ſome black Specks.

Places and Latitudes.			Bearings of the Places.	Diſtances Leagues	Depth Fathom	Latitude of the Ship.		What Manner of Grounds.
	D.	M.				D.	M.	
Renowes and	46	45	W.	44	44	46	45	Sand
Cape *Spear*	47	22	WNW.	30				
Fermowes and	46	48	W.	37	62	46	48	Fine white Sand
Cape *Spear*	47	22	WNW. N.erly	33				
Ferryland-head	46	50				46	59	
and Cape *Spear*	47	22	W. byNortherly	31	63	46	48	Fine Sand
and Bay *Bulls*	47	11		30				
Ferryland-head	46	50	W. by N.N.ly	29		46	17	
and Cape *Spear*	47	22	WNW.:N.ly	26	85	46	45	
Ferryland-head	46	50	W. by N. N.ly	28		46	30	
Cape *Broyle*	46	54				46	34	
Bay *Bulls* and	47	11	W. by N. N.ly	28	80	46	51	
Cape *Spear*	47	22				47	02	Oozy Ground
Ferryland-head	46	50	W. by N. N.ly	24	55	46	33	
and Bay *Bulls*	47	11				46	54	
Ferryland-head	46	50	W. by N.	17	52	46	40	
Cape *Broyle*	46	54	W. by N.	13		46	46	Fine Sand
Ferryland head	46	50	W. by N.	13	58	46	42	
and Bay *Bulls*	47	11				47	03	
Cape *Broyle*	46	54	W. by N. N.ly	12	80	46	45	
			WNW.	10	85	46	43	
Cape *Broyle* and	46	54	WSW. W.erly	6½	95	47	42	
Bay *Bulls*	47	11	NW. by W.	4½		47	03	[ſmall Stones
Bay *Bulls*	ditto		W. by N. ¼ N.ly	65	64	46	14	Black Sand and ſome
	ditto		W. by N. N.ly	60	57	46	27	Rough Ground
	ditto		W. by N. N.ly	50	50	46	34	Fine Sand and Stones
Whitleſs Bay and	47	08	WNW.	55	45	46	05	Fine Sand
Cape *Spear*	47	22	NW. by W.	34		46	45	
Torbay	47	33	WNW.	66	64	47	17	Rough Ground

The

(32)

Rocks called Virgins.   The *Virgins* are Rocks lying about 23 Leagues Eaſt from Cape *Race :* They lie ENE. about 4 Miles in Length, and the ſhoaleſt is about 20 Feet Water. Sometimes the Sea breaks very high upon them, which renders them very dangerous, beſides a very ſtrong current often ſets about them. Ships ſometimes anchor on them a-fiſhing, in about 12 and 14 Fathom Water.

As to the Bank of *Newfoundland,* there are Soundings from the outer Edge of the main Bank to the Height of the Ground, where generally Ships lie to catch Fiſh, and which is about 40 Leagues diſtant from the Land, and then the Soundings in along are uncertain. The Bank goes quite to the Land to the Northward of Cape *Ballard,* where the Bank falls more to the Eaſtward, and the Water is deeper, and ſo increaſes along to the Northward. To the Southward of Cape *Race,* and to the Weſtward is ſhoal Water 2 Leagues off the Shore, not above 20 or 22 Fathom Water; and to the Weſtward of Cape *Pine* it is ſtill ſhoaler, at the ſame Diſtance.

The outer or falſe Bank is about 110 or 115 Leagues from the Land, and is thought to be about 14 or 16 Leagues broad in the Middle; and from the inner Edge of it to the main Bank are near 30 Leagues, and no Soundings between them. In the Spring of the Year many Iſlands of Ice lie between theſe Banks, very dangerous, when foggy. The beſt Part for Fiſhing is from 100 to 140 Miles off the Shore, which is the ſhoaleſt Part of the Bank.

From *Miſtaken* Point to the *Powles* or entering of *Trepaſſey* is WNW. 5 Leagues: there is a deep Bay on the Back-ſide or Eaſt Side of *Powles,* and a Neck of Beach, ſo that you ſee the Ships Maſts over it, but very dangerous to be imbayed in that Place, the Sea commonly falling in there, and no Current to help you out; therefore, if you intend for *Trepaſſey,* ſtand over to Cape *Pine* till you ſee the Harbour open, and then bear into the Harbour according as you have the Wind, Cape *Pine* being ſafe and bold to ſail along that Side, &c. By Mr. *Stone*'s Deſcription of it to me, it is a very good Harbour, and large, and very fair Shoalings at the Entering of 8, 7, 6, and 5 Fathom, and turning may ſtand into 4, 3¼, or 3 Fathom, as I was informed.

DIREC-

DIRECTIONS
FOR NAVIGATING THE
BAY OF *PLACENTIA*
ON THE
South Coast of *Newfoundland*,

From *Cape Chapeau Rouge* to *Cape St. Mary's*.

Surveyed by Order of Commodore SHULDHAM, Governor of *Newfoundland, Labradore*, &c. by MICHAEL LANE.

N. B. The BEARINGS and COURSES are true Bearings and Distances, and not by Compass, the Variation of the Compass being 19° 30' W. this present Year 1774.

CAPE *St. Mary's* to the East, and *Cape Chapeau Rouge* to the West, form the Entrance of *Placentia Bay*: They lie East and West of each other in the Lat. 46, 53, N. distant from each other 16 Leagues.

Cape Chapeau Rouge is already described in Mr. *Cook's* Directions. From it Sauker Head. to *Sauker Head* (which is a high Hill, in the Shape of a Sugar Loaf,) the Course is E.N.E. distant three Miles ; between them lie the Harbours of *Great* and *Little St. Laurence*, which have also been already described in Mr. *Cook's* Directions.

From *Sauker Head* to *Small Point* (which is the lowest Land hereabouts) the Small Point. Course is N. 63° E. two Miles : And from *Small Point* to *Corbin Head* (which Corbin Head. is a very high Bluff Head) is N.E. 2 ¼ Miles : There are many high Headlands betwixt them which form several Coves, the Bottoms of which may be seen in sailing along Shore. The Coast is clear of Rocks, and thirty Fathom close to the Shore, but no Shelter for any thing. From *Corbin Head* to *Shalloway Point* the Course is N.N.E. ¼ E. 4¼ Miles. Betwixt them, and nearly on Corbin Island. the same Course, lie two very high round Islands, called *Corbin* and *Little Bu-* Little Burin *rin* ; *Corbin* Island has very much the Appearance of *Chapeau Rouge* when Island. coming in with the Land, and seen through the Fog. These Islands are high, and are little more than a Cable's Length from Shore.

From *Corbin Head* to *Cat Island*, the Course is N.E. 4 Miles nearly ; this is Cat Island. a high round Island near the South End of *Great Burin Island*.

About a Mile to the Northward of *Corbin Head*, in a Bight, lies *Corbin* Corbin Har-*Harbour*, which is very good for small Vessels. The best Anchorage is in bour.

A   the

the N. Arm, at about ¼ of a Mile within the Entrance, opposite a Cove on the Starboard Side. A Quarter of a Mile to the Eastward of this Harbour, and two Cables Length from the Shore, is a sunken Rock, on which the Sea breaks in bad Weather, and has not Depth sufficient at low Water for a Boat to go over it. Vessels bound for this Harbour must avoid a Shoal which lies ¼ of a Mile to the E. of the S. Point of the Entrance to the Harbour, on which is only 2 Fathom Water. Between the two high round Islands aforementioned and the Main, there is from 7 to 1 ; Fathom, and no Danger but what may be seen : In case Ships should fall close in with the Land in the Fogs, they may occasionally sail within them, although the Passage is little more than a Cable's Length wide.

Great Burin Island.   *Great Burin Island* lies nearly North and South, is 2½ Miles in Length, and high Land ; near the North End is another high Island, about ¼ Mile in *Pardy's Island* Length, called *Pardy's Island*. On the Main within these Islands lie the Harbours of *Great* and *Little Burin*.

Shalloway Island.   *Shalloway Island* lies N.W. ¼ W. 1 Mile from *Cat Island*, and N.E. by N.
Burin Harbours.   ¼ E. ¼ Mile from *Little Burin Island :* the Passage into *Burin Harbours* from the Southward is to the Westward of *Shalloway Island*, between that and the *Neck Point*, take Care to give *Poor Island* a Birth on your Larboard Hand ; after you are within *Shalloway Island* you may anchor in Safety between that and *Great Burin Island* from 12 to 18 Fathoms Water. The best *Ship Cove.*   Anchorage in *Great Burin Harbour* is in *Ship Cove*. The Course up to it after you are within *Neck Point* is North about 1¼ Mile, and is better than ½ Mile wide ; to sail up to it, keep the West Shore on Board, in Order to avoid a sunken Rock on the Eastern Shore at about half the Way up, and about half a Cable's Length from the Shore, directly off, is a remarkable Hole in the Rock on the same Side, and a remarkable Gully in the Land, from the Top to the Bottom, on the Western Shore. There is another Rock, on which is only 2½ Fathom Water ; it lies better than a Cable's Length to the Southward of *Harbour Point*, which is a round green Point, of a moderate Height, joined to *Great Burin Island* by a low narrow sandy Neck.

Burin Bay.   After passing *Little Burin Island* 1 Mile N. you come into *Burin Bay*, which is a clear Bay, about a Mile broad every Way, and where Ships may occasionally anchor safely, being almost land-lock'd. The Course into this Bay from *Little Burin Island* is North. All the Land about this Bay is very high. In it are 2 Islands, one a low barren Island, called *Poor Island* ; the other, which runs to the North, is high and woody, and lies before the Mouth of *Burin Inlet*, on the other Side of which Vessels may pass up the Inlet. A little within the Entrance on the E. Side, half a Cable's Length from the Shore, is a Rock covered at ¼ Flood, at 1¼ Mile from the Entrance ; near the Middle is another Rock, to the W. of which is very good Anchorage.

S.W. Entrance into Burin Harbour.   The *S.W. Entrance* into the Harbour, which is a Quarter of a Mile wide, is formed by *Shalloway Island* and the *Neck Point*, in which there is no Danger,

ger, giving a Birth to *Poor Island* on the Larboard Side. When in *Burin Bay* the Courfe through the S.W. Entrance into the Harbour is E.N.E. and when paſt the Points that form the Entrance, the Courſe is North up the Harbour, which is better than a Quarter of a Mile wide, and a Mile and a half long up to *Ships Cove*, where it is full half a Mile wide every Way. This is the beſt Anchorage.

There are only two Dangers within this Harbour that do not appear above Water; the firſt is a ſmall Shoal on the Starboard Side, about half Way up the Harbour, directly off a remarkable Hole in the Cliff on the Starboard Side, going up, called *the Oven*; and about half a Cable's Length from the Shore there is alſo on the other Side, directly oppoſite, a remarkable Gully in the Land, from the Top to the Bottom. The long Mark to keep to the Weſtward of this Rock is, not to bring *Little Burin Iſland* to the Eaſtward of *Neck Point*. The other Shoal, on which there is three Fathom, is very ſmall, and lies about a Cable's Length SSW. from Harbour Point. Burin Harbour.

The *Eaſt Paſſage* is not very ſafe to ſail in without a commanding Gale, and that between the NNE. and SE. To ſail into this Paſſage, and coming from the Weſtward, come not within two Miles of the Shore on the Eaſt Side of *Burin Iſland* (becauſe of ſeveral Cluſters of Rocks), till you bring the North Point of *Pardy's Iſland* open to the Northward of *Iron Iſland*, then ſail right in for *Iron Iſland*, leaving it on your Larboard Side going in, then ſteer for the ſaid Point of *Pardy's Iſland*, and that will avoid all Dangers. It muſt be obſerved, with the afore-mentioned Winds there is commonly a great Swell ſets to the Shore on the Starboard Side going in, therefore, in caſe of little Winds (which often happens when you are paſt *Iron Iſland*), endeavour to borrow on *Pardy's Iſland*, except the Wind be from the NE. Eaſt Entrance into Burin Harbour.

At the Bottom of *Burin Bay* there is an Inlet, which runs in Land 5 Miles; there is a ſmall *Woody Iſland* juſt before the Entrance; Ships may ſail on either Side; the Eaſt Side is the wideſt. A little within the Eaſt Head that forms the Entrance, and half a Cable's Length from that Shore, there is a ſunken Rock, which is dry at low Water, therefore, in ſailing into the Inlet, keep the Weſt Shore cloſe on board, for about a Mile up; it lies North, and is about two Cables Length wide, then NNW. for a Mile, and is there half a Mile wide, with a ſunken Rock right in the Middle; to the Weſtward of that Rock there is good Room and good Anchorage, from 7 to 12 and 15 Fathom Water in the Entrance, and, in the Middle, two Miles up, is from 15 to 23 Fathom, and from thence up to the Head is from 10 to 5 Fathom. Burin Inlet. Woody Iſland.

Iron Iſland is a ſmall high Iſland, lying NNE. half E. one League from the SE. Point of *Great Burin Iſland* and SSW. half W. one Mile from *Mortier Weſt Head*, and E. 1¼ Mile from the North Part of *Pardy's Iſland*; Veſſels bound for the Harbours of *Burin* may paſs on either Side of *Iron Iſland*, the Iron Iſland.

A 2 only

The Brandys. only Danger paſſing to the Northward is the *Brandys*, which almoſt always break; they lie near ¼ Mile to Southward of a low Rock above Water, cloſe under the Land of *Mortier Weſt Head*. If the Wind ſhould take you a-head after you are within *Iron Iſland*, take Care to keep *Mortier Weſt Head* open to the Weſtward of *Iron Iſland*, in order to avoid *Gregory's Rock*, on which is only 2 Fathom Water. The Mark to carry you on this Rock is, to bring the *Flag Staff* on *St. George's Iſland* (in the Center of the Paſſage between *Great Burin* and *Pardy's Iſlands* and *Mortier Weſt Head*) on with the Weſt Side of *Iron Iſland*; this Rock almoſt always breaks; Veſſels may paſs with Safety between this Rock and *Iron Iſland*, taking Care to give *Iron Iſland* a Birth of one Cable's Length.

Gregory's Rock.

On the Main within *Pardy's Iſland* are two remarkable white Marks in the Rocks, the Northermoſt of theſe Marks brought on with the North Part of *Pardy's Iſland* and *Iron Iſland* N. by E. half E. will carry you on the *Galloping Andrew*, a Shoal, on which is 5 Fathoms Water.

Galloping Andrew.

SW. one Mile from *Iron Iſland* lies a Shoal, on which is 8 Fathoms Water, called the *White Horſe*.

White Horſe.

Dodding Rock.
Dodding Rock lies about ¼ Mile from the Eaſtermoſt Part of *Great Burin Iſland*.

MortierBank.
Mortier Bank lies E. by S. two Leagues from *Iron Iſland*, and N. 25 E. five Leagues frome *Cape Jude*; the Shoal Part of this Bank is about one League over. On it I had not leſs than 7 Fathom Water, but, by the Fiſhermens Account, there is not more than 4 Fathoms on one Part of it: in bad Weather, the Sea breaks very high on it.

Mortier Bay and Iſland.
About three Miles to the NNE. from *Iron Iſland* is the Opening of *Mortier Bay*, at the Entrance of which is a round Iſland, called *Mortier Iſland*, lying a Third of the Diſtance from the Weſt Side. Ships may ſail in on either Side of it. It is bold too all round. Cloſe to the firſt Point beyond the Iſland, on the Larboard Side going in, is another little Iſland, ſcarcely perceptible, as it lies cloſe under the Land; and, two Cables Length from it, in a direct Line towards the outer Iſland, is a ſunken Rock, on which the Sea breaks in bad Weather: there is no other Danger in this Bay. At the Bottom of it, a Mile and a half from *Mortier Iſland*, on the Eaſt Side, there is a Cove, called *Fox Cove*, wherein is good Anchorage, and Room for one Ship to moor in 9 Fathom, good holding Ground. They will lie two Points open to the Sea, that is, from SSE. to SE. A Ground Swell tumbles into the Cove in bad Weather, but no Anchor was ever known to come home here. Fiſhing Ships ſometimes ride here the Seaſon. On the Weſt Side of the Bay is the Harbour, which is ſmall and narrow, but a very good one for ſmall Veſſels, where they lie moored to the Shore. There is 7 and 8 Fathom through the Entrance, and 2 Fathom when in the Harbour, and ſufficient

Fox Cove.

sufficient Room for fifty Shallops at the Head of it. Off the Starboard Point going in is a Rock, which at high Water is always covered.

Croney Island lieth N. by E. nearly two Miles from *Mortier East Point*. Croney Island. This is a round Island, and lies close to the Shore.

Two Miles and a half from *Croney Island* is the Entrance into *Mortier Bay*; Mortier Bay. at the Entrance on the West Side is a small Harbour, called *Boboy*; in it is 9 Boboy. Feet Water at low Water. The Course into *Mortier Bay* is North for about two Miles, and is ¼ Mile wide, in which you have from 50 to 70 Fathom Water, the Land on each Side being high; it then runs to the Westward about two Miles, and is near two Miles wide. In the SW. Corner of the Bay is a River, which runs to the SW. about seven Miles. On the East Side, at about three Miles from the Entrance, is an exceeding good Harbour, called *Spanish Room*, in which you may anchor from 4 to 6 Fathom Water, Spanish good Bottom, and lie secure from all Winds. There is not the least Danger Room. in sailing into this Harbour, giving the low Rocks above Water, at the Entrance on the Larboard Hand, a Birth of one Cable's Length.

Two Miles to the NE. of the Entrance into *Mortier Bay* lies *Rock Har-* Rock Harbour, fit only for Boats, by Reason of the infinite Number of Rocks in it, both bour. above and under Water.

From *Mortier East Point* to *John the Bay Point* the Course is N. 25 E. John the Bay Distance eight Miles. Between *John the Bay Point* and *Rock Harbour* lie Point. two sunken Rocks, ¼ Mile from the Shore.

Two Miles to the NW. of *John the Bay Point* lies *John the Bay*, in which John the Bay. is tolerable good Anchorage, in about 8 Fathoms Water, with sandy Bottom.

The *Saddle-back* is a small Island lying N. 47 E. 8 Leagues from *Corbin Head*, Saddle-back. and N. 55 E. from *Mortier West Point*, and N. 83 E. 3 Leagues from *John the Bay Point*. Between it and the Main are a great Number of Rocks and Islands, which render this Part of the Coast very dangerous. There is a Chain of Rocks lying 1¼ Mile to the NE. by N. of the *Saddle-back*.

Cape Jude is an Island about two Miles and a half in Length, and two in Cape Jude. Breadth; it lies one Mile and a half to the NNW. of the *Saddle-back*; on the South End of it is a remarkable round Hill, which is called the *Cape*. Between this Island and the Main are a Cluster of Islands and low Rocks, with a great Number of sunken Rocks about them, called the *Flat Islands*, Flat Islands. the innermost of which lies about one Mile from the Main.

Audearn Island lies half a Mile to the Northward of *Cape Jude Island*, on Audearn the West Side of which is a tolerable good Harbour. Vessels bound for this Island and Harbour may pass between *Cape Jude Island* and *Audearn Island*, and between Harbour.

Crew

Crow and Pa- *Crow* and *Patrick's Island*, which are two small Islands, lying off the SW.
trick's Island. Point of *Audearn Island*. About one Cable's Length from *Audearn Island*,
to the Southward of the Harbour, is a sunken Rock; the Mark for avoiding
it in coming from the Southward is, not to haul in for the Harbour till you
open a remarkable green Point on the South Side of the Harbour. The best
Anchorage is on the North Shore, just within a small Island. There is a Spit
of Rocks stretches just off the *Green Point* on the South Shore, which are
covered at high Water.

Ford's Island. Off the East Point of *Audearn Island* is a small Island, called *Ford's Island*,
on the West Side of which is a sunken Rock, about one Cable's Length from
the Island, and another on the East Side, which almost always break.

Broad Cove. *Broad Cove* lies on the Main, W. ¼ N. 5½ Miles from *Ford's Island*; in
this Cove is exceeding good Anchorage, in 8 or 9 Fathom Water.

Cross Island. *Cross Island* lies 3 Miles to the NW. of *Ford's Island*, is about 1½ Mile in
Length, and 1 Mile in Breadth, is high woody Land; between this Island and
Bane Har- the Main are several other Islands. *Bane Harbour* lies on the Main. Within
bour. these Islands is an exceeding good Harbour for small Vessels; the Passage
into it is very narrow, and hath in it 2 Fathom Water, but when in, there
is sufficient Room to moor in 3 Fathom, good Bottom.

Boat Harbour. *Boat Harbour* lies about one Mile to the Northward of *Cross Island*, and
runs up NNE. one League, with deep Water to about half a Mile of the
Bay de Leau. Head; close round the Eastern Point of *Boat Harbour* lies *Bay de Leau*, which
runs in NNE. ¼ E. better than a League.

Long Island. *Long Island* is about 4 Miles long, and not half a Mile broad, is high Land
making in several Peeks; the South Point of it lies N. 37 E. 2 Leagues from
the *Saddle-back*, and E. by S. 3 Miles from *Ford's Island*.

NW. two Miles from the South Point of *Long Island*, and NE. by E. one
Green Island. Mile and a half from *Ford's Island*, lies a small *Green Island*, which has a
Shoal all round near one Cable's Length.

From *Green Island* NW. two Miles and a half, and N. 19 E. three Miles
Great Gal- from *Ford's Island*, lies *Great Gallows Harbour Island*, which is a high Land.
lows Harbour Vessels may pass on either Side of this Island into *Great Gallows Harbour*,
and Island. which lies one Mile to the NE. of the Island. In this Harbour is exceeding
good Anchorage in 7 Fathom Water on the Starboard Side, just within a
low stony Point, taking Care to give the Point a small Birth, in order to
avoid a Rock, which is covered at high Water.

Little Gal- *Little Gallows Harbour* lies close round to the Eastward of *Great Gallows
lows Harbour. Harbour*, and is only fit for small Vessels, which must lie moored to the
Shore.

Shore. Above a Rock above Water, on the Larboard Hand, *Little Gallows Harbour Island* lies, before the Mouth of the Harbour.

Cape Roger Harbour lies close to the Westward of *Cape Roger*, which is a high round barren Head, lying N. 15 W. three Miles and a half from the South Point of *Long Island*. There are several low Rocks and Islands lying off the East Point of the Entrance. In the Harbour, 1¼ Mile within the Entrance, on the West Side, lies a small Island; to the Northward of it, between that and the Main, is very good Anchorage in 7 or 8 Fathom Water; or you run farther up, and anchor in 6 or 7 Fathom.

One Mile and a quarter to the Eastward of *Cape Roger Harbour* lies *Nonsuch*; there are several Islands lying in the Mouth of it, and no safe Anchorage till you get within all of them.

Petit Fort is a very good Harbour, having in it from 14 to 7 Fathom Water, good Bottom. The Entrance into it is better than a Quarter of a Mile wide, and lieth NNE. 5 Miles from the South Point of *Long Island*, and N. by W. 2 Miles and a half from the North Point of *Long Island*. There is not the least Danger in sailing into this Harbour; the best Anchorage is on the Starboard Side, the SE. Winds heaving in a great Swell on the West Shore, when they blow hard.

One Mile to the Eastward of *Petit Fort* lies the Entrance into *Paradise Sound*, which runs up NE. by E. 4 Leagues and a half, and is about one Mile broad; in it is very deep Water, and no safe Anchorage till you get near the Head of it. Just within the Entrance, on the East Side, is a Cove (in which are several Rocks above Water), is 10 Fathom Water, but not safe to anchor in, the Bottom being rocky.

From *Corbin-head* to *Marticot Island* the Course is N. 48 E. 11 Leagues and a half nearly; this Course will carry you just without the *Saddle-back*. Between *Marticot* and the Main is *Fox Island*; there is a safe Passage for Vessels between these Islands, with not less than 9 Fathom Water, but no Passage between *Fox Island* and the Main. On the Main, within *Marticot Island*, lie the Harbours of *Great* and *Little Paradise*. The Harbour of *Great Paradise* is only fit for Boats. The Harbour of *Little Paradise* lies one Mile to the Northward of the East Point of *Marticot Island*; the only safe Anchorage is in a Cove, at the Head, on the Larboard Side; here they lie moored to the Shore, and are entirely land-locked.

One Mile to the Eastward of *Little Paradise* lieth *La Perche*, in which is no safe Anchorage, the Ground being bad, and lies entirely exposed to the SE. Winds.

ENE. 2 Miles from *Marticot Island* is a Rock above Water, called the *Black Rock*; ¼ Mile within this Rock lies a sunken Rock; NNE. half E. 2 Miles

Prefque. Miles from this Rock lies *Prefque*; in it is very deep Water, but no fafe Paffage into it, by Reafon of a Number of Rocks, both above and under Water, lying before the Entrance.

Merafheen Ifland. Eaſt 4 Miles from *Prefque*, and NE. by E. 6 Leagues from the *Saddle-back*, lies the Weſt Point of *Merafheen Island*. This Ifland is high, and runs to the NE. by N. better than 6 Leagues, and is very narrow, the broadeſt Part not being more than 2 Miles. At the South Part of the Ifland, near the Weſt End, is a very good Harbour, but fmall, in which is from 6 to 10 Fathom Water. To fail into it, keep the Starboard Shore on board, in order to avoid a funken Rock, that lies one Cable's Length off a ragged rocky Point on the Larboard Hand going in.

Indian Harbour. *Indian Harbour* lies on the Eaſt Side of *Merafheen Island*, at about three Leagues from the South Point; this Harbour is formed by a fmall Ifland, on either Side of which is a fafe Paffage into it; the only Anchorage is to the Weſtward of the Ifland, between it and the Main, and here the Ground is uncertain.

Little Ifle of Valen. Great Ifle of Valen. N. 20 W. 2½ Miles from the Weſt Point of *Merafheen Island* is the *Little Isle of Valen*; this is high and round, and lies within about ¼ Mile of the Main : ¼ Mile from *Little Isle of Valen* lies the *Great Isle of Valen*, on the SE. Part of which is a fmall Harbour.

Clatife Harbour. On the Main, within the *Great Isle of Valen* lies *Clatife Harbour*; the Entrance into it is about ¼ Mile wide; in it is 40 or 50 Fathom Water. The beſt Anchorage is in the Weſt Cove, which is 1 Mile long, but not ½ Mile broad; in it is from 17 to 20 Fathom Water, good Bottom.

Grammer's Rocks. *Grammer's Rocks* are low Rocks above Water, and lie 1¼ Mile from the North End of *Great Isle of Valen*.

Little Sandy Harbour. *Little Sandy Harbour* lies on the Main, and is a tolerable good Harbour; in it you have 6 and 7 Fathom Water, good Bottom; in the Mouth of which is a low Rock above Water. Veffels bound for the Harbour muſt pafs to the Northward of this Rock. This Harbour may be known by the Bell Ifland. Ifland called *Bell Island*, which lies ESE. ½ E. 1¼ Mile from the Mouth of it, and N. by E. ½ E. 13 Miles from the Weſt Point of *Merafheen Island*; off the South Point of the Ifland is a remarkable Rock, refembling a Bell with the Bottom upwards.

Great Sandy Harbour. *Great Sandy Harbour* lies ¼ Mile to the Northward of *Little Sandy Harbour*; the Paffage into it is narrow, but in it you have 6 or 7 Fathom Water. There are two Arms in this Harbour, one running to the SW. which almoſt dries at low Water; the other runs to the NE. in which is tolerable good Anchorage. There are feveral low Rocks and Iflands lying before this Harbour.

Barren

Barren Island is about 3½ Miles long, and 1 Mile broad, is high Land, and lieth better than 1 League from the North Part of *Merafheen Island*, and about ¼ Mile from the Main. On the East Side of this Island, near the South End, is a Cove, in which is tolerable good Anchorage from 10 to 16 Fathom Water. Along the West Side of this Island, between it and the Main, is very good Anchorage.

On the Main, opposite the North End of *Barren Island*, lies *La Plant*, a Harbour only fit for Boats.

From *Barren Island* are a String of Islands quite to *Piper's Hole*, which lies 3 Leagues from the North Part of *Barren Island*. These Islands are about ¼ Mile from the Main, having from 17 to 7 Fathoms Water, good Anchorage all the Way to *Piper's Hole*.

Cape St. Mary's is the East Point of the Entrance into *Placentia Bay*, and lies in the Latitude of 46° 52' N. is a pretty high bluff Point, and looketh much like *Cape St. Vincent* on the Coast of *Portugal*; a little to the Northward of the Cape is a small Cove, where fishing Shallops shelter from the Easterly and Southerly Winds. The Land from *Cape St. Mary's* to *Placentia* is pretty high and even. S. by W. 7½ Miles from the Cape lie *St. Mary's Keys*, which are two Rocks just above Water, and on which the Sea almost always breaks.

From the *Virgin Rocks* to *Cape St. Mary's* the Course is South, Distance eight Leagues and a half; between *Green Point* and *Cape St. Mary's* there is no Shelter for Ships or Vessels. The Land from *Placentia Road* to *Cape St. Mary's* is of a moderate, and appears nearly of equal Height all the Way; but over *Placentia*, and to the Northward of it, the Land is very high and uneven, with many peaked Hills.

Bull and Cow Rocks are a Cluster of Rocks above Water, lying SE. by E. 2 Leagues from *Cape St. Mary's*, about one Mile from the Main, and SW. by W. from *Point Lance*, which is a low ragged Point, and is the West Point of the Entrance into *St. Mary's Bay*; at about ½ of the Distance from the Main to the *Bull and Cow Rocks* is a sunken Rock, which shews above Water at half Ebb.

From *Cape St. Mary's* to *Point Breme* the Course is N. by W ½ W. 8 Miles.

From *Point Breme* to the *Virgin Rocks* the Course is NNE. Distance 10 Miles; these Rocks shew above Water, and lie about one Mile from the Main.

Three Leagues S. from *Green Point*, and a League from the Shore, lie the *Virgin Rocks*, which are a Cluster of Rocks above Water. A little to
B the

(10)

the Southward of thefe Rocks there are fome whitifh Cliffs in the Land, by which that Part of the Coaft may be known, on coming in with it in thick Weather.

Point Verd. From *Virgin Rocks* to *Point Verd* the Courfe is N. 38 E. Diftance 5½ Miles. This is a low green Point, and is the South Point of the Entrance into the Road of *Placentia*.

Placentia Road and Harbour. Placentia Road and Harbour is fituated on the Eaft Side of the Great Bay of that Name, at eleven Leagues Diftance from *Cape St. Mary's*. To fail into the Road, and coming from the Southward, you muft keep a League *Gibraltar Rock.* from the Shore, to avoid the *Gibraltar Rock*, which lies WSW. from *Point Verd*, till you bring the *Caftle-hill* open to the Northward of *Green Point*. The *Caftle-hill* is on the North Side of the Road on which ftands the Caftle, *Green Point.* and is diftinguifhable far out at Sea. *Green Point* is a low level Point, which forms the South Side of the Road. The *Gibraltar Rock* has fixteen Feet Water upon it, and lies W. ½ S. Diftant 2½ Miles from *Green Point*, and 2 Miles from Shore. The Mark afore mentioned will carry you ¼ of a Mile without it, and when you have the faid Mark open, you may fteer in for the *Caftle*, keeping your Lead going; there is regular Sound on both Sides. Along the South Side is a Flat, to which you may borrow into four Fathom. The beft Anchorage is in fix or feven Fathom Water, under the *Caftle-hill* at ¼ of the Diftance over from that Side, where you lie in good ground, and open about four Points to the Sea. At the Bottom of the Road is a long Beach, which terminates to the North in a Point, on which ftand the Inhabitants Houfes and a Fort. Between this Point and *Caftle-hill* is the Entrance into *Placentia Harbour*, which is very narrow, in which is 3¼ Fathom Water, but within the Narrows it widens to one third of a Mile broad, and runs up NNE. above a Mile and a half, where Ships may lie in perfect Security, in fix or feven Pathom. To fail in you muft keep neareft to the Starboard Side.

Near the Bottom of *Placentia Road*, on the North Shore, at the Top of a Hill, ftands a Caftle; when you have this Caftle open to the Northward of *Point Verd*, you may haul in for the Road in Safety, taking Care to give *Point Verd* a Birth of near two Cables Length. The beft Anchorage in the Road is under the *Caftle-hill*, in about 6 Fathom Water. The Entrance into the Harbour is very narrow, in it you have 3¼ Fathom Water; after you are within the narrows it is about ¼ Mile broad, and about 1½ Mile long; here you may anchor in perfect Safety in 6 or 7 Fathoms Water.

Remarks for knowing the Land on the Weft Side of Placentia Bay. This coaft is eafily known, in clear Weather, by the *Chapeau Rouge*, and other remarkable Head-Lands. The beft Directions that can be given on coming in with it in thick Weather, are, to obferve, that, between *Burin* and *Loun*, there are no Iflands except *Ferryland Head*, which is very near the Main, fo as not to be diftinguifhed as an Ifland till very clofe to the Shore; alfo alſo that the Iſlands about *Burin* are large and full as high as the main Land; thoſe about *Laun* are ſmall, and ſcarce half the Height of the Main Land, and the *Lamilines* are two low flat Iſlands. There are ſeveral ſmall Rocks juſt above Water between *Laun* and *Lameline*, and there are none ſuch any where elſe along the Coaſt.—The Land from *Mortier Head* up the Bay is high, rocky, and uneven; with ſeveral Iſlands near the Coaſt, which forms many Capes and ragged Points.

From *Mortier Head* to *Red Iſland* the Courſe is N.E. by E. Diſtance 16 Leagues. This Iſland is high, and may be ſeen in clear Weather 12 Leagues from the Decks. The South End of it bears from *Placentia Road*, N. W. diſtance 4 Leagues and ¼. Red Iſland.

Red Iſland is high barren Land, about 5 Miles long and 3 Miles broad. The South Point lies N.W. 11 Miles from *Placentia Road*. On the Eaſt Side near the North End is a ſmall Harbour, which is only fit for Shallops.

Point Latina lies about 5 Miles to the Northward of *Placentia Road*; between theſe Places the Land is low and even near the Sea, but juſt within it high and ragged; there are ſeveral ſunken Rocks lying along the Shore about ¼ a Mile off. Point Latina.

Point Roche lies better than one Mile to the Eaſtward of *Point Latina*; there is a Shoal ſtretches off *Point Roche* better than ¼ Mile. Point Roche.

S.E. by S ¼ E. 1 ¼ Mile from *Point Roche* is the Entrance into the Harbour of *Little Placentia*, which runs up S. W. by W. ½ W. about 1½ Mile, and is near ½ Mile broad; there is exceeding good Anchorage in this Harbour in a Cove on the North Shore; this Cove may be known by the Weſt Point being woody, the Land to the Eaſtward being barren; off the Eaſt Point of the Cove lies a Shoal for near ⅓ of the Diſtance over to the South Side of the Harbour, in this Cove is 7 and 8 Fathom Water. LittlePlacentia Harbour.

From *Point Latina* to *Ship Harbour*, the Courſe is E N.E. Diſtance 5½ Miles; this Harbour runs up North 2¼ Miles, and is about ¼ Mile broad; the beſt Anchorage is in a Cove on the Weſt Side in about 10 Fathom Water, at about one Mile from the Entrance. Ship Harbour.

Fox Island is a ſmall round Iſland lying N. by E. ¼ E. 3 Miles from *Point Latina*, and W. by N. one League from *Ship Harbour* Point, which is a low ſtony Point, lying about 1¼ Mile to the Weſtward of *Ship Harbour*; between *Fox Iſland* and this Point are a Range of Rocks, which in bad Weather break almoſt quite acroſs. Fox Iſland.

N.W. 1¼ Mile from *Fox Iſland* is a ſteep Rock above Water, called *Fiſhing Rock*; North 1¼ Mile from *Fiſhing Rock* lies a ſunken Rock, which almoſt always breaks. Fiſhing Rock.

(12)

Ram Iflands. The *Ram Islands* are a Clufter of high Iflands, lying about 3 Miles to the N. N. E. ¼ E. of *Fox Island*. E. N. E. 3 Miles from the South Point of *Ram Islands* is the Entrance into *Long Harbour*; there is not the leaft Danger in failing into it; the beft Anchorage is on the North Side to the Eaftward of *Harbour Island* between it and the Main; here you will lie fecure from all Winds in 7 or 8 Fathom Water.

Little Harbour. From *Ram Islands* to *Little Harbour* is North about 5 Leagues; there are feveral low Iflands and Rocks along fhore; between thefe Places, which I had not an Opportunity of examining, but was well informed there is not the leaft Shelter for Veffels, nor fcarcely for Boats along that Coaft. *Little Harbour* is fmall, with 7 Fathoms Water; the Ground is bad, and lies entirely expofed to the S.W. Winds, which heave in a very great Sea.

Long Ifland. From *Point Latina* to the South Point of *Long Ifland* the Courfe is N. by W. ¼ W. 4½ Leagues; this Ifland is near 3 Leagues long, in high Land, the South Point being remarkable high fteep Rocks. On the Eaft Side of the Ifland, about one League from the South Point, lies *Harbour Buffet*; a tolerable good Harbour; the Entrance into it is narrow, but hath 13 Fathom Water in it. There are two Arms in this Harbour, one running to the Weftward, the other to the Northward; the beft Anchorage is in the North Arm, in about 15 Fathom Water. This Harbour may be known by the Iflands that lie in the Mouth and to the Southward of it, and by *Harbour Buffet* Ifland, that lies E. N. E. ¼ E. 1 Mile from the Entrance. To fail into it, you muft pafs to the Northward of the Iflands in the Mouth.

Harbour Buffet.

Mufcle Harbour. About 4 Miles from the South Point of *Long Island*, on the Weft Side, lieth *Mufcle Harbour*; Veffels bound for this Harbour may pafs between *Long Island* and *Barren Island*, which is a high barren Ifland about one Mile long, and about ¼ of a Mile from *Long Island*. The Entrance into the Harbour lies oppofite the North End of *Barren Island*, and is between a low green Point on your Starboard Hand, and a fmall Ifland on your Larboard Hand; this Harbour is near two Miles long, and one broad; in it is from 10 to 22 Fathoms Water, rocky Bottom.

Little South Harbour. *Little South Harbour* lies one Mile to the Weftward of *Little Harbour*; before the Mouth of it are feveral rocky Iflands: in failing into the Harbour you muft leave all the Iflands on your Starboard Hand except one, on either Side of which is a fafe Paffage of 15 Fathoms Water. On the Eaft Shore within the Iflands is a funken Rock about one Cable's Length from the Shore, which generally breaks: nearly oppofite on the Weft fhore are fome Rocks about half a Cable's Length from the Shore, that fhew at ¼ Ebb. This Harbour is about 1½ Mile long, near ½ Mile wide, with 7 Fathom Water, good Bottom.

Great

Great South Harbour lies about one Mile to the Northward of *Little South* Great South Harbour; there is no Danger in failing into it; near the Head is very good Harbour. Anchorage in 6 or 7 Fathoms Water.

One Mile to the Westward of *Great South Harbour* is *Isle au Bourdeaux*, Ile au Bor- a high round Island near the Main. deaux.

The Entrance into *Come by Chance* lies North 4 Miles from *Isle au Bour-* Come by *deaux*, and runs up N. E. by N. 3 Miles: in it is from 20 to 3 Fathom Wa- Chance. ter, sandy Bottom, is intirely expofed to the S.W. Winds, which heave in a very great Swell.

North Harbour is N.W. 2½ Miles from *Come by Chance*, and S.E. by E. North Har- 2¼ Miles from *Piper's Hole*; about 2 Miles from the Entrance is good An- bour. chorage in 7 Fathoms Water, and no Danger failing into it.

For Navigating Part of the

COAST of NEWFOUNDLAND,

FROM

APE St. MARY TO CAPE SPEAR,

INCLUDING

St. Mary's and Trepassy Bays.

Surveyed by Order of Commodore SHULDHAM, Governor of Newfoundland, Labradore, &c. by MICHAEL LANE, in 1773.

N. B. All BEARINGS and COURSES hereafter mentioned are the true Bearings and Courses, and not by Compass.

THE Entrance of *St. Mary's Bay* is formed by *Cape Lance* on the West, and *Cape Pine* on the East Side. The Land from *Point Lance* lies E. by N. ¼ N. 3 Leagues to a high *bluff Cape*, from which the Land along the West Side of the Bay lies N.E. by N. and S.W. by S. 10 Leagues up to the Head of the Bay.— From the aforementioned *bluff Cape*, to *Cape English*, on the East Shore, the Course is S.E. ½ E. Distance 5 Leagues.

Cape St. Mary's. *Cape St. Mary's* is a pretty high bluff Point, makes in all Directions much like *Cape St. Vincent* on the Coast of *Portugal*; and the Land along Shore from it, for a considerable Distance, appears even, and nearly of equal Height with the Cape itself, which lies due W. Distance between 17 or 18 Leagues from *Cape Chapeau Rouge*, and is in the Lat. 46. 52. N. A little to the Northward of this Cape is a small Cove, where Fishing Shallops shelter with Southerly and Easterly Winds.

Bull and Cow. From *Cape St. Mary's* S.E. by E. Distance 5 Miles and a half, lie the *Bull and Cow Rocks*, which are two flat Rocks, and very near together, with several smaller Rocks about them, all above Water; they may be seen 4 Leagues from the Deck when open from the Land, but when shut on with the Land, they are not distinguishable so far. They bear W. Dist. 3 Miles from *Point Lance*, which is a low ragged Point which forms the Entrance on the West Side of *St. Mary's Bay*. The *Bull and Cow* lie one Mile from the nearest Part of the main Land; at two thirds of the Distance from them to the Main, is a

small

(15)

small Rock that appears above Water at Half Tide; there is 10 Fathom between this Rock and the Main, and 15 Fathom between it and the *Bull and Cow*. Ships may safely pass within the *Bull and Cow* occasionally.

St. Mary's Rocks lie S. by W. Distance 7½ Miles from *Cape St. Mary's*, and S. W. by W. from *Point Lance*, and S. W. ¼ W. from the *Bull and Cow*. These are two Rocks that appear just above Water, upon which the Sea almost always breaks very high. They lie S. E. and N. W. from each other, Distance about 3 Cables Length; in the Middle between them is a Channel of a Cable's Length broad, in which is 15 Fathoms Water; there is also 15 Fathoms at a Cable's Length all round them, except to the S. E. at 2 Cables Length; Distance is 6 Fathoms. Between these Rocks, and *Cape St. Mary's* is 25 and 30 Fathoms Water, and all about *Cape St Mary's* at 2 and 3 Leagues Distance, is the same Depth of Water. <small>St. Mary's Rocks.</small>

Point Lance is a low Point near the Sea, but the Land within it is high, and is the West Point of the Entrance into the Bay of *St. Mary's*. It lies in the Latitude of 46° 50′ N. <small>Point Lance.</small>

From *Point Lance* to the Eastern Head of *St. Shot's*, (the East Point of the Entrance into *St. Mary's Bay*) the Course is S. E. by E. ¼ E. distant 22 Miles. This Bay runneth 9¼ Leagues to the N. E. with several very good Harbours in it, the Land on each Side being moderately high, and mostly barren. <small>Eastern Head of St. Shot's. St. Mary's Bay.</small>

From the Eastern Head of *St. Shot's* to the Western Head the Course is N. 41 W. Distance 2 Miles; this Bay is entirely open to the Sea, and about one Mile deep.

From the Western Head of *St. Shot's* to *Gull Island* the Course is N. 20 W. distant 4 Miles. This Island is small, of the same Height with the main Land, and so near it, that it cannot be distinguished, unless you are close in Shore. <small>Gull Island.</small>

From *Gull Island* to *Cape English* the Course is N. 7 W. distance 2 Leagues; this Cape is high Table Land, terminating in a low rocky Point, forming a Bay about a Mile deep to the Southward of it; at the Bottom of this Bay is a low stony Beach, within which is a Pond, called *Holy Rood Pond*, running to the N.E. for about 7 Leagues, and is from ¼ Mile to 2 or 3 broad; this Pond makes *Cape English* appear from the Southward like an Island. <small>Cape English.</small>

From *Cape English* to *False Cape* the Course is N. 20 E. one Mile. <small>False Cape.</small>

From *Cape English* to *Point le Haye*, the Course is N E 3 Leagues. This is a low Point, off from which there runs a Ridge of Rocks ¼ of a Mile to the Sea, and above a Mile along Shore, on which the Sea breaks in bad Weather. This is the only Danger in all *St. Mary's Bay*, that will take a Ship up. <small>Point le Haye and Rocks.</small>

From

Double Road Point.	From *Point le Have* to the South Point of the Entrance into *St. Mary's Harbour* (called *Double Road Point*), the Courfe is NE. Diftance 1¼ Mile; the Land between thefe Points is low and barren.
St. Mary's Harbour.	From *Point le Have* to the low Point on the Starboard Side going into *St. Mary's Harbour*, called *Ellis's Point*, the Courfe is NE by E. 2 Miles, and from *Point Lance* to *St. Mary's Harbour* is E. ¼ N. Diftance 9 Leagues. The Entrance to this Harbour is above a Mile wide. Within the Points that form the Entrance, it divides into two Branches, one to the ESE. the other to the NE. When you are paft *Ellis's Point*, haul in to the Southward, and anchor abreaft of the Fifhing Stages and Houfes, upon a Flat, in 4 or 5 Fathoms. Here you will be land-locked. This Flat runs off about ¼ a Mile from the Shore; without it is from 15 to 40 Fathoms Water over to the other Side; but the beft Anchorage in this Harbour is about 2 Miles above the Town, where it is above ¼ a Mile wide, oppofite *Brown's Pond*, which is on the Starboard Side, and may be feen over the low Beach; here you will lie land-locked in 12 Fathoms, and excellent Ground all the Way up to the Head of the Harbour. One Mile above the faid Pond, on the oppofite Shore, is a Beach Point, clofe to which is 4 Fathoms, where Ships may heave down; and here is Plenty of Wood and Water. The NE. *Arm* of *St. Mary's Harbour* runs up 2 Miles from the Entrance; about half Way up, it is a Mile broad, and above that it is half a Mile broad, where Ships may anchor, but being open to the Sea, this Place is not reforted to by Ships.

Two Leagues above *St. Mary's Harbour*, lie two Iflands, the largeft of which is about two Leagues long. There is a good Paffage for Ships between thofe Iflands, alfo between them and each Shore. The Paffage on the Weft Side is 2½ Leagues wide. Above thofe Iflands, are many good Anchoring-places on each Shore, and at the Head of the Bay is a frefh Water River, which is navigable 2 or 3 Leagues up.

Mall Bay.	*Mall Bay* lies to the Weftward of *North Eaft Point*, and is about one mile broad, and better than 2 miles deep. There is no good Anchorage in this Bay, being open to the Sea, and generally a heavy fwell fetting into it: Veffels may occafionally anchor near the head in 5 or 6 Fathom Water, good Ground.
Great Colinet Ifland.	From *Cape Englifh* to the South part of *Great Colinet Ifland* the Courfe is N. 10 W. Diftance 3 leagues. This Ifland is of a moderate Height, about one league long, and one mile broad. On either fide of this Ifland is a fafe paffage up the Bay, taking care to give *Shoal Bay Point* a birth of ½ of a mile, there being feveral funken Rocks lying off this Point.
Shoal Bay Point.	*Shoal Bay Point* lieth one mile diftant off the Eaft fide of *Great Colinet Ifland*. On the North fide of *Great Colinet Ifland* is a ftony Beach, from off which lieth a Bank for about ¾ of a mile, on which is from 7 to 17 fathom Water, rocky bottom.

Little

(17)

Little Colinet Island lieth 1 ¼ Mile from *Great Colinet Island*; is above one Mile long, and ½ a Mile broad. *Little Colinet Island.*

The Entrance into *Great Salmon River* lieth N. 50 E. Distance 2 Leagues from the North Part of *Little Colinet Island*, is about ¼ of a Mile broad, and runs to the N. E. 7 or 8 Miles; in it is very good Anchorage; the best is about 3 miles from the Entrance on the North Side, in a sandy Cove, in 5 or 6 Fathom Water. *Great Salmon River.*

North Harbour lieth N. by W. ¼ of a Mile from the North Part of *Little Colinet Island*, is about a Mile broad at the Entrance, and runs to the Northward about 3 Miles: in it is very good Anchorage, in about 6 or 7 Fathom Water, at about 2 miles from the Entrance, where it is not above ½ a Mile wide; or you may run up the Narrows, which are formed by two low sandy Points, about ½ a Cable's Length asunder, taking care to keep the Starboard Point close on board, and anchor close within the Point on the Starboard Shore. *North Harbour.*

Colinet Bay lies N. N. E. ¼ E. 5 Miles and ½ from the North Part of *Little Colinet Island*: in it is very good Anchorage from 5 to 12 Fathom Water. *Colinet Bay.*

From the Eastern Head of *St. Shot's* the Land to the Eastward tends a-way E. by S. ¼ S. for about one Mile, then E. ¼ S. one Mile to *Cape Freels*. *Cape Freels.*

From *Cape Freels* to *Cape Pine* the Course is E. N. E. one Mile and ½. The Land about *Cape Pine*, to the Eastward and Westward, is moderately high and barren. *Cape Pine.*

From *Cape Pine* to *Mistaken Point* the Course is E. ¼ N. distant 4 ½ Leagues. Between these Points lies *Trepassey Bay*, in which is *Trepasse Harbour*. *Mistaken Point.*

The Entrance of this Harbour lies 2 Miles to the N. E. of *Cape Pine*, is about ¾ Mile wide, and runneth nearly the same Breadth for about 2 ½ Miles, and is here little more than ¼ of a Mile wide, but afterwards increases to ¼ of a Mile wide; here Vessels generally ride. The Dangers in sailing into this Harbour are a small Rock that lieth on the East Shore, about a Mile within the Entrance, and is about ¼ Cable's Length from the Shore; and on the West Shore, within the Harbour, off a stony Beach, lieth a Shoal, and runs along Shore, up the Harbour, to a low green Point. *Baker's Point*, on with a low rocky Point in the Entrance of the Harbour, will carry you clear off this Shoal. When you are nearly up with the low green Point, you may borrow more to the Westward, and anchor either in the N. W. or N. E. Arm, there you will be very handy for Wooding and Watering. *Trepassey Harbour.*

From the *Powles* (the East Point of the Entrance into *Trepassey Harbour*) to Cape *Mutton* the Course is E. ¼ N. Distance one Mile. Between these *Mutton Bay.*

C Points

Points lieth *Mutton Bay*, and is about 2 Miles deep; in it is from 12 to 3 Fathom Water, rocky Bottom. The North-weſt part of the Head of this Bay is ſeparated from the Harbour of *Trepaſſey* by a low narrow ſtony Beach, over which may be ſeen the Veſſels in the Harbour.

Biſcay Bay.   *Biſcay Bay* lieth about 1½ Mile to the Eaſtward of *Mutton Bay*, the Entrance of which is about one Mile wide, and about two Miles deep; in it is from nine to three Fathom Water, ſandy Bottom, but is quite open to the Sea.

French Miſ-
taken Point.   From *Miſtaken Point* to *French Miſtaken Point* the Courſe is N. 80 W. Diſtance 2 Miles.

Powles.   From *French Miſtaken Point* to the *Powles* the Courſe W.N.W. Diſtance 8 Miles.

Cape Race.   The Land from *Miſtaken Point* to the Eaſtward tends away E.N.E one League, then N. E. by E. 1½ Mile to Cape *Race*, which is Table Land, of a moderate Height, having a high black Rock lying cloſe off the Cape, with ſeveral ſmall low Rocks to the Northward of it. This Cape lieth in the Latitude of 46° 42′ N.

Cape Ballard.   From *Cape Race* to *Cape Ballard* the Courſe is N.E. by N. Diſtance three Leagues : nearly one Mile to the Southward of *Cape Ballard*, lieth a high black Head, called *Chain Cove Head*. Between theſe Points is a Cove, and to the Weſtward of *Chain Cove Head* lieth *Chain Cove*, before which lieth a black Rock above Water.

New Bank.   Due Eaſt from *Cape Race*, and S. by E. ¼ E. from *Cape Ballard*, lieth a Fiſhing-Bank, called *New Bank*, about 5 Miles long, and nearly 2 Miles broad ; on it is from 9 to 25 Fathom Water.

Renowe's
Rocks.   From *Cape Ballard* to *Renowe's Rocks* the Courſe is N. 20 E. Diſtance 2 Leagues. Theſe Rocks are ſmall, of a moderate Height, and lie one Mile from the Main-Land, and are bold too.

Renowe's
Harbour.   From *Renowe's Rocks* to the *Harbour of Renowe* the Courſe is N. by W. ½ W. Diſtance 2¼ Miles. This is but a ſmall Harbour, and hath not above 15 or 16 Feet at Low Water; it is but an indifferent Harbour, having ſeveral Rocks in the Entrance, and the South-Eaſt Winds heave in a very great Sea. To ſail into it, you muſt keep the North Shore on board.

Fermouſe
Harbour.   *Fermouſe Harbour* lieth about 3½ Miles from *Renowe's*; between theſe Harbours lieth *Bear's Cove*, off of which lieth a ſunken Rock, about a Cable's Length from Shore. *Fermouſe Harbour* is an exceeding good Harbour, there being no Danger in ſailing into it. The Entrance is not more than a Cable's

Length

(19)

Length wide; juſt within the Entrance, on the North Shore, is a ſmall Cove, in which a Fiſhery is carried on, but no ſafe Place for anchoring. About ¼ of a Mile farther in, on the ſame Side, lieth another Cove, called *Admiral's Cove*. In this Cove the Merchants Ships generally ride, in 7 or 8 Fathom Water, land-locked. About one Mile farther up the Harbour is a Cove, called *Vice-Admiral's Cove*. On the South Side is the beſt Anchorage for large Ships, in 12 or 15 Fathom Water, muddy Ground; here you will be handy for wooding and watering. Farther up, on the ſame Side, lieth a Cove, called *Sheep's-Head Cove*. Directly off this Cove, near the Middle of the Paſſage up the Harbour, lieth a Shoal, on which is only 9 Feet Water. This is the only Danger in this Harbour.

Bald Head lieth N. 30 E. one Mile nearly from *Fermouſe Harbour*.   Bald Head.

From *Bald Head* to *Black Head* the Courſe is N. by W. one Mile.   Black Head.

From *Black Head* to the Entrance into the Harbour of *Aqua Fort*, the Courſe is NW. by N. one Mile nearly; in the Entrance is a high Rock above Water. The Paſſage into the Harbour is to the Northward of this Rock, in which you have 15 Fathom Water. This Harbour lieth in Weſt about 3 Miles: at about 2¼ Miles from the Entrance it is very narrow, where you have 4 Fathom Water; but juſt within the Narrows, on the North Shore, is a ſmall Cove, in which you will have 7 Fathom Water; this is a good Place for Veſſels to heave down, the Shore being ſteep. To ſail up through the Narrows, take Care to give the ſtony Beach, on the North Shore, without the Narrows, a Birth, it being a Shoal along that Beach, except at the Point of the Narrows, which is bold too.   Aqua Fort Harbour.

Ferryland Head lieth ENE. ¼ E. diſtant 2 Miles from *Aqua Fort*, and N. 30 E. diſtant 3¾ Miles from *Fermouſe*. *Ferryland Head* is moderately high, having two high Rocks above Water lying cloſe off the Head, called the *Hare's Ears*. This Head is not eaſily diſtinguiſhed, by Reaſon of the Main-Land within it being much higher. The Entrance into *Ferryland Harbour* lieth to the Northward of *Ferryland Head*, between it and *Iſle Bois*, and is little more than ¼ a Cable's Length wide; but, after you are within *Iſle Bois*, it is better than ¼ Mile wide, and tolerable good Anchorage, in 8 or 10 Fathom Water; but the North-Eaſt Winds heave in a very great Sea over the low Rocks that run from *Iſle Bois* to the Main.   Ferryland Head. Ferryland Harbour.

From *Iſle Bois* to *Gooſe Iſland* the Courſe is N. ¾ E. diſtant half a Mile; and from *Gooſe Iſland* to *Stone Iſland* the Courſe is N. 5 W. diſtant half a Mile.   Gooſe Iſland. Stone Iſland.

Caplin Bay runneth in NW. by W. diſtant 2¼ Miles from *Gooſe Iſland*, is a tolerable good Bay, with a ſafe Paſſage into it on either Side of *Gooſe Iſland*.   Caplin Bay.

C 2   To

To the Northward of *Goose Island*, between it and *Stone Islands*, there is not the least Danger, the Island being bold too. If you pass to the Southward of *Goose Island*, between it and *Isle Bois*, be sure to keep the Point of *Ferryland Head* open to the Eastward of *Isle Bois*, in Order to avoid a sunken Rock, on which is only 2 Fathom Water, and lieth nearly Midway between *Goose Island* and *Cold East Point*; after you are within this Rock, there is not the least Danger in sailing up the Bay. The best Anchorage is abreast of a Cove on the Larboard Hand, about ½ a Mile within *Scogin's Head*, in 16 or 17 Fathom Water.

Cape Broyle. From the *Hare's Ears*, off *Ferryland Head*, to *Cape Broyle*, the Course is N. ¼ W. distant 2½ Miles. This Cape is high Table Land, and maketh in a Saddle, either coming from the Northward or Southward. From the
Old Harry. North Part of the Cape, ESE. ¼ of a Mile, lies a small Rock, called *Old Harry*, on which is only 3 Fathom Water; but between it and the Main is upwards of 20 Fathom Water. About ¼ of a Mile to the NE. of the North
Horse Rocks. Part of *Cape Broyle* lieth a Ledge of Rocks, called *Horse Rocks*, on which you have from 7 to 14 Fathom Water. In bad Weather the Sea breaks very high on these Rocks. The Mark for these Rocks is a white House on *Ferryland Downs*, open with *Stone Islands*, and the Head of *Cape Broyle Harbour* open will carry you on them.

Brigus Head. From the North Part of *Cape Broyle* to the South Part of *Brigus Head*, the Course is NW. by N. Distance 1½ Mile. These Points form the En-
Cape Broyle trance into *Cape Broyle Harbour*, which runs 3½ Miles up. About 1¼ Mile
Harbour. within the Entrance on the North Shore, is a Cove, called *Admiral's Cove*, in which you may anchor in about 12 Fathom Water, good Ground; but here you will lie open to the South-East. The best Anchorage is above the Narrows, in about 7 Fathom Water. The only Danger in sailing up the Harbour is a Ledge, called *Saturday's Ledge*, and lieth about a Cable and a ½ Length without the Narrows, on the North Shore; if you are coming in from the Northward, keep the Saddle on *Brigus Head* open with the Point of *Admiral's Cove*, it will carry you clear off this Ledge. After you are above the Narrows, you may anchor in about 7 Fathom Water, good Ground. Here you will be very handy for wooding and watering.

Brigus by *Brigus by South* is a small Harbour, only fit for Boats, and lieth close to
South. the Northward of *Brigus Head*.

Cape Ned- *Cape Neddick* lieth N. 5 Miles from *Cape Broyle*, and N. 2 W. Distance
dick. 7½ Miles from the *Hare's Ears* off *Ferryland*. This Cape is Table Land, of a moderate Height, and steep towards the Sea.

From

(21)

From *Cape Neddick* to *Baline Head* the Courſe is N. 15 E. Diſtance 1¼ Baline Head.
Mile. *Baline Cove* is about ¼ Mile to the Northward of *Baline Head*. This
is but a ſmall Cove, fit only for Boats.

From *Cape Neddick* to the outer Point of *Great Iſland* the Courſe is N. 40 Great Iſland.
E. Diſtance 2¼ Miles. This Iſland is about ½ a Mile in Length, and of a
moderate Height.

From *Baline Head* to *Iſle Spear* the Courſe is N. ½ E. Diſtance one Mile. Iſle Spear.
Nearly within this Iſland a Fiſhery is carried on, but no ſafe Anchorage, the
Bottom being rocky.

Toad's Cove is a ſmall Cove, about 1 Mile to the Northward of *Iſle Spear*, Toad's Cove.
and is only fit for Boats.

About 1¼ Mile from *Iſle Spear* lieth the South Point of *Momable's Bay*; Momable's
from this Point to the North Point of the ſaid Bay, being the South Point Bay.
of *Witleſs Bay*, the Courſe is NE. by E. Diſtance 1¼ Mile. *Momable's Bay*
is an open Bay, about 1 Mile deep.

Green Iſland is a ſmall round Iſland, about ¾ of a Mile from the South Green Iſland.
Point of *Witleſs Bay*. From this Point lieth a Ledge of Rocks, about ¼ of
the Diſtance over to *Green Iſland*.

The South Point of *Gull Iſland* lieth about ¼ Mile to the Northward of Gull Iſland.
Green Iſland, and is about 1 Mile long, and ¼ of a Mile broad, and is pretty
high Land.

Witleſs Bay runneth in about 2 Miles from *Gull Iſland*. In it is a mode- Witleſs Bay.
rate Depth of Water, good Ground, but open to the Sea. About half Way
up, on the North Shore, lieth a Ledge of Rocks; Part of theſe Rocks ſhew
above Water at about half Tide.

One Mile and ¼ to the Northward of *Gull Iſland* lieth the South Point of Bay of Bulls.
the Entrance into the *Bay of Bulls*; from this Point to the North Point of
ſaid Bay, called *Bull Head*, the Courſe is NE. ¼ E. Diſtance 1 Mile. The
beſt Anchorage in this Bay for large Veſſels is about ¼ a Mile from the Head,
in about 14 Fathom Water; but ſmall Veſſels may anchor higher up, and
moor to the North Shore, and will then lie land-locked. The only Dangers
in this Harbour are, a ſmall Rock off *Bread and Cheeſe Point*, but is not
above 20 Yards off, and a Rock on which is 9 Feet Water, lying off
Magotty Cove, about half a Cable's Length off Shore.

From

(22)

From *Bull's Head* to the South Point of *Petty Harbour* the Courſe is NNE. Diſtance 8¼ Miles. From this Point runs a Ledge of Rocks for about ¼ of a Mile.

Petty Harbour.
From the South Point of *Petty Harbour* to the North Point, the Courſe is N. by E. ¼ E. Diſtance 2¼ Miles. Between thoſe Points lieth *Petty Harbour Bay*, which runneth in about 2 Miles. At the Bottom is a ſmall Cove, where a Fiſhery is carried on.

Cape Spear.
From the North Point of *Petty Harbour* to *Cape Spear* the Courſe is NNE. ¼ E. Diſtance 2 Miles. This Point is rather low and ragged, and may be known by the Land to the Northward tending away to the WNW.

F I N I S.

SAILING DIRECTIONS

FOR THE

GULF of St. LAWRENCE.

FROM *Cape North*, in the Island of *Cape Breton*, to *Cape Ray*, in *Newfoundland*, the Courſe is ENE. 19 or 20 Leagues.
From *Cape North* to the Middle of the Iſland of *St. Paul*, the Courſe is ENE. ¼ North, Diſtance 4 Leagues.
From *St. Paul's Iſland* to *Cape Ray* the Courſe is ENE. ¼ E. 16 Leagues.
All theſe Bearings are by Compaſs, and the Variation 16 or 17° Weſt; and the Diſtances are found by trigonometrical Calculation by ſeveral Bearings taken, &c.
From *Cape North* to the *Bird Iſlands* the Courſe is North 9° Weſt, 17 or 18 Leagues.
From *St. Paul's Iſland* to the *Bird Iſlands* the Courſe is North 24° Weſt, Diſtance 15¼ Leagues.
From *Cape Ray* to the *Bird Iſlands* the Courſe is Weſt 26° North, Diſtance 22 Leagues.
From the *Bird Iſlands* to the North Part of Iſle *Brion* is Weſt ¼ South, 5 or 6 Leagues.—All the above Courſes are by Compaſs.

REMARKS.

The *Bird Iſlands* are but ſmall, and not far aſunder; the Paſſage between is a rocky Ledge. They are of a moderate Height, and white at Top, the Northernmoſt being the largeſt, from the Eaſt End of which runs a ſmall Ledge of Rocks.
The Paſſage between *Little Bird Iſland* and the Iſle of *Brion*, is about 5 Leagues.

SOUNDINGS.

Body of the Iſland *Brion* S. and S. ¼ W. 4 Leagues, 35 Fathom, brown Sand.
N. End of Ditto SW. by S. 36 Fathom, ſame Ground.
NW. End of Ditto S. 40 Fathom, rocky with ſmall Shells.
Body of Ditto S. by E. 7 or 8 Leagues, 45 Fathom, Sand and Stones.
From *Iſland Brion* to *Cape Roſiere* the Courſe is NW. by W. 39 Leagues. Here the Variation is 17 Degrees.
From *Cape Roſiere* to the NW. End of *Anticoſti* the Courſe is NNW. 20 Leagues. Here the Variation is 17° 30′.

REMARKS.

The Channel between *Anticoſti* and the Main-Land of *Nova Scotia*, is about 14 or 15 Leagues, and in the Middle is very deep Water, ſometimes no Ground with 180 to 200 Fathom Line. To the Weſtward of *Anticoſti* is a Bank, the Extent of which is not known.

B   LATI-

(2)

LATITUDES.

	North	
	°	′
Cape North	47	6
St. Paul's Island	47	14
Cape Ray	47	40
Bird Island	47	52
North Part of Brion Island	47	50
Cape Gaspee	48	44
N. W. End of Anticosti	49	46

The Islands of Mingan are 10 Leagues N. E. from the Island of *Anticosti*, in Latitude 50° 15′ North.

REMARKS.

The Harbour of *Mingan* is very secure for Ships in all Weathers: there is good Anchorage all within the *Parokett* and other Islands, and great Plenty of Cod-fish. It appears to be very convenient for the Cod, Seal, and Salmon Fishery, and has the additional Advantages of a level, good Soil, and profitable *Indian* trade. It flows here Full and Change, at 3 o'Clock rises about 10 or 12 Feet; but much of the Tides depends on the Weather.

The Bay of *Seven Islands* is on the North Side of the River *St. Lawrence*, being a very secure Harbour for a Number of Ships in any Wind. It lies in Latitude 50° 20′ N. and lies N. from *Mount Lewis*, and WNW. 25 Leagues from the NW. End of *Anticosti*, by the Compass.

N. B. It flows SSW. rises 18 or 19 Feet Spring, and 10 at Neap Tides.

⁂ The Settlement here was one of the *French* King's Posts for trading with the *Indians*.

Directions for sailing up the RIVER St. LAWRENCE.

FROM the NW. End of *Anticosti* to Cape *Chat* the Course is WSW. 36 or 38 Leagues.

REMARKS.

From Cape *Chat* it is best never to stand so far Northward as *Mid-Channel*, particularly when a-breast of *Manicouagan* Shoal, where are some very strong and irregular Eddies that will set you on that Shoal. Several Sail of Men of War have been catched in them in a fresh Breeze of Wind, when not a single Ship could answer its Helm; some of them drove on board each other, and it was not without much Difficulty that very great Mischief was prevented by their running foul of each other, and the Danger of driving on the Shoals of *Manicouagan*.

From Cape *Chat* to the Island of *St. Barnaby* the Course is WSW. ¼ W. Distance 28 Leagues.

SOUNDINGS

SOUNDINGS.

N. W. End of *Anticosti* E. ¼ S. 6 Leagues, and the *Lady's Mountains* S. W. by W. ¼ W. in 58 Fathom.
N. W. End of *Anticosti* E. by S. 7 or 8 Leagues, 44 Fathom.
Mount *Camille* ——— ——— S. W. by W.
Uppermost of the *Lady's Mountains* ——— S. E. ¼ E.
Two little Paps near the Shore ——— ——— S. W. ¼ W.
About 2 Leagues from the South Shore, 98 Fathom, soft Mud.
Mount *Camille* ——— ——— S. W. ¼ S.
Westermost *Lady's Mountain* ——— ——— S. 50° E.
170 Fathom, soft Mud.

REMARKS.

This being nearest to the North Shore, the Current was so strong, that it was with Difficulty the Ships were kept from driving on board one another.

About 2 Leagues off the South Shore, 80 Fathom, soft Mud.
Mount *Camille* ——— ——— S. 50° W.
Westermost *Lady's Mountain* ——— ——— S. 59° E.
Two little Paps on the South Shore ——— S. 20? E.
Nearest the North Shore, 160 or 170 Fathoms, soft black Mud.
Mount *Camille* ——— ——— S. 28° W.
River *Manicouagan* ——— ——— N. by W. ¼ W.
West Point of Ditto *Low Land* — —— N. 65? W.

REMARKS.

A strong Current here which sets towards the North Shore, and is a Demonstration that the South Shore is properest to keep on, as it is a clear Coast, and no visible Current there.

About a League from South Shore, 17 Fathoms, muddy Bottom.
Mount *Camille* ——— ——— S E. ¼ E.
East Part of the Isle of *St. Barnaby* ——— S W. by S.
Father Point — ——— ——— S.
38 Fathom, muddy Ground.

ANCHORAGE.

In 17 Fathom, muddy Bottom, 4 or 5 Miles from Shore, the Bank shoals gradually to 10 Fathom within 2 ¼ Miles of the Shore.
Father Point ——— ——— S S E.
East Point of the Isle *St. Barnaby* ——— S W. ¼ S.
Isle Bic ——— ——— W. by S.

The higheſt of *Bic* Hills, in a Line with the outer Part of *St. Barnaby's* Iſland, bearing W. ¼ S. 7 ¼ Fathoms.

Ditto Mountain on the Middle of the Iſland, about Half a Mile from Shore, 6 Fathoms.

The outer Part of *Bic High Land*, juſt without the Iſland, 5 Fathom, all ſoft Mud.

From *St. Barnaby* to the Iſle of *Bic* the Courſe by Compaſs is W. ¼ S. Diſtance 3 Leagues, in moſt Places 16 Fathom Water.

ANCHORAGE
At *Bic* in 12 Fathom Water.

South End of *Bic* Iſland	——	W. by S.
North Part of Ditto	——	W. by N.
St. Barnaby's Iſle	——	E. ¼ N.
Mount Camille	——	E. ¼ S.
Eaſt Part of *Bic Hills*	——	S.
At the upper End of *Bic Iſlands*, about 2 Miles from the Iſland, in 9 Fathom Water.		
Bicquet Iſland	——	N. ¾ E.
Weſtermoſt Rock of *Bicquet* in Sight	—	N. by W.
Rocks off the Eaſt End of *Bic*	—	NE. ¾ E.
Weſt Part of *Bic* Iſland	—	N. by E. ¼ E.

REMARKS.

Bic is a low woody Iſland, about 4 Miles from the South Main Land, and is 3 Leagues W. ¼ S. from the Iſle *St. Barnaby*; all the Way is good Anchorage in 14 and 16 Fathom Water. Between *Bic* and the Main Land is 10 and 12 Fathoms. Off the SE. End of *Bic* is a Ledge of Rocks which appear above Water, and are very ſteep too.

To the North Weſtward of *Bic* lies a ſmall Iſland called *Bicquet*, from the Weſt End of which lies a Ledge of Rocks that may be ſeen at leaſt 2 Miles, and perhaps they run further under Water. Off the Eaſt End of this Iſland are likewiſe Rocks, as there are to the Weſtward of *Bic*; ſo that there can be no Paſſage between theſe Iſlands, except for Boats or very ſmall Craft.

From the Iſland of *Bic* to *Baſque* the Courſe is WSW. 7 Leagues. Between theſe Iſlands are two very ſmall Iſlands near the South Shore, called the *Razade Iſlands*; they are about 5 Leagues from *Bic*, and 2 Leagues from *Baſque*.

Paſſing Southward of *Bic* ſteer W. by S. in 9, 10, to 16 Fathom, when almoſt a-breaſt of the *Razade Iſlands* ſteer W. S. W. and you will have from 20 to 22, 24, and 26 Fathoms at High Water, 'till a-breaſt of the Iſle of *Baſque*, Diſtance 4 Miles, all ſandy Bottom.

REMARKS.

Although the Courſe from *Bic* to *Baſque* is W. S. W. yet if you come to the Southward of *Bic* (eſpecially in little Wind) you will run on the Main Land by ſteering that

Courſe,

Courfe, therefore you fhould at firft fteer W. by S. until you deepen to 18 and 20 Fathom, and then W. S. W. if you are not as high as the *Razade Iflands*, for if you are, you will then be too near the Shore.

ANCHORAGE.

About 4 Miles off *Bafque Ifland* in 26 Fathom (at High Water), a fandy Bottom.

Red *Ifland*	—— ——	W. ¾ S.
Eaft Point of *Green Ifland*	—— ——	S. W. ¼ W.
North Point of *Green Ifland*	— —	S. W. by W.
Middle of *Apple Ifland*	—— ——	S. S. W. ¾ W.
Entrance of *Saguenay River*	——	W. by N. ¼ N.
Wefternmoft Rocks between *Bafque* and *Apple Iflands*		S. by E.
Weft End of *Bafque Ifland*	—— ——	S. S. E. ¼ E.
Eaft End of *Bafque Ifland*	—— ——	S. E. ¼ E.
Weftern *Razade Ifland*	—— ——	E. ¼ S.
High Land of *Bic*	—— ——	E. N. E. ¼ N.

N. B. Bafque Ifiand, Apple Ifland, the Rocks between them, Middle of *Green Ifland*, and the outermoft Land in Sight (when on *Apple Ifland*), are in a Line W. S. W. and E. N. E. by Compafs.

REMARKS.

The Ebb Tide runs here 4¼ Knots, and much ftronger near the Ifland, as in 17 Fathom Water, at the fame Time it runs 6 Knots an Hour.

Although the Ebb Tide is fo ftrong here, and the Tide rifes much by the Shore, yet the Flood is fcarce perceivable.

Within a Cable's Length of *Bafque Ifland* is 10 Fathom, and very near the Rocks that lie between *Bafque* and *Apple Iflands* is 6 Fathom. Thefe Rocks are always above Water.

Green Ifland is about 3 Leagues W. S. W. from the Ifle of *Bafque*, the Ebb Tides of *Green Ifland* are exceeding ftrong, fo that it requires a frefh Gale of Wind to ftem it with all Sails. The Tide of Ebb fets directly toward the Ifland, as do the Floods (which are but little here) towards the *White Ifiand* Ledge; therefore great Care fhould be taken to anchor here in Time, in cafe it fhould fall calm, and you be near the Ifland, for there is 25 Fathom almoft clofe to the Rocks, and foul Ground.

REMARKS.

Off the NE. End of *Green Ifland* is a Ledge of Rocks about a Mile and an Half in Length, which partly fhew themfelves; there is likewife a Ledge of Rocks off the Weft End of the Ifland, which lie right out from it.

From a little below *Green Ifland*, till you are near the Length of *Hare Ifland*, there is a conftant and very ftrong Ebb, occafioned by the great Difcharge of the Waters from *Saguenay River*; and even at the Eaft End of *Hare Ifland*, the Flood is not of more than four Hours Continuance, and runs fo weak, that, if it blows but a moderate Gale

Wefterly,

Westerly, the Ship will not *tend* to it: In failing up, it is necessary to keep well to the Southward of *Red Island*, and to the Westward of it, before you cross over for the East End of *Hare Island*, to avoid getting into the Stream of *Red Island*; for should it fall little Wind, the Ebb Tide would set you on the Shoals of that Island, and there is no safe Anchoring to prevent driving upon them.

Red Island is a low flat Island, and is about 2¼ Leagues NW. by N. with the Middle of *Green Island*. There are great Shoals off *Red Island*, as yet not quite discovered. Being a-breast of *Green Island* you will see the East End of *Hare Island*, and the *Brandy-Pot Islands* (which are two little Islands a small Distance from it) bearing about W. by S. or WSW. from you, Distance about four Leagues from the West End of *Green Island* to the *Brandy-Pots*.

When past *Green Island* you should steer for the *Brandy-Pot Islands*. There is likewise another small Island off the NE. End of *Hare Island*, called *White Island*. Between these Islands is a Ledge of Rocks that extends at least 2¼ Leagues from the East End of *Hare Island*; this Ledge is dry at Low Water. Coming away from the upper End of *Green Island*, and steering W. by S. you have 18 Fathom a little Distance from *Green Island*, and afterwards 16 and 14 Fathom: In passing *White Island*, going towards *Brandy-Pot Islands*, you may go to 10 or 12 Fathom, far enough from all Danger, and anchor, being all good holding Ground, clayey Bottom.

Anchorage in 11 Fathom clayey Ground.

White Island ———	———	NNW. ¼ W.
Brandy-Pot Islands	———	WSW. ¼ S.
East End of *White Island* Ledge in Sight	—	N. by E. ¼ E.
Green Island ———	———	ENE. ¼ N.
East Point of *Hare Island* ———	———	NW. by W.
S. W. Point of *Hare Island*	———	WSW. ½ S.
N. Easternmost *Pilgrim Island*	———	SSW. ¾ W.
Westernmost *Pilgrim Island*	———	SW. ¼ S.

The *Pilgrims* are high rocky Islands, a-breast the upper End of *Hare Island*, and are near the South main Land. Between *Hare Island* and the South Shore is a long Bank near the Middle of the Channel, which is now called the *Middle Bank*, and it lies in the following Direction. Plate X. Fig. 1. is the Appearance of the Land, a Mountain on the Main Land at the Letter *a*, (it is the first Hill remarkable from the Eastward for a good Way); when this Mountain is brought almost on the East Hummock of the North-East *Pilgrim* at the Letter *b*, or to rest on it in the same Manner it does in the above Representation over the West Hummock of the said Island, at the Letter *c*, you will then be on the Middle of the Bank, and by sailing along with the said Mountain and Hummock in one, you will keep on it.

REMARKS.

The true Extent of this Bank is not yet known; there is in some Places more Water than in others; in one Place, at the East End of it, there is no more than Ten Feet at Low Water.

There

(7)

There is likewife a Bank or Shoal off the S. W. End of *Hare Ifland*, which extends almoft to the Middle Bank, and makes the Paffage very narrow, in which there is Depth enough at Low Water for a Ship of great Draught.

Paffing by *Brandy-Pot Iflands*, which have 10 Fathom very near them, and keeping along by *Hare Ifland*, at about $1\frac{1}{4}$ Mile Diftance from it, is all along regular Sounding 14 and 16 Fathom, till you come to $\frac{1}{4}$ of the Length of *Hare Ifland*, and then coming over for the *Pilgrims* you have Shoal Water all at once from 7 Fathom to 6, $5\frac{1}{2}$, 5, and $4\frac{1}{4}$ (at $\frac{1}{4}$ Flood) you muft heave the lead as faft as poffible; *White Ifland* will be almoft in a Line with the Eaft End of *Hare Ifland* (between it and *Brandy-Pot Ifland*) and a White Houfe on the South Shore near the River Side, almoft fhut in with the Rocks off the Eaft End of the N. E. *Pilgrim*.

Though the ftrong Flood Tide here will fet you very faft towards the Shoal off the S. W. End of *Hare Ifland*, yet be very cautious how you fteer your Ship to the Weftward, becaufe the Water fhoals very much, but haul up to the Southward, and you will directly get into 5 or 6 Fathom Water. The aforementioned White Houfe being juft in a Line with the Rocks of the Eaft End of the N. E. *Pilgrim*, and *White Ifland* juft open of the Eaft End of *Hare Ifland*; it is fhoal near the N. E. *Pilgrim*, therefore it is not proper to come too near it. Being above the N. E. *Pilgrim*, you may approach the others pretty near, and fteer away directly for the great Ifland of *Kamourafca*, which you will fee about S. W. from you, and all along in this Direction are regular Soundings from 10 or 12 to 14 or 16 Fathoms, till near the greateft and N. Eafternmoft *Kamourafca*; when a-breaft of it, (and very near) you will have very deep Water; but at fome Diftance is a very good Bank to anchor on, in any Depth, from 9 to 14 or 16 Fathom, and good holding Ground.

To efcape the Danger of the *Middle Bank*.

Coming away from *Brandy Pot Ifland* (which you may pafs very near to), fteer along by *Hare Ifland* in fuch a Manner that you may fee *White Ifland* open within *Brandy-Pot Iflands*, between them and *Hare Ifland*. Keep along in this Pofition until you have a Mountain at the Letter *a* (in *Plate* X. *Fig.* 1.) brought in a Line with the fecond *Pilgrim* at the Letter *d*, and then fteer directly for them. They will bear about S. by W. $\frac{3}{4}$ W. and with this Direction you may crofs the Bank with Safety; then fteer away for the *Kamourafca Iflands* as before.

N. B. It is not fafe to crofs this Bank with a large Ship till it is half Flood.

Anchorage in 22 Fathom High Water.

The *Lower Pilgrim Ifland*	E. N. E. $\frac{1}{4}$ N.
The *Lower Kamourafca Ifland*	E. by N. $\frac{1}{4}$ N.
Goofe Cape	W. by S. $\frac{1}{2}$ S.
Middle of *Coudre Ifland*, about fix Leagues	W. by S. $\frac{3}{4}$ S.
Cape Torment	W. S. W. $\frac{1}{4}$ S.

Anchorage in 14 Fathom, Sand and Clay Bottom.

Pilgrim Iflands	N. E. by E.
Goofe Cape	W. $\frac{3}{4}$ S.

Lower

Lower Kamouraſca	E. N. E. ¼ N.
Hare Iſland	N. E. ¼ N.
Cape Torment	W. S. W. ¼ S.
Mal Bay River	N. N. W. ¼ W.
Middle of *Coudre Iſland*	W. by S. ½ S.
Upper Kamouraſca Iſland	E. by N.

Anchorage in 24 Fathom.

Gooſe Cape	W. N. W.
N. E. End of *Coudre Iſland*	W. by S.
S. W. End of Ditto	W. S. W.
Mal Bay River	N. ¼ W.
Hare Iſland	N. E. ¼ E.

Soundings in 39 Fathom Water.

When *Cape Gooſe* bore	W. S. W. ½ S.
Cape Torment	S. W. by W.
Hare Iſland	E. N. E. ½ N.

When the Land to the Weſtward of *Cape Gooſe* is juſt open of it, and a little Mountain on the South Shore near the Eaſt Point of the Weſternmoſt *Kamouraſca Iſlands*, you have 25 Fathom.

When the Land to the Weſtward of *Cape Gooſe* is open about a Sail's Breadth of *Cape Gooſe*, *Cape Salmon* juſt open of *Cape Eagle*, and the Hill and Iſland as before, you have 25 Fathom.

When the South Mountain is quite open to the Weſtward of the Weſternmoſt *Kamouraſca Iſland*, and the Land to the North-Eaſtward juſt open of *Cape Salmon*, you have 19 Fathom, ſoft Ground.

When the Weſt Point of *Mal Bay River* is juſt opening of *Gooſe Cape*, and the South Part of the Iſle of *Coudre* bears S. W. by W. you will have 41 Fathom.

When the North Part of the Iſle of *Coudre* bears W. by S. ½ S. about 2 Miles off the Iſland, you will have 35 Fathom.

When the South Part of the Iſland of *Coudre* bears W. by S. and *Cape Gooſe* N. W. by W. you will have 14 Fathom.

When *Gooſe Cape* is N. W. by W. 4 or 5 Miles, and *Mal Bay River* N. by E. ½ E. you will have 10 Fathom.

When the South Part of *Coudre* is W. by S. ¾ S. and *Gooſe Cape* W. N. W. 2 or 3 Miles, you will have 15 Fathom, the Water deepening to the Northward.

When the South Part of *Coudre* is S. W. and the North Part of ditto W. ¾ S. about 2 or 3 Miles from the Eaſt Part of the Iſland, the great Rock bearing N. N. E. ¼ E. 17 Fathoms.

Anchorage in 25 Fathom, rocky Ground.

Cape Torment	S. W. by W.
South Part of *Coudre*	W. S. W. ½ S.
North Part of *Coudre*	W. by S.
Cape Gooſe	N. ½ E.

Bearings

(9)

Bearings by Compafs.

Goofe Cape and *Cape Salmon* ——— N. E. ¼ N. and S. W. ¼ S.
South Part of *Coudre* and *Cape Torment* N. E. ¼ E. and S. W. ¼ W.

You may moor at *Coudre* in 17 Fathom coarfe Sand. *Cape Goofe*, juft open of the Land to the Weftward of it, bearing E. by N. ¼ N. a confiderable *Fall of Water* on the North Shore N. by W. ¼ W. and the Eaft End of *Coudre* E. ¼ S. In this Place the Tide runs very ftrong, which caufes the Ship always to fwing round with the Sun.

You may alfo moor at *Coudre* in 17 Fathom at Low Water, Sand and Mud.

Cape Goofe ——————— ——————— E. by N. ¼ N.
Cape Torment ——————— ——————— S. W. ¼ W.
Eaft Point of *St. Paul's Bay* ——————— W. by N. ¼ N.
Water-Stream on the N. Shore ——————— N.

Five Fathom Water, Half a Mile from *Coudre*, till almoft clofe to the Shore, and then 3 ¼ Fathom at Low-Water Mark, all clear Ground.

The Tides at *Coudre*, both Ebb and Flood, are very ftrong, yet at the Meadows is good Anchorage, but not near the North Shore. It is High Water at *Coudre* by the Shore at ¼ paft 4, at the Full and Change of the Moon, and it runs off in the Road an Hour longer. There is a very long Reef of Rocks runs off the N. W. of the Ifland, which are all covered at High Water.

Bearings from the End of the Ledge that is dry at Low Water.

St. Paul's Church (juft open) ——————— N. 41° W.
E. Bluff Point of *St. Paul's Bay* (called *Cape Diable*) N. 27 W.
The *Water-Fall* on the North Shore ——————— N. 27 E.
N. W. Bluff Point of the Ifland ——————— S. 22 W.
The N. E. Bluff of Ditto, off which is a Reef of Rocks E. 9 N.

N. B. The Part of this Reef which is dry at Low Water lies to the Weftward about S. W. and N. E. and to the Eaftward about Eaft and Weft. Near the Length of a Cable farther out is 5 Fathom at Low Water.

The Tides, both Ebb and Flood, fet into *St. Paul's Bay*, which is fhoal and rocky fome Diftance off (from whence the *French* have given it the Name of the Whirlpool), fo that, paffing either up or down the River, it is proper to go as nigh the Reef as you can, to keep out of the contrary Current; and, for the greater Safety, it is proper to buoy the End of the Ledge in about 5 Fathom at Low Water, and it fhoals out afterwards pretty gradually. If you pafs it in about 8 Fathom (which is far enough off, with a Breeze of Wind to command the Ship), you will be much nearer the Ifland than the Main Land, and being paffed the End of the Ledge you will have 16 and 18 Fathom at a convenient Diftance from the Ifland.

There is a Shoal or Ledge of Rocks off the North Shore all the Way from the W. Point of *Paul's Bay*, or *Cape Raven*, to *Cape Hog*, which is about a League above *Cape Maillerd*. This Shoal lies not a great Way off, but farther in fome Places than others. In coming away from *Coudre* and failing up the River it is proper to keep three Capes,

C   which

(10)

which you will fee to the Weftward, open one of another all the Way from *Coudre*, till you come paft the little River Settlement, or to bring the Church of it to bear about N. W. by N. is a very rocky Bottom, and then begins good Ground.

Anchorage in 16 Fathom, Sand and Mud.

Cape Maillard, Diftance about 1¼ Mile	——	N. W. by N.
South Part of *Coudre*	——	N. E. ¼ E.
Pillar Ifland	——	S. E. ¼ E.

Anchorage about 1 Mile from the North Shore, in 9 Fathom at Low Water, Sand and Mud.

Pillar Ifland, in one with a * rocky Ifland	——	E. ¼ N.
Goofe Cape, almoft one with the S. E. Part of *Coudre*	——	N. 48 E,
Cape Torment, a little open with *Burnt Cape*	——	S. 72 W.
The South Part of *Orleans Ifland*	——	S. 63 W.
Cape Raven, juft open of *Cape Maillard*	——	N. 30 E.
North Part of *Coudre*	——	N. 36 E.

Obferved the Latitude here to be 47. 04.

* Bearings taken from the faid rocky Ifland.

Goofe Cape, a Sail's Breadth open of the S. E. Part of *Coudre*		N. 50 E.
North Part of *Coudre*	——	N. 40 E.
Cape Corbeau, or *Cape Raven*	——	N. 35 E.
Cape Maillard	——	N. 22 E.
Cape Torment —	——	S. 65 W.
South Part of *Orleans* in Sight —	——	S. 55 W.

In one with the Eaft End of the rocky Ledge,

Pillar Ifland —	—	E. 1 N.

This rocky Ifland is about Half a Cable's Length dry at Low Water, and very craggy; it is never covered, although the Sea may break all over it in bad Weather.

Soundings having the Rock and *Pillar Ifland* in one, from the North Shore to the rocky Ifland, according to the following Marks, by *Coudre* are, (See *Plate* II. *Fig.* 1.)

Ifland of *Orleans* juft fhut in with *Burnt Cape* and very near the Shore		10 Fathom.
a—the N. W. End of *Coudre* in one with *d*	——	9
a—on with the Valley at *x*	——	10
c—on with the Mountain at *c*	——	9
a—on with the Valley at *n*	——	5¼
a—on with the Mountain at *b*	——	3¼

And very fhoaly quite to the rocky Ifland, and when on it *(a)* was on with *f*.

On the Eaft Part of *Rocky Ledge*, at Low Water, *(a)* will be on with *b*. And a Bluff to the Weftward a good deal open of *Cape Torment*.—*Pillar Ifland* E. ¼ N.

Coming

(11)

Coming away from the laſt-mentioned Anchorage for the Traverſe, keep the Letter *(a)* chiefly on with *x* in 9 Fathom Water, and ſometimes leſs.

Being a-breaſt of *Burnt Cape*, and very near the Shore in 11 Fathom, *(a)* will be on with *(a)*. The high Part of *Orleans* (or a-ſlope on it) is juſt open with *Cape Torment*.

A White Houſe on the South Shore open of the Eaſt End of the Iſle of *Madame* (and when it is quite ſhut in) being very near the North Shore, you will have 11 Fathom.

A little Mountain open of the Weſt End of *Rot Iſland*, being near the North Shore, you will have 9 and 8 Fathoms.

The ſame Mountain on the Eaſt End of the Iſle of *Madame*, about $\frac{1}{4}$ of a Mile from the Shore, you will have 10 Fathom. Then haul over for the *Traverſe*.

Directions for paſſing the TRAVERSE.

BEING paſt *Burnt Cape*, or when it bears N. N. E. from you, haul over for the Traverſe, which ought to be paſſed in a very clear Day. If the Points of the Shoals are not buoyed, which for greater Safety ſhould be done, becauſe in hazey Weather the Land-Marks cannot be ſeen, which are three Mountains very far in Land ; and a little round Hill to the Weſtward may likewiſe be made uſe of ; which, after you are paſt *Burnt Cape*, and croſſing in the Traverſe, muſt always be kept to the Weſtward of the Eaſt End of *Madame*, or otherwiſe you will certainly be on a Sand Shoal, which extends itſelf from *Burnt Cape Ledge*. This Mountain, in clear Weather, may always be ſeen, and keeping it a Ship's Length to the Weſtward of the Eaſt End of *Madame* is the beſt Mark for the Traverſe ; and this Courſe ſhould be continued until two Points on the South Side of *Orleans* are opened a good Ship's Length off each other, that is, *St. John's Point*, with the Point of *Dauphine River*, and then you may bear up and ſteer up along with the Point *St. John*, ſtill a little leſs open, as you go farther up towards the Iſland of *Orleans*, to avoid a little Shoal that is off the Eaſt End of *Orleans*, on which is not quite three Fathom at Low Water, of which there is no Danger for any Ship, except it ſhould be dead Low Water ; yet *St. John's Point* ſhould not be ſhut in with *Dauphine Point* (or elſe you may be on the Shoal that reaches from the Eaſt End of *Orleans*) till you are almoſt a-breaſt *Cape Torment*, or until it bears North. There is another Mark to know when you are far enough over from *Burnt Cape*, and that you may bear up, obſerve on the South Shore a little round Mountain (there being no other near) when you have brought this little Mountain open to the Weſtward of the *Two-Head Iſland*, you may bear up for *Orleans*, &c. (As the *Two-Head Iſland* cannot be well diſtinguiſhed by a Stranger from the other Iſlands, ſo may it be ſuppoſed a Stranger will not attempt paſſing the Traverſe without firſt acquainting himſelf with it.) This little Mountain, when open of the *Two-Head Iſland*, will bear S° 69′ E, there is no Danger in ſtanding farther to the Southward as the Channel is pretty wide ; but, as there is a Shoal between you and *Rot Iſland*, on which is but 9 Feet at Low Water, and uneven Rocks, to avoid this Shoal you ſhould obſerve the Point of *Orleans* for Marks as aforeſaid.

(12)

There is a Mark to know when you are coming on the Edge of this Shoal, which is: Observe to the Eastward, on the South Main Land, a Mountain which appears to have three Points of an equal Distance, when this Mountain is brought on the East Point of *Cance Island* you are coming on the Edge of this Shoal; there is likewise a little rocky Island off *Burnt Cape*, which, when you are on the Edge of this Shoal, will be about 2 Ships Length open of *Goose Cape*. When you are on the Shoal the Island will be nearly in a Line with *Goose Cape*, and the *Three-pointed Mountain* with *Cance Island*.

To make use of the 3 Mountains aforesaid.

In coming up past *Burnt Cape*, when you have brought the West End of the Westernmost Mountain on with the East End of *Rot Island*, you may steer over with them in one Line until you open *St. John's Point* as aforesaid. Nor is there any Danger in bringing the East End of the Westernmost Mountain on with the East End of *Rot Island*, but it should not be brought to the Westward of it until you have opened *St. John's Point*. You might by this last Mark go over near *Rot Island*, and go up to the Southward of the Middle Shoal, with *St. John's Church* just open of the Point; in this Channel is deep Water, but it is narrow; it is called the *Old Traverse*, and the other is called the *New Traverse*. It is not proper for the Old Traverse to be made use of, as the Passage between the Middle Shoal and the Sand off *Burnt Cape Ledge* is narrow, and you will be so much the longer going a-cross the Tide, which may carry you out of the Way if you are not very attentive to the Marks. The Middle Shoal reaches up the River until you have got *Belickase Church* a good deal open of the West End of *Rot Island*, but as a Mark of this Kind is very deceiving, it reaches until you have brought the East End of the Middle Mountain on the West End of *Rot Island*, and then you will be past it, and have the Channel open from near the Island of *Orleans*, to very near the West End of *Rot Island*, and may anchor between *Orleans* and *Madame Islands*, or proceed up the River at Pleasure. If it should be thick Weather and you would pass the Traverse and the Mountains cannot be seen, nor the Ends of the Shoals buoyed, it might be done by keeping one or two Houses open of the East End of *Rot Island*, or the third House may be brought in a Line with it, but should not be opened; and these Marks may be observed until you have opened *St. John's Point* as aforesaid.

But as these Houses may be mistaken for others, even by a Person who is acquainted with the Traverse, it is not safe to use them. It is certain, the greatest Difficulty of the Traverse is in coming over from *Burnt Cape* to open *St. John's Point*, as the Channel is but narrow, and you are so long going a-cross the Tide; and at *Burnt Cape* the Channel is not above ¾ of a Mile wide between the Cape and the Point of the Ledge. You should likewise observe here, to keep clear of the Ledge, to keep a Part of the *Butt* (which is a high Spot of Land in the Middle of *St. Joachim's Meadows*, and appears like a Platform or Island) always shut in behind *Cape Torment*, that is, you must not open it all of the Cape until *Burnt Cape* bears North of you, or you will certainly be on the Ledge. The Soundings at the Edge of this Ledge are very uncertain, for at one Cast you will have 6 Fathom, and at the very next Cast (heaving the Lead fast) you may be on Shore; it may be observed, that just as you have *St. John's Point* opening, there is not any more Water any where in the Channel, between *Orleans'* Shoal and the Shoal off *Burnt Cape*, than 5 Fathom at Low Water; but after you have bore up for *Orleans* is 6 and 7 Fathom at Low Water, within a Ship's Length of the Sands that dry.

Soundings

(13)
Soundings in the *Traverfe*.

A breaft of *Burnt Cape*, a little round Mountain to the Weftward, on with the Eaft End of *Madame*, 5 Fathom.
The fame Mountain between *Rot-Lland* and *Madame* 4 and 4 ½ Fathom.
The E. End of the firft W. Mountain on the W. End of *Groffe Island*, and the little one to the Weftward, a little to the Weftward of the E. End of *Madame* 5 ¼ Fathom.
The W. End of the fecond Mountain on the W. End of *Groffe Island*, and Little Mountain on the E. End of *Madame*, 2 ¼ Fathom.
Little Mountain on the E. End of *Madame*, and the E. End of the fecond Mountain on the W. End of *Groffe Island*, 2 ¼ Fathom.
The Little Mountain a little to the Weftward of the E. End of *Madame*, and the W. End of *Groffe Island* in the Middle, between the fecond and Eaftermoft Mountain, 6 Fathom.
A White Houfe juft open of *Madame*, and the Hill a little to the Weftward of the E. End of *Madame*, and the E. End of the 3d, and Eaftermoft Mountain on with the W. End of *Groffe Island*, 6 Fathom.
The W. End of the firft Mountain on the E. End of *Rot Island*, *St. John's Point* well open 5 ½ Fathom. (Steer by it.)
The Middle of the firft Mountain on the E. End of *Rot Island*, the Little Mountain juft to the Weftward of the E. End of *Madame*, *St. John's Point* well open 4 ¼ Fathom.
N. B. Keep the Little Mountain always to Weftward of the E. End of *Madame*.
The E. End of the firft Mountain on the E. End of *Rot Island*, 2 White Houfes open of *Madame*, the Little Mountain juft opening to the E. End of *Madame*, 4 ¾ Fathom (never open the Little Mountain). The W. End of the firft Mountain on the *Vifta* in *Rot Ifland*, *St. John's Point* well open 5 Fathoms.
The E End of the firft Mountain on the *Vifta*, *St. John's Point* well open 5 Fathom.
The fecond Mountain on the *Vifta*, and another little Hill near the other on the W. End of *Madame*, *St. John's Point* well open 6 ¼ Fathom.
Marks on the little Shoal near the E. End of *Orleans*.
The W. End of the fecond Mountain on the W. End of *Rot Ifland Shoal*, and the W. Trees of *Rot Ifland*, about the Middle of the fame Mountain; the W. Part of the *Three-Pointed Mountain* on the E. Part of *Canoe Ifland*; *St. John's Point* a good deal open of *Dauphine*.
The E. Point of *Orleans* on the *Little Valley* at the W. End of the *Saddle Mountain*.

Bearings on the Eaft End of *Orleans Ledge*, in 4 Fathom at Low Water.

The *Little Rocky Ifland*	N. 68 E.
Cape Torment	N. 2 E.
W. End of *Rot Ifland*	S. 30 W.
E. End of *Rot Ifland* and E. End of the *Second Mountain*	S. 13 ¼ E.
W. End of *Groffe Ifland*	S. 28 E.
W. End of the *Two-Head Ifland* and the *Little Mountain* juft to the Weftward of it	S. 69 E.
W. Part of the *Three-Pointed Mountain* on the W. Part of *Grofe Ifland*	N. 83 E.

St. John's.

St. John's Point a good deal open	S. 52½° W.
W. End of *Madame*	S. 40½ W.
E. End of *Madame*	S. 34½ W.
E. End of the *First Mountain*, about ½ the Distance of *Rot Island* from the E. End	S. 6 E.
Goose Cape	N. 52½ E.

Bearings near the Edge of the *Middle Ground*.

E. End of *Orleans*	N. 63 W.
A Buoy on a little Shoal near *Orleans*	N. 54 W.
St. John's Point	S. 53½ W.
St. Francis's Church	S. 72½ W.
West End of *Rot-Island*	S. 6 E.

Bearings taken near the upper End of the Land (off *Orleans*) dry at Low Water.

The W. End of *Rot-Island*	S. 3½ W.
E. End of *Rot-Island* with the W. End of *Grosse Island*	S. 55½ E.
Cape Torment	N. 31 E.
St. Joachim's Farm	N. 12½ W.
St. Joachim's Church	N. 52 W.
E. Point of *Orleans*	N. 71 W.
N. E. Point of *Orleans*	W.
The *Little Island*	N. 60 E.

Bearings from another Station near the East End of the said Sand, dry about 1½ Mile N. 63° E. from the Last.

W. End of *Rot Island*	S. 22 W.
E. End of *Rot-Island*	S. 25½ E.
W. End of *Grosse Island*	S. 36 E.
Little Island	N. 63 E.
Burnt Cape	N. 39 E.
Cape Torment	N. 14 E.
E. End of *Orleans*	S. 64½ W.
Point of *Dauphine River*	S. 52 W.
St. Joachim's Farm	N. 53½ W.
The Shoal to the Eastward	N. 51½ E.

Bearings from the West End of *Rot Island*.

Cape Torment	N. 18 E.
St. Joachim's Farm	N. 3½ W.
E. Part of *Orleans*	N. 32½ W.
S. W. End of *Grosse Island*	S. 89 E.
Little Mountain	S. 82 E.
East End of the Third	S. 27 E.

E. End

E. End of the Second	S. 18° E.
E. End of D°.	S. 12 E.
Weftward of the *Firft Mountain*	S. 7 E.
Middle of *Bellchafe Ifland*	S. 19 W.

Bearings from the Eaft End of *Rot-Ifland.*

St. Thomas's Church	S. 53 E.
W. End of the *Firft Mountain*	S. 2 E.
E. End of Ditto	S. 7 E.
E. End of the 2d Ditto	S. 14½ E.
Bellchafe	S. 27 W.
Middle of *Bellchafe Ifland*	S. 36½ W.
The *Mark Windmill*	S. 43 W.
St. Valier's Church	S. 47 W.
N. E. Part of *Groffe Island*	N. 83 E.
N. E. Part of *Crane Island*	N. 80 E.
S. W. Part of the *Two-Heads*	N. 78 E.
Little Island	N. 33 E.
Houfes below *St. Joachim's*	N. 28½ W.
W. End of the *Butt*	N. 51 W.
E. End of *Saddle Hill*	N. 64 W.
Two Points off *Orleans*	N. 75½ W.
St. Francis's Church	S. 86½ W.

Bearings for the Weft End of *Madame.*

St. John's Church	S. 71° W.
Port St. Lawrence	S. 68 W.
St. Valier's Church	S. 28¼ W.
The *Mark Church*	S. 17½ W.
St. Thomas's Church	S. 86 E.
Bellchafe Church	S. 40 E.
The Middle of *Bellchafe Ifland*	S. 25 E.
E. End of the *Firft Weft Mountain*	S. 18½ E.
Dauphine River	N. 60 W.
Little Mountain	E.
South Part of *Crane Ifland*	N. 79 E.
South Part of *Groffe Ifland*	N. 70½ E.
S. Part of *St. Margaret*, on the *Three-Pointed Mountains*	N. 73½ E.
Cape Raven	N. 40½ E.
Cape Torment	N. 29 E.
E. Point of *Orleans*	N. 19 E.
St. Francis's Church	N. 5 E.

From *Point St. John* to *Point St. Lawrence* there is no Danger, and about a Mile from the Shore of *Orleans* you will have 9, 7, 10, 13, 16, and 18 Fathoms, rocky Ground.

At

At *Point St. Lawrence* you muſt (in order to avoid the Shoals of *Beaumont*) keep the Starboard Shore till you have paſſed the *Falls* of *Beaumont*, which are on the South Shore, and then ſteer up in the Middle of the Stream, till near the Weſt End of *Orleans*, when, to avoid the *Morandas Rocks*, keep neareſt to the South Shore, and you may anchor at ¼ of a Mile from the South Shore, in 9 Fathom Water, *Point Levy* bearing W. S. W. and the Weſt Point of *Orleans* N. N. E. rocky Ground, or you may proceed with the Tide directly for *Quebec*, and anchor within 2 Cables Length of the Town, in 15 Fathom muddy Ground, *Cape Diamond* bearing S. W. ¼ W. N. E. End of the *Barbet Battery*, W. by N.

The Tide flows Full and Change,

At *Quebec*, Half an Hour after 8.
Iſle Madame, at 8.
Cape Maillard, at 7.
Iſle of *Coudre*, at 6.
The *Kamouraſcas*, at ¾ paſt 5.
The *Pilgrims* and *Hare Iſland*, at 5.
Bic, ¾ paſt 3, but not regular.

N. B. From *Coudre* to *Quebec* the Water falls 4 Feet before the Tide makes down. At Iſle of *Coudre*, in Spring Tides, the Ebb runs at the Rate of 9 Knots. The next ſtrongeſt Ebb is between *Apple* and *Baſque Iſlands*—the Ebb of the River *Sanguina* uniting here, it runs full ſeven Knots in Spring Tides.

Directions for Sailing from Quebec *down the River* St. Lawrence.

FROM *Point Levy* to *Point St. Lawrence*, the Courſe is E. ¼ N.
From *Point St. Lawrence* to *St. John's*, the Courſe is N. E. by E.
From *St. John's* to *St. Francis*, N. E. ¼ N. keeping upon the Iſland Side, all the Way having from 10 to 16 Fathom.
When a-breaſt of *St. Francis*, ſteer N. N. E. until you bring *St. John's Point* a Handſpike Length open with *Dauphine Point*, with that Mark ſteer N. E. ¼ E. at which Time a round Rock will be right a-head of you; continue this Courſe until a high Hill on the South Shore will be juſt on with the Eaſt End of *Rot Iſland*, at which Time the Trees on the ſaid Iſland will be juſt a-breaſt of you, and then ſteer N. by E. for *Cape Torment*: Keep very near *Burnt Cape*, on Account of *Burnt Cape Ledge* that lies oppoſite to it.

Anchorage on the Edge of *Burnt Cape Ledge*, in 4 Fathom.

Eaſt End of *Rot Iſland*	—	—	S. 14° W.
Weſt End of *Groſſe Iſland*	—	—	S.
Weſt End of the *Firſt Mountain*, about a Sail's Breadth to the Eaſtward of *Groſſe Iſland*	—	—	

Middle

Middle of *Little Ifland* ——— ——— E. 3° S.
Burnt Cape ——— ——— N. 25 W.

The *Butt* almoſt all open of *Cape Torment*, and the *Little Mountain* on *Canoe Ifland*, *Cape Maillard*, and the Land behind, will appear as repreſented in *Plate* II. *Fig.* 2.

REMARKS.

The *Little Hummock*, or Riſing on the High Land of *Coudre* at *a* muſt never be open of *Cape Maillard* till you are below *Burnt Cape*, nor all the *Butt* by any Means kept open of *Cape Torment*, if you would keep the Channel, which is but ¼ of a Mile wide at *Burnt Cape*.

Bearings taken from the Weſt End of *Little Ifland*, or *Gooſeberry Ifland*, which lies about N. 55 E.

Weſt End of the *Butt* ——— ———	S.	77 ¼ W.
Cape Torment ——— ———	S.	85 W.
Burnt Cape ——— ———	N.	69 ¼ W.
Cape Maillard ——— ———	N.	36 ¼ E.
Cape Raven ——— ———	N.	37 E.
Gooſe Cape ——— ———	N.	52 E.
Neptune Rock ——— ———	N.	52 ¼ E.
The Middle of *Three-Pointed Mountain* on the Eaſt End of *Gooſe Ifland* ——— ———	N.	84 E.
The Weſternmoſt Rock dry ———	S.	58 E.
The *Little Mountain* ——— ———	S.	57 E.
Weſt End of *Crane Ifland* ——— ———	S.	30 E.
Eaſt End of the *Firſt Mountain* ———	S.	4 E.
Weſt End of *Groſſe Ifland* ——— ———	S.	15 ¼ W.
Eaſt End of *Rot Ifland* ——— ———	S.	29 ¼ W.
Weſt End of *Madame* ——— ———	S.	46 W.

You muſt then ſteer N. E. for *Cape Maillard*, keeping the N. Shore on Board, which is very bold.

From *Cape Maillard* to go clear of *Coudre Spit* N. E. by N.

In ſailing from *Cape Maillard* to *Coudre* with the Tide of Ebb, you muſt go as near as poſſible to the Point of the Shoal which lays off the N. W. End of the Ifland, till you come in 8 Fathoms Water.

The firſt of the Tide ſets directly on *Cape Diable* from this Point; ſo that if you have but little Wind you muſt anchor before you get within two Miles of the Point. At half Ebb the Tide runs truer through the Channel. The Moment you get to the Eaſtward of the Point (if you intend to anchor) haul up for the Meadows, otherwiſe you will not be able to get in good Ground.

The Courſe from *Coudre* to the *Kamouraſcas* and *Pilgrims* is N. E. by E.
From the Middle of the *Pilgrims* to the *Brendy-Pots*, the Courſe is N. E. ¼ N.
From the *Brandy-Pots* to the Iſle of *Bic* is N. E. by E. ¼ E.

(18)

Directions for the South Channel from St. John's Point *of* Orleans, *to the South-West End of* Crane Island, *opposite the South River.*

THERE is a Ledge of Rocks lies off the SW. End of *Madame*, about S. 60° W. from it, and in a Line for a Point on the South Shore, thefe Rocks are very dangerous and dry at Low Water. To know when you are at the End of it, and that the Channel is all clear, obferve on the High Land by the Water-fide on the South Shore a Windmill and three mountains, a great Way back in the Country (the fame three Mountains taken Notice of for the Traverfe); when this Windmill is brought in a Line with the Eaft End of the Wefternmoft of the three Mountains, you are juft off and on of the Weft End of the Shoal. But as it may be often hazey that the Mountains cannot be feen, the Windmill will then bear S. 22° E. *St. John's Church* S. 85° W. *St. Francis's Church* NNE. *Bellchafe Islands* E. 10° S. and the North Part of *Rot Island* about two Ships Length open of the North Part of *Madame :* Therefore to be quite clear of the Ledge, the Windmill fhould bear S. 30° E. then *St. Valier's Church* (which is the next Church to the Weftward of it) will bear about S. 12° E.. and the Middle of a little Wood by the Water-fide on *Orleans* NW. Being below the End of the Ledge going down, a Part of *Rot Island* fhould always be kept open to the Southward of *Madame* (as in the North Channel *Rot Island* fhould always be kept quite open to the Northward of *Madame*, whilft you are between the Ledge and *Orleans Island*); and if you have a fair Wind, you may fteer away directly for the South Part of *Crane Island*, the Channel being clear and open, until you bring *St. Francis's Church* to bear N. 70° W. or the Eaft End of *Rot Island* N. 38° W. for in that Direction begins a Shoal off the South Shore, a little above a Point called *Quail Point*. This Shoal is very wide, and extends Half the Breadth of the Channel of *St. Thomas's Church*, and the South River. And to keep clear of this Shoal, you fhould always fee a Part of the *Goofe Islands* open to the Northward of *Crane Island*. The Channel is very near *Crane Island*; here is every where good Anchorage, Clay Bottom, and in the Channel, in moft Places, 7 Fathom Water. The South Shore is every where elfe pretty bold too, and there is deep Water very near *Bellchafe Islands*. In turning between *St Margaret's Island* and the Shoal, you may ftand to the Southward until the *Goofe Islands* are almoft fhut in by the North Part of *Crane Island*. And to the Northward, until the *Goofe Islands* are quite fhut in (to the Northward) by the South Part of *Moiac Island*, or until *Canoe Island* is almoft all open to the Northward of *Moiac Island*, but not any farther, nor even fo far with a large fhip. The Ifland *St. Margaret* is pretty bold, only a few Rocks lie off of it, and thofe not far; the fartheft off is a fingle Rock off the S. W. End, and therefore it is not proper to come too near the Ifland here. There are likewife fome few Rocks off *Groffe Island*, and not far off *Rot Ifland* is a Flat or Sand-Bank, which lies above half a Mile into the Channel, it is likewife fhoal to the Southward of *Madame*, but not far off, but as it is bold toward the South Shore, it is not proper to come too near thofe Iflands. *Crane Ifland* is bold too, and the beft of the Channel is very near to it. On the N. W. End of *Crane Ifland*, (the *South River*

River Falls S. 4° E. *St. Thomas's Church* S. 22° W. *Bellchase Church* S. 60° W. West End of *Grosse Island* S. 85° 30' W.) a Base Line of one Mile was measured to the South Part of the Island called *La Pointe au Pain*, or *Bread Point*, by which the Breadth of the Channel and the Extent of the Shoal off the South River (on the Edge of which a Sloop was anchored) were determined as follows:

From the West Part of *Crane Island* to *St. Thomas's Church*, 3 Miles. From ditto to the *South River Falls*, 3 Miles and ¼. From ditto to the Edge of the Shoal in a Line with *St. Thomas's Church*, 1 Mile and ¼.

N. B. For a greater Certainty of keeping in the Channel, you may keep a high Mountain (at a pretty great Distance on the South Shore) in a Line with the South Part of *Crane Island* or *Bread Point*. This Mountain bears with the said Point N. 71° E. and S. 71° W. and then you will have all along about 7 Fathom Water and exceeding good holding Ground, Clay Bottom; nor are the Tides near so strong as in the North Channel.

These Observations on the South Channel were made on board his Majesty's Sloop Zephyr; *but as she went no lower down in this Channel than the West End of* Crane *Island, it is thought proper to add the following Directions taken on board a Vessel that went quite through the South Channel, below* Coudre.

The first Danger is the Reef of *Madame*, which runs off S. W. by W. 2 ¼ Miles from the West End of it, to avoid which, in sailing round the Island do not haul to the Southward, 'till you have brought the East End of the Westernmost Mountain on the South Shore, a Sail's Breadth to the Westward of the Windmill on *Bellchase*, (See *Plate* III. *Fig.* 1) with which Mark you will pass to the Westward of the Shoal in 5 Fathom at Low Water; steer for *Bellchase*, until you open the Isle of *Rot* to the Southward of *Madame*; then you may steer E. by N. or E. N. E. along Shore, in any Depth from 5 to 9 Fathom. There is no Danger 'till you come a-breast of the Middle of the *Isle Madame*; to the Southward of which about a Mile lies a Bank of Sand, that runs almost as far as the Isle of *Grosse*; this Bank is dry in many Places, but as it shoals gradually to the Northward it may be avoided, by keeping the Lead going.

There is however a Mark that will carry you in the best of this Channel, if the Weather is so clear as to distinguish it; (See *Plate* III. *Fig.* 2.) which is to keep the Mountain A just open with the S. W. Part of *Crane Island*.

In this Direction, you will not have less than 6 and 7 Fathom to *Crane Island*, 2 Miles to the Southward of which there is a Bank of Sand, which has not above 2 Fathoms on it at Low Water. This Bank begins a little above *St. Thomas's*, and runs down as far as the *River Ovill*. From *Crane* and *Goose Islands*, you will have 8, 9, and 10 Fathoms strong Clay Ground; these Islands are joined by an Isthmus, and make the best Road in this River. The Breadth of the Channel, from the Island to the Bank, is about a Mile and a Half, the Ground good, very little Tide, and sheltered from all Winds but E. N. E.

From *Goose Island* steer for the Southermost Rock of the Pillars, which you may pass at 2 Cables Length, in 5 and 6 Fathom at Low Water. When past the Southernmost Pillar steer N. E. by E. for the Eastermost. About 2 or 3 Miles, S. E. by S. off of the East Pillar about a Quarter of a Mile, there is a Rock which covers and uncovers with the Tide, and has 5 Fathom close to it; to avoid which in sailing down,
keep

keep the Southernmoſt Pillar open to the Northward of *Crane Iſland*, 'till you are a-breaſt of the Eaſternmoſt Pillar; then ſteer N. E. by N. for *Cape Gooſe* 7 Leagues, keeping the Paps (P) in the Valley over *Gooſe Cape*, or Point of *Little Mal Bay*, as will appear in *Plate* III. *Fig.* 3.

In this Direction you will have the beſt of the Channel, from 5, 7, to 12 Fathom, the Ground very uneven, but no leſs than 5 Fathom at Low Water, till you bring the Weſt End of *Coudre* on the Weſt End of *St. Paul's Bay*, you will then find the Channel run more to the Eaſtward, ſo as to be obliged to bring P on A, with theſe Marks on, you will have the ſame Kind of Soundings and Ground when a-breaſt of the Middle of *Coudre*; P muſt ſtill be brought more open, *viz*. about $\frac{1}{7}$ of the Diſtance from A to B; this is the narroweſt Part of the Channel, from hence to the Eaſt End of *Coudre*, for anchoring the Sloop in 2 and $\frac{1}{4}$ Fathom at Low Water, on the North Banks; the Water to the Southward is gradually deeper, to 5, 7, 8, 9, and 10 Fathom, and ſhoals ſuddenly to 4 and 3 $\frac{1}{4}$ Fathoms, all within the Diſtance of about a Mile, or a Mile and a Quarter. The E. End of *Coudre* will bear N. 25 W. and the Weſt End N. 73 W. The Banks to the Southward ſeem to make a Point here, as in the *Chart*, and ſtretch E. by S. or E. S. E. to the Point of *Ovell*. When on the Eaſt End of this Bank, you will have the Mountain M on the Point of *Ovell*, as in *Plate* III. *Fig.* 4. On the Edge of this Bank is 13 Foot at Low Water 3 Miles from the Shore; to anchor to the Eaſtward of it, the Mountain M ſhould be brought at leaſt a Mile to the Eaſtward of the Point of *Ovell*. The Bank to the Northward is very uneven and rocky, and has from 3 to 15 Fathom, which, in a Quarter of a Mile, will ſhoal to 5, 4, and 3; however, by keeping the Paps P, as above directed, till the Eaſt End of *Coudre* is brought N. W. by W. you will be clear of the North Bank, and may ſteer down N. E. by E. or E. N. E. for the *Kamouraſcas*. This Channel, from the *Pillar Iſlands* to the Eaſtward, ought not to be attempted with Ships of above 16 or 17 Foot, without being buoyed, as it runs nearly in the Middle of the River. Between *Coudre* and the South Rock, the Marks are at too great a Diſtance to be ſeen diſtinctly, but in clear Weather.

F I N I S.

www.ingramcontent.com/pod-product-compliance
Lightning Source LLC
Chambersburg PA
CBHW031459160426
43195CB00010BB/1030